GASKELL AND THE LAW

This is the first ever study of law in the fiction of Elizabeth Gaskell.

Elizabeth Gaskell is best known today as a novelist of social realism. Until now, however, her use of law, which is crucial to her portrait of society, has never been systematically explored. This book shows that Gaskell's fiction is rich with insights into the law of her time, and that reading her work with a lawyer's eye deepens and enriches the reading experience.

The book explores Gaskell's work as a whole. It gives careful attention to her most famous novels, but also engages with the lesser-known novels and the shorter fiction, showing that these often overlooked works contain a wealth of original ideas and legal interest. Gaskell's fiction is shown consistently demonstrating a skilled, accurate and critical handling of legal rules and a sensitivity to law's personal and social effects. She does not limit herself to mid-nineteenth century issues, but enters into such fundamental questions as the individual's obligation to obey the law, and the relation between law and fiction. The book shows that a hitherto unappreciated aspect of Gaskell's genius as writer is that she integrates this sophisticated engagement with law seamlessly, so that it contributes to the cumulative artistic effect of her work.

As a leading scholar of Victorian legal history, Paul Mitchell brings an in-depth knowledge of the law to his close readings of Gaskell. He brings out the richness and sophistication of Gaskell's engagement with the law, and proposes both new readings and new valuations of this important novelist's work.

Gaskell and the Law

Paul Mitchell

• HART •
OXFORD • LONDON • NEW YORK • NEW DELHI • SYDNEY

HART PUBLISHING

Bloomsbury Publishing Plc

Kemp House, Chawley Park, Cumnor Hill, Oxford, OX2 9PH, UK

1385 Broadway, New York, NY 10018, USA

Bloomsbury Publishing Ireland Limited, 29 Earlsfort Terrace, Dublin 2, D02 AY28, Ireland

HART PUBLISHING, the Hart/Stag logo, BLOOMSBURY and the Diana logo are trademarks of Bloomsbury Publishing Plc

First published in Great Britain 2025

A catalogue record for this book is available from the British Library.

A catalogue record for this book is available from the Library of Congress.

Library of Congress Control Number: 2025945676

ISBN: HB: 978-1-50993-973-2
ePDF: 978-1-50993-975-6
ePub: 978-1-50993-974-9

Typeset by Compuscript Ltd, Shannon

For product safety related questions contact productsafety@bloomsbury.com

For Susan, Ben and Amelia

ACKNOWLEDGEMENTS

I gratefully acknowledge comments on the development of this project from Paul Raffield and Marco Wan, and on earlier draft chapters from Emily Gordon, Anthony Julius and Steven Vaughan. I am also grateful to participants at seminars where some of the material in this book was presented – in particular, the UCL Faculty of Laws Staff Seminar Series and the King's Private Law Forum. Kate Whetter at Bloomsbury Publishing could not have been more encouraging, patient or supportive in bringing this book to fruition, and Verity Stuart, Claire Banyard and Linda Goss have skilfully guided it through production.

Paul Mitchell
May 2025

TABLE OF CONTENTS

1

Introduction

I

In the course of a relatively short career (beginning with *Mary Barton* in 1848 and ending with *Wives and Daughters* in 1865), Elizabeth Gaskell produced an extraordinary range of writing. She remains best known for her novels – particularly those engaging with industrial life (*Mary Barton*, *North and South*) and small rural communities (*Cranford*, *Wives and Daughters*) – and for her biography of her friend and fellow-novelist Charlotte Brontë. The importance of her shorter fiction – which highlights her versatility, and virtuosity across genres, is also coming to be recognised.[1] Her standing in the literary pantheon is secure.

And yet, there remains a nagging sense of critical deficit, and an impression that, when her work does receive attention, critics feel that they have to make the case for attending to it.[2] No such justification is required for, say, Dickens. Part of the explanation for this felt need is, undoubtedly, the earlier general neglect of female writers. But part of it may also be linked to the perceived nature of Gaskell's work itself. Henry James struck a note that has still not entirely died away when, reviewing *Wives and Daughters*, he commented that:

> Mrs Gaskell's genius was so very composite as a quality, it was so obviously the offspring of her affections, her feelings, her associations, and (considering that, after all, it *was* genius) was so little of an intellectual matter, that it seems almost like slighting these charming facts to talk of them under a collective name, especially when that name is a term so coarsely and disrespectfully synthetic as the word genius has grown to be. But genius is of many kinds, and we are almost tempted to say that that of Mrs Gaskell strikes us as being little else than a peculiar play of her personal character. In saying this we wish to be understood as valuing not her intellect the less, but her character the more.[3]

As the final sentence here makes clear, James was not setting out to be hostile, or dismissive, but his valuation of the work in such personal terms inevitably slights

[1] See particularly S Foster, *Elizabeth Gaskell A Literary Life* (Palgrave Macmillan, 2002).

[2] See eg P Stoneman, *Elizabeth Gaskell* (Harvester, 1987). There is a helpful sketch of the critical history in JL Matus, 'Introduction' in JL Matus (ed), *The Cambridge Companion to Elizabeth Gaskell* (Cambridge University Press, 2007) 1 at 1–2.

[3] H James, review of Elizabeth Gaskell, *Wives and Daughters* in H James, *Literary Criticism Volume 1* (Leon Edel ed, Library of America, 1984) 1018 at 1018–19.

it as a potential subject of literary criticism. What, beyond the merely biographical, could there be to say? From this Jamesian perspective, a study of law, lawyers and legal institutions in Gaskell is a peculiarly unpromising project.

However, if this book has a central thesis, it is that it is a mistake, and a misvaluation, to prize Gaskell's work solely for its undoubted wit, fluency, lightness of touch and acute social observation. There is far more to it than that; not least that she makes brilliantly insightful, original and perceptive use of all aspects of law: its rules, its assumptions, its personnel, its systems.[4]

II

Gaskell's engagement with law is so sustained that it almost amounts to a preoccupation. Only religion can claim a similar centrality in her work. Religion played a fundamental part in her life: not only was she herself a committed Unitarian, her husband, William, was a Unitarian minister (at Cross Street Chapel, in Manchester, where a plaque commemorates Gaskell's attendance). The exploration of Christian, often specifically Unitarian, ideas in her fiction is, therefore, hardly a surprise.[5] But with law it is different. Gaskell has been very well served by biographers, and it is remarkable quite how very little there is to say about her connection with the law.[6] We can infer that she must have mixed with lawyers socially, as the Cross Street Chapel had a largely middle-class congregation;[7] and she once dined with the judges at an assizes (when it is tempting to imagine her being at her most alert and observant).[8] But these biographical minutiae are no explanation for the sophistication and originality of her law-related material.

She was, also, nearly a litigant. The occasion was the publication of her biography of Charlotte Brontë, and the potential litigation a claim for libel, in which she would have been the defendant. Gaskell seems to have approached the risk of being sued for libel with a kind of jaunty recklessness. She wrote to the publisher, George Smith, asking him if he 'minded the law of libel', and listing three people in respect of whom she intended to settle scores.[9] Smith replied with a calmness

[4] The key critical monograph on Gaskell's work remains Stoneman's *Elizabeth Gaskell* (n 2).

[5] See eg M Wheeler, 'Elizabeth Gaskell and Unitarianism' (1992) 6 *Gaskell Society Journal* 25, and J Chapple, 'Unitarian Dissent' in Matus (ed), *Cambridge Companion* (n 2) 164; note also the strong emphasis on Unitarianism in Patsy Stoneman, 'Gaskell, gender and the family' in Matus (ed), *Cambridge Companion* (n 2) 131.

[6] The leading biography is J Uglow, *Elizabeth Gaskell* (Faber, 1993).

[7] Uglow (n 6) at 87 describes the members and trustees of the Chapel as 'the millocracy … bankers and barristers.'

[8] JG Sharps, *Mrs Gaskell's Observation and Invention* (Linden Press, 1970) 367.

[9] Letter to George Smith: letter 314 in E Gaskell, *The Letters of Mrs Gaskell* (ed JAV Chapple and A Pollard, Manchester University Press, 1966). Uglow's comment (n 6) at 405 that 'Reading Elizabeth's letters, one cannot help feeling that she knew the risks, yet was fully determined to press ahead' seems an understatement. Marnie Jones notes the 'bantering tone' ('George Smith's Influence on *The Life of Charlotte Brontë*' (1984) 18(4) *Brontë Society Transactions* 279 at 280).

that it is difficult to imagine even the most composed of publishers attaining today. He insisted on removing the identity of a publisher who had exploited the Brontë sisters; but he left in Gaskell's denunciation of a reviewer of *Jane Eyre* who had impugned Charlotte Brontë's character, and her singling out of a married woman who had, allegedly, seduced Charlotte's brother Branwell. Smith was, perhaps, distracted by the suggestions in the manuscript that he had had a mildly flirtatious relationship with Charlotte (suggestions which he sought to tone down); he may also have been lulled into a false sense of security by Gaskell's letter, and assumed that only the people she named were potential claimants.[10]

In the event, after publication of the biography, Branwell's supposed seducer threatened to sue, and there was an unanticipated response from a clergyman who had been in charge of the Cowan Bridge School – where Charlotte Brontë had been a pupil. Gaskell's biography spelled out that the Lowood Institution in *Jane Eyre*, where the young heroine experiences bitter cold and semi-starvation, and is subjected to an unjustified public humiliation by the school's pompous, hypocritical founder, was the Cowan Bridge School. The now elderly clergyman, William Carus Wilson, professed himself indifferent to the attacks, though he denied the allegations. His relatives were more energetic, and their threats to sue prompted Smith to recall those copies that he could, and to amend the text for a revised edition. The result was a revision, but not a retraction.[11] Gaskell had, she explained, received letters confirming her account and others countering it; the revised version omitted some details and somewhat softened the portrait of Carus Wilson, but it left the sense of neglect and hypocrisy firmly in place. The Gaskells (William became involved when there was the threat of legal action) seem here to have had the great good fortune to have been advised by William Shaen, a family friend and leading solicitor.[12] Shaen seems to have calculated that, with some factual concessions made, Wilson would not risk a libel action; that turned out to be correct.

The episode was a painful one, and Gaskell emerged from the experience of writing the biography with a bitter sense that the law suppressed the truth. Thus, in response to Smith's insistence that the exploitative publisher should not be named, she says, *in the text of the biography* – 'I understand that truth is considered a libel in speaking of such people.'[13] She 'understand[s]', ie, has had to be told, because 'truth is considered a libel' is a flat contradiction in terms, a perverse reversal of the basic legal doctrine that truth is not a libel. In similar vein she writes in a letter,

[10] On the possible distraction see Jones (n 9).

[11] cf Smith's approach to the threat from Branwell's supposed seducer, where the allegation was publicly retracted (Uglow (n 6) 427). Angus Easson persuasively argues that 'It seems that there was something between Mrs Robinson and Branwell' which fell short of seduction: 'Introduction' in E Gaskell, *The Life of Charlotte Brontë* (A Easson ed, Oxford University Press, 1996) xvii–xviii.

[12] Shaen married Elizabeth Gaskell's friend Emily Winkworth in 1851, with William Gaskell performing the marriage ceremony. See Shaen's entry by Judy Slinn in the *Oxford Dictionary of National Biography* (online ed) for an overview of his wide influence and impressive career.

[13] Gaskell, *Life of Charlotte Brontë* (n 11) 268.

after the affair is concluded, that 'for the future I intend to confine myself to lies (i.e. fiction). It is safer.'[14] These angrily epigrammatic, paradoxical remarks can usefully be set alongside a passage in the biography which reflects on Charlotte Brontë's position:

> Miss Brontë more than once said to me, that she would not have written what she did of Lowood in 'Jane Eyre', if she had thought the place would be so immediately identified with Cowan Bridge, although there was not a word in her account of the institution but was true at the time when she knew it; she also said that she had not considered it necessary, in a work of fiction, to state every particular with the impartiality that might be required in a court of justice, nor to seek out motives, and make allowances for human failings, as she might have done, if dispassionately analyzing the conduct of those who had superintendence of the institution. I believe she herself would have been glad of an opportunity to correct the over-strong impression which was made upon the public mind by her vivid picture, though even she, suffering her whole life long, both in heart and body, from the consequences of what had happened there, might have been apt, to the last, to take her deep belief in facts for the facts themselves – her conception of truth for the absolute truth.[15]

Whether on her own behalf, or as a proxy for Brontë, Gaskell paints a troubled picture of the triangular relationship between the law, the writer and the truth. At its starkest there is direct conflict – as with identifying the exploitative publisher, where legal costs and the risk of litigation silence a writer who might otherwise expose the truth about wrongdoing. The 'lies' of fiction are safer, because fiction is – at least generally – beyond the reach of defamation law.[16] But Gaskell is a realist novelist. As we shall see, in the very striking preface to her first novel, *Mary Barton*, she wrote 'I have tried to write truthfully'.[17] Thus, for her to speak of the 'lies' of fiction is for her to describe the artistic method by which she aspired to communicate a more profound, valuable and worthwhile truth than a merely banal replication of fact. The apparent retreat to 'lies' is in fact a claim to a superior truth. The sense of different kinds of truth clashing and painfully competing is particularly vivid in her imagining of Charlotte Brontë's attitude. Here Gaskell acknowledges that Brontë's account could not pass muster judged by a legal standard – it is her 'conception of the truth' not 'the absolute truth'. That might perhaps make Brontë's position seem weak, but that is not so. It has the irrefutability and integrity of being Brontë's own experience, imprinted on her by continuing physical suffering, and heightened and intensified by novelistic recasting. By contrast, the law's pretensions to impartial and absolute truth frequently fall short in practice. Gaskell shows us the self-censorship that inevitably follows when 'the truth is considered as a libel' and, as we shall see, elsewhere

[14] Letter 358, to William Fairbairn in Chapple and Pollard (ed), *Letters* (n 9).
[15] Gaskell, *Life of Charlotte Brontë* (n 11) 51.
[16] It may be helpful to recall here that strict liability in defamation was a creation of the early twentieth century: P Mitchell, *The Making of the Modern Law of Defamation* (Hart Publishing, 2005) ch 5.
[17] See ch 2, s I.

in her work the law's failure to establish the truth is a constant refrain. Indeed, her acute sense of the rivalry between law and fiction in the pursuit of truth inspired much of her most incisive writing.

III

In seeking to demonstrate Gaskell's ongoing engagement with law, this book takes a broadly chronological approach. Generally it focuses on one work per chapter, which, it is hoped, will allow readers who are, as yet, only interested in a particular work or works to find everything they need in one place. It has very occasionally been desirable to treat aspects of works outside 'their' chapters; and inevitably some themes are repeated, varied and redeveloped, for which cross-referencing is provided. Ultimately, however, it is only by entering into Gaskell's work as a whole that it is possible to understand the range, the diversity and the imaginativeness of her uses of law.

If the book shows that Gaskell's engagement with law is an important aspect of her work, it should also be emphasised that law was not an obsession. Not everything she wrote can be illuminatingly seen in relation to law; nor, for the same reason, does every major work deserve its own chapter. The conclusion analyses work where law is touched on, and brings out the extent to which these moments confirm, or elaborate on, the uses of law featured in earlier chapters.

Finally, it may be helpful to explain the methodological assumptions and techniques on which the book is based. It is an interdisciplinary work, in which law, and, particularly, legal history, is brought into relationship with literary criticism. Gaskell's work has been read with close attentiveness to its legal moments. In these moments law in a broad sense – including legal rules, legal professionals, the legal system – is invoked, frequently for telling literary effect. The book's main aim is to bring out, illuminate and reflect on the significance of these legal moments, and, in doing so, to piece together Gaskell's strikingly distinctive, often subversive, attitude to law. It has often seemed particularly valuable to anchor the legal analysis in a rigorously accurate legal history: reconstructing the precise legal context against which Gaskell was writing brings out more vividly, and precisely, the full richness and sophistication of her meaning.

2

Mary Barton

I

Gaskell's remarkable debut opens with a remarkable Preface. The novel is set in Manchester, in the 1840s, and is very largely focused on working-class characters. The setting, timing and subject-matter all seem to demand of the novelist an understanding of the political and economic forces that had shaped Manchester in the early industrial revolution. Gaskell's bold, indeed, provocative, response to this demand is immediately to refuse it: 'I know nothing of Political Economy, or the theories of trade. I have tried to write truthfully.'[1]

Reviewers and critics have been duly provoked. For some, Gaskell's statement has been taken as a virtual admission of her unsuitability to write on her chosen topic.[2] Others have explored whether the claim was quite accurate – she must have been familiar with some writings on political economy, not least her father's; it has also been suggested that 'Political Economy' might have a narrower, more technical meaning than has generally been assumed.[3] These points are important. But surely what is more important is Gaskell's emphasis on truth, with the implication that theories of political economy and trade offer no access to that truth. Gaskell is, in other words, firmly pushing aside rival discourses which might have plausible pretensions to truth, and appointing the novelist's perspective as sovereign. She does the same thing, more subtly, with poetry in the first chapter: 'It was an early May evening – the April of the poets' – the poets miss the mark too![4]

As the novel unfolds, the characters are seen struggling to find the truth, to accept it, and to prove it. The struggles are not confined to the characters: even the narrator's confident generalisations and explanations are vulnerable to being undermined by the characters' outspokenness and intransigence.[5] In the midst of this contest for truth Gaskell introduces legal elements. There are legal personnel: attorneys, barristers, judges, police officers; there are legal institutions such as magistrates' cells and court rooms; there is legal terminology – particularly 'alibi' – and

[1] E Gaskell, *Mary Barton* (Thomas Recchio ed, Norton, 2008) 6.
[2] See eg Lord David Cecil, *Early Victorian Novelists: Essays in Revaluation* (Constable, 1934) 235.
[3] P Stoneman, *Elizabeth Gaskell* (Harvester Press, 1987) 42.
[4] Gaskell, *Mary Barton* (n 1) 8.
[5] See especially C Lansbury, *Elizabeth Gaskell and the Novel of Social Crisis* (Elek, 1975) 9, 25 and 36.

legal documentation.[6] There is also, pervasively, a framework of legal ideas of guilt, responsibility, rights and obligations. These legal elements recurrently come into conflict with the novel's commitment 'to write truthfully'. The resulting depiction of law is nuanced, multifaceted and in many (but not all) ways troubling.

II

In its first few chapters the novel suggests that, with one important exception, the law has little to offer people like John Barton, a Manchester weaver, and his family. It is a fine May evening, and they are enjoying a walk in Green Heys Fields, but a shadow is cast over their holiday by the mysterious disappearance of Esther, Barton's sister-in-law. Barton describes his desperate attempts to find her: 'I even went to a policeman, a good enough sort of man, but a fellow I'd never spoken to before because of his livery …'.[7] The police have seen a woman matching Esther's description, but for all their '[a]cuteness'[8] they fail to find her. Barton's instinctive mistrust, both of the office and uniform, will later be amplified through the narrator.[9]

A similar sense that law offers little practical help can be seen when Barton's daughter Mary becomes apprenticed to a dressmaker:

> she had engaged herself as apprentice (so called, though there were no deeds or indentures to the bond) to a certain Miss Simmonds … where Mary was to work for two years without any remuneration, on consideration of being taught the business; and where afterwards she was to dine and have tea, with a small quarterly salary (paid quarterly because so much more genteel than by week), a *very* small one, divisible into a minute weekly pittance. In summer she was to be there by six, bringing her day's meals during the first two years; in winter she was not to come till after breakfast.[10]

As Gaskell's legally knowledgeable narrator highlights, the law going back to Elizabethan times required indentures or deeds for an apprenticeship to be fully legally effective.[11] The main consequence of the lack of such formalities was that the apprentice could not acquire settlement in the parish where she worked; settlement was crucial for establishing a person's right to financial or other relief in the case of poverty.[12] For Mary, however, this poses no problem since she could establish settlement through her father's residence in the parish, and, as we shall see

[6] On the significance of alibi in this novel see Jonathan H Grossman, *The Art of Alibi: English Law Courts and the Novel* (Johns Hopkins University Press, 2002) ch 5.
[7] Gaskell, *Mary Barton* (n 1) 13.
[8] ibid.
[9] ibid 193–94 (discussed further below in s VI).
[10] ibid 26–27.
[11] J Chitty, *A Practical Treatise on the Law Relative to Apprentices and Journeymen, and to Exercising Trades* (London, 1812) 26ff.
[12] W Cornish et al, *Law and Society in England 1750–1950*, 2nd edn (Hart Publishing, 2019) 393–97.

shortly in connection with the Davenport family, questions of settlement seem to have been becoming less important anyway. What is, surely, more significant here is the absence of any promises by the dressmaker, whether by deed or otherwise. A master's express covenants to apprentices typically included the duty to instruct and the duty to care for them in sickness; apprentices also had the right of recourse to justices of the peace in the event of mistreatment by their master.[13] None of these protections seem to be available to Mary. The general impression is one of legal provisions being completely overtaken by social changes and unmitigated economic inequalities: we are told that Barton has inquired about dressmaking apprenticeships at other establishments but has been deterred by the high premiums demanded.[14] The law here insists on certain forms (deeds, indentures) for the sake of anachronistic and increasingly irrelevant purposes, while doing nothing to protect workers like Mary against exploitation and abuse.

A fire at a mill a couple of chapters further into the novel illustrates other ways in which the law falls short. Two men are trapped in the mill by the spread of the fire: evidently there are no fire escapes or alternative exit routes required by law. The fire also prompts some astute critical observations by John Barton: 'much Carsons [the owners] will care, for they're well insured, and the machines are a'th'oud-fashioned kind. See if they don't think it a fine thing for themselves. They'll not thank them as tries to put it out.'[15] Barton is proved right: the Carsons are not 'over-grieved'. Indeed, they regard the destruction of the factory as 'an excellent opportunity', both to refit the factory and to save expenditure on wages during what is a slack period in trade.[16] It is worthwhile pausing for a moment to reflect on the role of law in this situation. Insurance is, of course, prudent, but the terms of the typical policy – which do not, it seems, encourage, let alone require, safety measures to be installed[17] – invite and encourage wasteful and, in the absence of insurance, irrationally destructive, conduct. By operation of insurance law, however, loss is transformed into gain. But the spell only works for the insured: for the workers at Carsons' mill, who will receive no wages until the mill is operational again, loss remains insistently loss. It is also worth noticing the laconic economy with which Gaskell constructs the situation: we never find out how the fire starts, and we do not need to know. All we need to be shown is that it is perfectly legitimate for Carsons to stand aside and let their mill burn.

Exceptionally, Gaskell then depicts law intervening to assist the victims of the loss of their livelihoods. One of Carsons' workforce, Ben Davenport, has become gravely ill, and has no money for food or medicine. John Barton and his friend

[13] Chitty (n 11) 74–76 (master's covenants); ch iv (jurisdiction of justices of the peace).

[14] Gaskell, *Mary Barton* (n 1) 26. The theme continued to concern Gaskell: she returned to it in *Ruth* (see below, pp 25–26).

[15] ibid 46.

[16] ibid 53.

[17] P Atiyah, *Vicarious Liability in the Law of Torts* (London, 1967) at 15–17 draws attention to the connection between insurers' practices (such as the inspection of insured premises) and insureds' levels of accident-consciousness.

James Wilson try to help him. Wilson asks Mrs Davenport if they 'had no money fra' th' town?'. Mrs Davenport's reply is revealing: 'No, my master is Buckinghamshire born; and he's feared the town would send him back to his parish, if he went to the board; so we've just borne on in hope of better times.'[18]

Wilson seeks out Mr Carson, in order to have Davenport admitted immediately to hospital. Carson grants only an out-patient order, and Davenport dies. Mrs Davenport, however, fares better than she had feared: 'The board, not so formidable as she had imagined, had inquired into her case; and instead of sending her to Stoke Claypole, her husband's Buckinghamshire parish, as she had dreaded, had agreed to pay her rent.'[19]

The subtlety and significance of this vignette can only be appreciated with a full understanding of the legal context. From Elizabethan times responsibility for those unable to provide for themselves had rested with parishes; parishes were responsible only for those who had settlement in the parish. A man had settlement in the parish of his birth; his wife and children were settled in the same parish. Parishes were entitled to remove people without settlement – hence the Davenports' fears that if they presented themselves to the authorities as being in need, they would be removed to Buckinghamshire.[20] The Poor Law Amendment Act 1834 would, on the face of it, have made the Davenports' position more precarious: by that Act the possibility of acquiring settlement by residence was abolished, and workhouses were established.[21] In the Davenports' case it is noticeable that Mrs Davenport never fears being sent to the workhouse in Manchester, and here Gaskell very accurately reflects the attitudes of the authorities in northern cities who exercised a discretion to provide 'outdoor relief' (ie, payments to support paupers), despite the strong legislative steer towards workhouses.[22] The incident is particularly noticeable in the novel as an example of thoughtful, humane intervention going beyond the law's strict requirements. It is an all too rare example of the kind of conduct that Gaskell, at the very end of the novel, hopes to see become 'the regulating law' between employers and workers.[23]

III

Examples of the law being incomplete or inadequate invite reflections on how the law might be changed, and on this topic the novel is not encouraging.

[18] Gaskell, *Mary Barton* (n 1) 59.

[19] ibid 67.

[20] Cornish (n 12) 394–95 (describing the 'skirmishing' between parishes over responsibility for paupers.

[21] Cornish (n 12) 403. The Poor Law Amendment Act 1834, s 64 abolished the possibility of settlement through residence.

[22] ibid 405.

[23] *Mary Barton* (n 1) 335.

One of the most crushing experiences to which Barton is subjected is his membership of the delegation bearing a Chartist petition to Parliament. Parliament refuses to receive it, rendering otiose proposals about shorter hours for factory work and employment of children. The only character to retain any optimism about law reform is the prickly, odd-tempered wife of James Wilson, Jane. In reply to the wishful suggestion that her articulate son, Jem, would 'speak a word to th' Queen, about factory work for married women', Jane says:

> 'I say it's Prince Albert as ought to be asked how he'd like his missis to be from home when he comes in, tired and worn, and wanting some one to cheer him; and maybe, her to come in by-and-by, just as tired and down in th' mouth; and how he'd like never for her to be at home to see to th' cleaning of his house, or to keep a bright fire in his grate. Let alone his meals being all hugger-mugger and comfortless. I'd be bound, prince as he is, if his missis served him so, he'd be off to a gin-palace, or summut o' that kind. So why can't he make a law again poor folks' wives working in factories?'
>
> Mary ventured to say that she thought the Queen and Prince Albert could not make laws, but the answer was, 'Pooh! Don't tell me it's not the Queen as makes laws; and isn't she bound to obey Prince Albert? And if he said they mustn't, why she'd say they mustn't, and then all folk would say, oh, no, we never shall do any such thing no more.'[24]

The dialogue is simultaneously comical and touching: comical in Jane's assumption that Victoria and Albert live like an ordinary working couple; touching in its belief that the royal couple would understand the difficulties, and intervene to protect family life. Jane's final observation is a lovely combination of legal truisms – the queen as monarch; a wife's duty to obey her husband – that could hardly give a less accurate account of the true sources of power, both political and economic, that might bring about legal change. The idea that the law might ameliorate the destructive effects of industrialisation is here shown to be laughable.

IV

In her depiction of legal rules and the prospects for their reform, Gaskell portrays a legal system undeserving of the faith or commitment of those governed by it. Thus, when characters contravene the law, or thwart its procedures, we are not invited to be shocked or to disapprove. This point is especially striking in the scenes immediately following Harry Carson's assassination by John Barton. Esther makes her way to the crime scene, discovers a crucial piece of evidence and takes it away with her. She shows it to Mary, telling Mary that she 'would never leave a thing about, as might help, ever so little, to convict.'[25] Mary realises that the paper incriminates her father and promptly destroys it. Before doing so, she insists that

[24] ibid 108.
[25] ibid 210.

Esther must not 'tell'. Esther's response is illuminating: '"Nay, Mary" said Esther rather reproachfully, "I am not so bad as that. Oh! Mary, you cannot think I would do that …"'.[26]

It says a lot about the moral landscape of the world Gaskell creates that a character is insulted by the suggestion that she might help the authorities to identify a murderer. The text offers the rather weak explanation that 'The murder, shocking though it was, was an absent, abstract thing;' but the real explanation is clearly that Esther wants to protect Mary, her niece, from being summoned to give evidence.[27] Similarly, Mary has no hesitation, or doubts, about destroying the paper that incriminates her father. Her plan succeeds – Barton never stands trial; and what is really striking about this is that the novel makes no criticism of the fact. Barton eventually confesses, on his death-bed. Harry Carson's father is determined to bring a prosecution, but changes his mind after overhearing an incident in the street where a little girl forgives a boy who has hurt her; the girl says '*He did not know what he was doing*', a phrase which prompts Carson to read, and be moved by, the famous Biblical passage where Christ uses very similar language.[28] The only 'tribunal' that inquires into Carson's murder is the informal gathering convened by the elder Carson, at which Jem Wilson and Job Legh attempt to cast some light on events. At the very beginning of the tribunal's proceedings Gaskell underlines their legal insignificance by having Carson remind Jem that 'you are aware that the law allows no one to be tried twice for the same offence.'[29] It is only by putting legal procedures entirely out of the question that there is any hope of accessing the truth.

Mary's destruction of evidence and Esther's removal of it from the crime scene would not, at that date, have amounted to criminal offences – the crime of attempting to pervert the course of justice is not recognised until the late nineteenth century.[30] But in a novel, and with a novelist, where conscience, duty and moral obligation are so prominent, it is remarkable that these characters should act as they do without a second thought, and not suffer any consequences. The explanation lies in Gaskell's portrayal of a legal system that has no moral authority, and does not deserve the allegiance of those to whom it applies. Law's central failing, like the failing of 'Political Economy and theories of trade', to which she alluded in the preface, is its failure to 'write truthfully'. The different ways in which 'writing truthfully' can be understood – and the corresponding ways in which law fails to achieve or promote truth – are the key to understanding Gaskell's depiction, and distrust, of law.

[26] ibid 211.
[27] ibid 207, 210.
[28] ibid 318. Luke 23: 34.
[29] ibid 329.
[30] *R v Vreones* [1891] 1 QB 360; JF Archbold, *Archbold Criminal Pleading Evidence and Practice* (Sweet & Maxwell, 2023 edn) 28-1.

V

At its simplest, the failure to write truthfully involves direct factual inaccuracy. Jane Wilson's unintentionally comical, legally accurate, description of Victoria and Albert is a light-hearted and unthreatening example – unthreatening because most people, like Mary, know that it is not true, and nothing turns on it anyway. When there are serious consequences at stake, however – as when Jem Wilson is wrongly accused of Carson's murder and faces the death penalty, the law's failure to identify the truth is profoundly disturbing.

Wilson, of course, does not help himself: he remains silent in order to avoid incriminating John Barton. We have, however, been led to have high expectations of the law's ability to establish truth. As the trial approaches, and Mary receives a subpoena, she goes to consult Job Legh. Legh, as has been recognised, is far more significant than his minor role in the plot might suggest – he is an epitome of intelligence, perceptiveness and good judgement.[31] When he tells Mary, to her dismay, that 'Truth's best at all times … and for sure it is when folk have to do with lawyers; for they're [a]cute and cunning enough to get it out sooner or later', we anticipate high-level forensic courtroom skills.[32]

The reality is rather different. In Gaskell's description of Jem's trial the plea of not guilty is a standardised, essentially meaningless formality – 'but one answer was expected, – was customary in all cases.'[33] The plea has no effect on the spectators at the trial, who, as connoisseurs of crime, have already decided that Jem looks like a murderer; his haircut, it seems, is particularly incriminating.[34] One powerful reason for the presumption of guilt here is the convenient narrative of motive – 'you see it was a fixed idea in the minds of all that the handsome, bright, gay rich young gentleman [Harry Carson] must have been beloved in preference to the serious, almost stern-looking smith, who had to toil for his daily bread.'[35] Jem is typecast as the jealous, spurned rival for Mary's affections.

Counsel for Jem, who has been given no instructions,

> had little hope of establishing anything like a show of defence, and contented himself with watching the case, and lying in wait for any legal objections that might offer themselves. He lay back on the seat, occasionally taking a pinch of snuff, in a manner intended to be contemptuous; now and then elevating his eyebrows, and sometimes exchanging a little note with Mr. Bridgenorth behind him.[36]

This is heavily acted theatre, verging on pantomime. When the barrister is given crucial information about Jem's alibi, which can be proved by the sailor Will

[31] K Tillotson, *Novels of the Eighteen-Forties* (Oxford University Press, 1956) 219.
[32] Gaskell, *Mary Barton* (n 1) 226.
[33] ibid 277.
[34] ibid 278.
[35] ibid 280.
[36] ibid 284.

Wilson, we might hope for a change of approach. But the moment provides the opportunity for Gaskell to show the legal profession at its worst:

> The barrister who defended Jem took new heart when he was put in possession of these striking points to be adduced, not so much out of earnestness to save the prisoner, of whose innocence he was still doubtful, as because he saw the opportunities for the display of forensic eloquence which were presented by the facts; 'a gallant tar brought back from the pathless ocean by a girl's noble daring,' 'the dangers of too hastily judging from circumstantial evidence,' &c. &c.; while the counsellor for the prosecution prepared himself by folding his arms, elevating his eyebrows, and putting his lips in the form in which they might best whistle down the wind such evidence as might be produced by a suborned witness, who dared to perjure himself. For, of course, it is etiquette to suppose that such evidence as may be given against the opinion which lawyers are paid to uphold, is any thing but based on truth; and 'perjury,' 'conspiracy,' and 'peril of your immortal soul,' are light expressions to throw at the heads of those who may prove (not the speaker, there would then be some excuse for the hasty words of personal anger, but) the hirer of the speaker to be wrong, or mistaken.[37]

The exposure of lawyers' utterly cynical lack of integrity is merciless. Counsel for the defendant is buoyed not by the prospect of clearing his client, but by the chance to display his 'forensic eloquence'. This proves to be hackneyed, clichéd and formulaic – one lazy narrative trope ('the gallant tar') replacing another ('the jealous lover'). Counsel for the prosecution is no better – he reverts to the kinds of crude, tired theatrics in which his opponent had previously indulged. He, like other lawyers ('it is etiquette') has no compunction about making the most insulting and baseless aspersions about a person's integrity as a matter of course. This final point is perhaps Gaskell's most devastating one: in these proceedings everyone is pretending to be trying to establish the truth, but allegations of lying have become so routine, so much an expected part of the action that it is a breach of politeness *not* to make them. When legal professionals mindlessly label everything false, establishing the truth becomes a matter of sheer luck.

Jem is lucky. The jury acquit, and Gaskell briefly takes us behind their verdict:

> The verdict they had come to was unsatisfactory to themselves at last; neither being convinced of his innocence, nor yet quite willing to believe him guilty in the teeth of the *alibi*. But the punishment that awaited him, if guilty, was so terrible, and so unnatural a sentence for man to pronounce on man, that the knowledge of it had weighed down the scale on the side of innocence, and 'Not Guilty' was the verdict that thrilled through the breathless court.

The jury's reservations were not, of course, part of the verdict. 'Not guilty' is unqualified, absolute – as a matter of law. As a matter of social perception however, it is otherwise. Jem's co-workers shun him, and tell their employer they will no longer work under Jem. In the end Jem has to resign, with his employer

[37] ibid.

recommending him for a position at a Canadian agricultural college. At the end of the novel, Mary and Jem, together with Jane Wilson, emigrate. Critics have found this a powerful moment. For Raymond Williams, 'there could be no more devastating conclusion.'[38] Coral Lansbury adds that 'Manchester has defeated them … [it] will not tolerate those who have transgressed its iron laws.'[39] Both comments are telling; and both invite further reflection on the underlying legal causes of Mary and Jem's removal. The reason they cannot stay is precisely *not* because of a legal transgression – they are not being *transported*; rather, the legal system that has acquitted Jem of murder is held in such low esteem, there is so little confidence in its ability to establish the truth, that its pronouncements count for nothing. In other words, it is the legal system's failings, not Jem's, that precipitate his emigration, and that is, indeed, a devastating conclusion, because it implies a total failure of criminal law as a social institution.[40]

VI

In Jem's trial the law's inability to establish truth is at its starkest – we come precariously close to the law declaring a falsehood to be true. This is undoubtedly the most direct way in which Gaskell portrays law's problematic relationship with truth; but she also depicts more subtle incompatibilities. Two of the most interesting and suggestive of those are the role of the police in investigating Harry Carson's murder, and the arrest of Esther for disorderly vagrancy.

Gaskell's portrait of the police is wary and sceptical. The tone is set from the first chapter, when John Barton says that he has 'even' asked a policeman's help to find Esther. Barton had hoped that the police's '[a]cuteness' would help in the search, but they have failed to locate her.[41] As the novel develops, the detective police's acuteness proves to be a troublingly ambiguous quality, and only deployed intermittently. The police, for instance, never seem to secure or investigate the crime scene – leaving, literally, the field open to Esther to enter it and remove a crucial piece of evidence. Nor is their acuteness brought to bear on the basic narrative of romantic jealousy which is the essential foundation of the murder case. Instead, they seem to be worryingly complicit in the determination of Harry Carson's father to see Jem Wilson hanged.

Where the police do deploy their acuteness, it is less than edifying. In a passage which, in effect, introduces an example of the police in action, the narrator observes that

[38] R Williams, *Culture and Society 1780–1950* (Chatto and Windus, 1958) 98.

[39] Lansbury (n 5) 24.

[40] Contrast Dion Bouciclaut's stage adaptation of *Mary Barton*, *The Long Strike*, which ends with the jury immediately returning a verdict of 'Not Guilty!', followed by 'Loud shouts by the crowd. Lively music. CURTAIN' (*Mary Barton* (n 1) 420, 458).

[41] Gaskell, *Mary Barton* (n 1) 13.

> there is always a pleasure in unravelling a mystery, in catching at the gossamer clue which will guide to certainty. This feeling, I am sure, gives much impetus to the police … they enjoy collecting and collating evidence, and the life of adventure they experience.[42]

This enthusiasm for unravelling is then illustrated by an episode where a disguised policeman brings the murder weapon to Jane Wilson's (Jem's mother's) house, asking if it is Jem's. Jane immediately confirms that it is. Then,

> the policeman walked off with his prize, with an odd mixture of feelings; a little contempt, a little disappointment, and a good deal of pity. The contempt and the disappointment were caused by the widow's easy admission of the gun being her son's property, and her manner of identifying it by the ornaments. He liked an attempt to baffle him; he was accustomed to it; it gave some exercise to his wits and his shrewdness. There could be no fun in fox-hunting, if Renard yielded himself up without any effort to escape …[43]

The same ambivalence towards the police (which contrasts strikingly with the admiration of contemporaries like Dickens) is also visible in Gaskell's non-fiction essay 'Disappearances'.[44] The piece offers some examples where police investigation would have brought offences to light quickly, but also discusses situations where the tone is less celebratory. For instance, the essay begins with the whimsical Mr B, who 'charming as he is in many points, has the little peculiarity of liking to change his lodgings once every three months on an average.'[45] The narrator remembers that Mr B has moved to a village for the summer, but mislays his address. Her enquiries in the village are fruitless until a plainclothes detective gives her a complete description of B's appearance and daily habits, along with his full address. We can admire the feat of memory and observation while being somewhat disquieted by the note of surveillance, and the ease with which the information is disclosed to the narrator. Solving the 'mystery' is the only thing that matters here.[46]

The second example of the law's subtly problematic relationship with truth is Esther's arrest. Esther hears rumours of Mary's flirtation with Harry Carson; she is terrified that Mary will be seduced and suffer the same terrible consequences of poverty, sex work and addiction that have been visited on her. She therefore approaches John Barton in the street to warn him of the danger; Barton scornfully dismisses her, and she falls to the ground in despair. The police assume she is drunk and arrest her; she is quickly tried by magistrates and imprisoned. It is, we are told, 'a clear case of disorderly vagrancy.'[47]

[42] ibid 193–94.

[43] ibid 195.

[44] For Dickens' enthusiastic admiration of the Detective Police see eg 'A Detective Police Party [i]' (1850) 1 *Household Words* 409 (27 July 1850).

[45] 'Disappearances' in E Gaskell, *Gothic Tales* (L Kranzler ed, Penguin, 2000) 1 at 1.

[46] On 'Disappearances' see further R D'Agnillo, 'Elizabeth Gaskell's "Disappearances": Narratives of absence between mystery and empirical detection' in F Marroni, R D'Agnillo and M Verzella (ed) *Elizabeth Gaskell and the Art of the Short Story* (Peter Lang, 2011) 71.

[47] Gaskell, *Mary Barton* (n 1) 112.

It is worth pausing for a moment to consider why the police's activities and Esther's arrest are problematic. In the case of the police, they are, of course, establishing the truth about the ownership of the gun used to kill Carson. The trouble is that this small truth is being used to bolster a bigger falsehood (ie, that Jem is guilty of murder); this bigger falsehood is no more than a lazy, convenient assumption – a cliché which happens to fit the very limited facts they have. The police here reveal their own shortcomings, their inability, whatever their efficient practical skills, to imagine an alternative narrative with actors and motives different from the most obvious ones.[48] There is also a further concern, articulated by Jane Wilson shortly after the disguised policeman has left, when it is suggested to her that she might have been manipulated by the authorities: '[the police]'d never go for to do that, and trick me into telling on my own son. It would be like seething a kid in its mother's milk and that the Bible forbids.'[49] Jane Wilson is a complex character – by turns prickly, irascible and unsympathetic, she occasionally reveals hidden depths. Here the imaginative jump to the Biblical example is a surprise, and the sentiment behind it is striking. Jane is essentially protesting against the police's deployment of its mystery-solving acuteness without any moral or ethical restraints; the quickest, most ingenious route to the truth may well take its toll on the innocent.

In the case of Esther's arrest, the details are rather different, but the theme of the law's inability to grasp a complex underlying narrative continues to apply. Esther has been found in a despairing heap; she has no home; it is a 'clear case', so far as the law is concerned. But readers of the novel know differently, know better. They know that Esther is trying to prevent disaster; that her motives are altruistic. The law's 'clear case' is only part of the truth, and the least important part at that. The slightly pompous, lawyerly confidence in pronouncing the situation 'a clear case' is ironically undercut by what we know to be the true complexity of the situation. The law's truth – the only truth the law cares about – is shown to be outward and trivial; the inner, significant truth, which is the novelist's focus, is not the law's concern.

VII

The world of *Mary Barton* is a world in which the law is peripheral and morally marginal. But that is not at all to say that it is an anarchic world: certain rules are recognised as being authoritative, and occasionally the source of those rules is highlighted.

[48] Gaskell would return to this theme in 'The Manchester Marriage': see ch 9.
[49] ibid 198.

The rule which has the greatest structural significance in the plot of the novel is an extensive rule about 'responsibility to the lives of family members', as the critic Rosemarie Bodenheimer has happily put it.[50] The obligation to care for and protect others runs throughout the novel – it can be seen, for instance, in John Barton and James Wilson's attempts to help the unfortunate Davenport family, in Esther's attempts to save Mary from being seduced, in Jem Wilson's refusal to incriminate John Barton as Carson's murderer. These are presented as admirable, and wholly positive manifestations of the rule; but it also has a negative side. The negative side can be seen when characters' own life choices are said to be constrained by the impact those choices will have on others.

The first example concerns Esther – her disappearance at the very start of the novel causes great anxiety to her sister, John Barton's wife. The wife soon dies in childbirth. Barton, however, accuses Esther of being the fatal cause when she reappears.[51] It is not only Esther who is blamed in this way. After Mary has refused Jem's proposal of marriage he tells her:

> you'll maybe hear of me as a drunkard, and maybe as a thief, and maybe as a murderer. Remember! When all are speaking ill of me, yo will have no right to blame me, for it's your cruelty that will have made me what I feel I shall become.[52]

This is Jem's least sympathetic moment; and it is equalled by his mother's accusation to Mary: 'Thou'lt have much to answer for if he's hung. Thou'lt have my death at thy door too.'[53]

A reader's instinctive reaction to these allegations is to deny them, and to invoke straightforward legal analysis to do so. No-one is at fault in Mrs Barton's death. If Jem's unhappiness makes him an alcoholic or a criminal, that is his own choice – his own independent act. The idea that Esther has a duty to stay where she is, or that Mary has a duty to accept a proposal of marriage from someone whom she does not at that point care for, is repulsive. It is noticeable that those seen as owing these duties to conform, and to make traditional choices with their lives, are young women. It is as if their potential to be different, and to disrupt, is so unnerving that it has to be suppressed. Gaskell, interestingly, seems ambivalent. When, later, Esther mistakenly starts to blame herself for having unwittingly driven Jem to commit murder, the narrator is sympathetic – 'Poor diseased mind!' she comments, 'And were there none to minister to thee.'[54] No such intercession, however, is offered when Mary reproaches herself for having 'thought it a fine thing to have a rich lover.'[55] The oppressive sense that Mary is

[50] R Bodenheimer, 'Private Grief and Public Acts in *Mary Barton*' (1981) 9 *Dickens Studies Annual* 195, 204.

[51] *Mary Barton* (n 1) 111: 'it was thee who killed her, as sure as ever Cain killed Abel.'

[52] ibid 200.

[53] ibid 201.

[54] ibid 206.

[55] ibid 203.

somehow to blame is never completely dispelled – even the description of her at the murder trial compares her to a portrait of Beatrice Cenci, who notoriously, did commit murder.[56]

VIII

Where do the rules that the characters recognise, or should recognise, come from? Ultimately it is religion; but that general claim can be helpfully broken down. One of the earliest, and most intriguing, allusions to sources of authority in the book comes in the first chapter. It is holiday time, and John Barton and his family are out walking in Green Heys Fields. 'I do not know', says the narrator, 'whether it was on a holiday granted by the masters, or a holiday seized in right of Nature and her beautiful spring time by the workmen.'[57] One might, at first glance, be dismissive of the second alternative, but it hints at a kind of authority, and test of legitimacy, very different to the masters' permission. As William Blackstone explained in his *Commentaries on the Laws of England*, a classic institutional text with which Job Legh is familiar:[58]

> Man, considered as a creature, must necessarily be subject to the laws of his creator, for he is entirely a dependent being … This will of his maker is called the law of nature. For as God, when he created matter, and endued it with a principle of mobility, established certain rules for the perpetual direction of that motion; so, when he created man, and endued him with freewill to conduct himself in all parts of his life, he laid down certain immutable laws of nature, whereby that freewill is in some degree regulated and restrained, and gave him also the faculty of reason to discover the purport of those laws.[59]

Blackstone goes on to explain God's laws in terms of 'the eternal, immutable laws of good and evil'.[60] That does not quite explain the workmen's entitlement to 'seize' their holiday 'in right of Nature', and it seems that Gaskell here has a different kind of natural law in mind, a kind of irresistible, instinctive veneration for the natural environment which, as a response to God's creation, should be respected and given full expression.

[56] ibid 281. For literary treatment of the history of Beatrice Cenci see eg PB Shelley, *The Cenci* (first published 1820 – available in eg PB Shelley, *The Major Works* (ed Z Leader and M O'Neill, Oxford University Press, 2003) 84); Gaskell may, here, particularly be drawing on Dickens' rhapsodic description of the portrait of Beatrice Cenci in the Palazzo Berberini as 'a picture almost impossible to be forgotten. Through the transcendent sweetness and beauty of the face, there is something shining out …': C Dickens, 'Rome' in *Pictures from Italy* (Bradbury and Evans, 1846) 165 at 211–12.

[57] Gaskell, *Mary Barton* (n 1) 8.

[58] ibid 225.

[59] W Blackstone, *Commentaries on the Laws of England Book I of the Rights of Persons* (W Prest (gen ed) and D Lemmings (ed), Oxford University Press, 2016; first published 1765) 39–40 (pagination in original, appearing at 33–34 of the Oxford edn).

[60] ibid 40 (34 in Oxford edn).

In Gaskell's situation the entitlement to a day enjoying the beauty of the natural world is, happily, granted by both divine and human authority. What happens, however, if the two sources of law fail to coincide? Blackstone is very clear:

> This law of nature, being co-eval with mankind and dictated by God himself, is of course superior in obligation to any other. It is binding over all the globe, in all countries, and at all times: no human laws are of any validity, if contrary to this; and such of them as are valid derive all their force, and all their authority, mediately or immediately, from this original.[61]

Gaskell, to judge by her treatment of legal rules, would surely have agreed.

Natural law was discoverable by the exercise of reason, but reason itself had proved insufficient – it had, in Blackstone's terms, become 'corrupt' – and was therefore reinforced, and supplemented, by the direct revelation of divine law in the Bible.[62] 'Upon these two foundations, the law of nature and the law of revelation, depend all human laws' explained Blackstone; 'that is to say, no human law should be suffered to contradict these.'[63]

There is one particularly crucial moment in the novel where a Biblical text is invoked as laying down the truly authoritative, binding law. It has been touched on earlier – Jane Wilson's comment after she has identified the murder weapon as her son's, and it is suggested to her that the person she was speaking to was a police officer: 'It would be like seething a kid in its mother's milk and that the Bible forbids.'[64] In its immediate context, Jane's position seems very naïve, and there is never any suggestion that the police officer has acted unlawfully. Viewed in the wider perspective of Gaskell's attitude to law, however, the response can be seen to have a deeper significance. Jane is not able to rely on a text which expressly prohibits the use of disguises by law enforcement officials when interviewing close family members of a suspect, and we might, therefore, be tempted to dismiss her argument, saying that there is no conflict between the scriptural text and what the law permits. Such a dismissal, however, would not do justice to Jane's point: she is saying that her situation is analogous to the Biblical case. Who is to determine whether the analogy is sufficiently close for the Biblical rule to apply? The apparently simple idea that human laws contravening the law of nature and revelation are invalid quickly starts to bristle with difficulties. Then there is the further question of what, in practical terms, 'invalidity' means. The law remains valid insofar as it meets the conditions for validity imposed by the legal system (for instance by being set out in an Act of Parliament). In Jane's situation, then, she has no recourse – she can only protest ineffectually because the conduct to which she is subjected is legally permitted.

[61] ibid 41 (35 in Oxford edn).
[62] ibid.
[63] ibid 42 (35 in Oxford edn).
[64] *Mary Barton* (n 1) 198. The Bible verse is Exodus 23:19. The image recurs at a moment of high drama in *Sylvia's Lovers*, ch XXIII (E Gaskell, *Sylvia's Lovers* (F O'Gorman ed, Oxford University Press, 2014) 224).

If one of the underlying themes of the novel is the unhappy divergence of natural law and human law, its conclusion indicates the need to realign them; specifically, to make 'the Spirit of Christ … the regulating law' between employers and workers.[65] So far as the inadequacies and shortcomings of the legal system are concerned, we might well feel that the novel has made its case. Gaskell's proposed solution, however, is a radical and challenging one. In particular we should notice that she is not proposing that existing rules be interpreted in the light of Biblical precepts, or that exceptions to rules should be made on grounds of compassion. She goes further: the Spirit of Christ is *to be the law*.

The lawyer's instinctive response is to ask: 'how could that work?' It makes Jane Wilson's application of the 'kid in mother's milk' rule to police investigations seem a paragon of certainty and clarity. It may also prompt lawyers to think of Lord Atkin's famous speech in *Donoghue v Stevenson*, where he attempted to formulate a general principle by which duties of care in the tort of negligence could be identified. Lord Atkin started from the Christian precept to 'love thy neighbour'; but, as Lord Atkin explained, it was not feasible simply to stop there. Legal systems could not adopt all moral wrongs as legal wrongs; and some narrower, legal definition of 'neighbour' was needed. Lord Atkin offered 'those who are so closely and directly affected by my act that I ought reasonably to have them in contemplation as being so affected when I am directing my mind to the acts or omissions which are called in question.'[66] Even this lawyerly exposition has been found to be unworkable and has, to some extent, now been superseded.[67] Crucially, for our purposes, Gaskell seems not even to be proposing anything akin to Lord Atkin's formulation, and that must prompt us to ask what kind of law (and, perhaps, what kind of legal system and mechanisms of enforcement) she has in mind?

Her earlier treatment of Esther's arrest for disorderly vagrancy may offer us a clue. Where Gaskell shows the legal system failing is in its disregarding Esther's personal circumstances, history, motivations, etc. Esther's attempts to explain these to the drowsy attendant at the cells fall, literally and symbolically, on deaf ears.[68] The novelist shows us that the lawyer's 'clear case' is in fact complex and multifaceted. We might perhaps say that the criticism is particularly well-aimed at an offence like vagrancy, where the underlying causes often call for compassion, not punishment. But the logic of Gaskell's position may be wider – and more radical – for it can be applied to all general rules. Such rules, by their nature, do not take account of all personal circumstances, indeed, they cannot if they are to

[65] ibid 335.

[66] *Donoghue v Stevenson* [1932] AC 562, 580. On nineteenth century literary and legal ideas of neighbourliness see J-M Schramm, 'Wrongs: Negligence, Neighborliness, and the Duty of Care in Nineteenth-century Narrative' in I Ward (ed), *A Cultural History of Law in the Age of Reform* (Bloomsbury Academic, 2019) 129.

[67] *Caparo Industries plc v Dickman* [1990] 2 AC 605; *Robinson v Chief Constable of West Yorkshire Police* [2018] UKSC 4, [2018] AC 736.

[68] Gaskell, *Mary Barton* (n 1) 112.

function as general laws. By putting forward 'the Spirit of Christ' as 'the regulating law' Gaskell is, in effect, dethroning human law.[69]

IX

It is only by taking the full measure of Gaskell's engagement with law in this novel that we can appreciate its depth, its sophistication and its radicalism. Law, legal institutions and lawyers continued to preoccupy and trouble her; as we shall see, her later work eloquently elaborates on many of the ideas she first explored in this remarkable novel.

[69] See further, on the conflict between Love and Law as 'a constitutive theme in English literature' – A Julius, 'Love poetry and the art of advocacy' (1997) 39(2) *Critical Quarterly* 3.

3

Ruth

I could understand it mysel' … that were no law for me

I

'There is an assize-town in the eastern counties …' Thus begins *Ruth*. It is an undramatic opening. But, in specifying that the setting of the first few chapters of her novel is a place that derives its identity from being a centre for the enforcement of the criminal law, Gaskell hints at themes that will preoccupy her for the rest of the book. What does the law prohibit? What should it prohibit? How effectively is it enforced? What rules from sources other than the law should determine our conduct? Do those rules, ultimately, have a superior claim to our allegiance than rules of law? And what is 'law' anyway? Must it be understood exclusively in terms of positive legal rules? All these questions will trouble Ruth's story, and the opening chapter begins to suggest answers that are not encouraging. Immediately after telling us that we are in an assize-town, the narrator tells us that the town has seen better days: evidently legal importance does not translate into prosperity. Still on the first page, there is a glimpse of the law's power to affect the physical environment in a reference to 'the infinite variety of windows that had been crammed into the walls long before Mr. Pitt's days of taxation.' The tax on windows had been introduced in 1754, and the events which Gaskell goes on to depict in the next couple of chapters will invite the inference that the reduction in windows prompted by this change in tax law has brought a corresponding reduction of empathy and care for others.

The most direct way in which Gaskell problematises, and ironises, the town's assize status is in her brief, but shocking, sketch of the flourishing of criminal activity:

> [N]o regard was paid to the wants of the middle class, who neither drove about in coaches of their own, nor were carried by their own men in their sedans into the very halls of their friends. The professional men and their wives, the shopkeepers and their spouses, and all such people, walked about at considerable peril both night and day … at night, the only light was derived from the glaring, flaring oil-lamps hung above the doors of the more aristocratic mansions; just allowing space for the passers-by to become visible, before they again disappeared into the darkness, where it was no uncommon thing for robbers to be in waiting for their prey.[1]

[1] E Gaskell, *Ruth* (A Shelston (ed), Oxford University Press, 1985) 1–2.

Clearly the criminal law is an inadequate deterrent, even in the very location of its enforcement. It is particularly important to notice how blame is apportioned here: self-interested aristocrats look after themselves, thus enabling the victimisation of the middle class; the robbers are little more than an inevitable symptom of selfishness. The sketch dramatises the culpability of indifference to what is happening (literally) on our own doorsteps. It also, subtly, puts forward an analysis at odds with the law: as a matter of law the only guilty parties are, of course, the robbers. We are barely on the second page of the book and there is already a disquieting sense that the law is both ineffectual and misses the point.

The narrator then goes on to make an observation about 'the traditions of bygone times' contributing to 'the formation of character', adding that –

> The daily life into which people are born, and into which they are absorbed before they are well aware, forms chains which only one in a hundred has moral strength enough to despise, and to break when the right times comes – when an inward necessity for independent individual action arises, which is superior to all outward conventionalities.[2]

The sketch of the town concludes with a description of the grand aristocratic houses being converted into smaller dwellings, 'or even (bend your ear lower, lest the shade of Marmaduke, first Baron Waverham, hear) into shops!'[3]

Critics have found Gaskell's suggestions here about the formative influence of traditions on character unsatisfactory, in the sense that as the novel unfolds Ruth's character seems not to be explained by any such traditions.[4] But this is surely missing the point. The people who have power over Ruth, and who judge her most harshly after her sexual fall, are fundamentally self-centred and lacking in empathy – Gaskell's allusion to 'the old traditions' invites the conclusion that it is the selfish disdain shown towards their predecessors which has formed these people's attitudes towards Ruth. The apparently casual, mock-snobbish allusion to the rise of shopkeeping also carries powerful thematic force – indeed, it is the key to the book – because the mentality of the shopkeeper is that the world goes on by buying and selling at a profit. The central, and most sympathetic, characters in *Ruth* are defined by their resistance to that ideology.

II

When we first encounter Ruth herself, she is a teenaged apprentice to a dressmaker, Mrs. Mason, who embodies the worst qualities of the profit-fixated shopkeeper. All of the apprentices are being exploited to the point of physical collapse; our first glimpse of Mason comes as she is urging the girls to redouble their efforts, so that everything will be ready for a ball. As if parodically combining the roles of wicked

[2] ibid 2.
[3] ibid 2–3.
[4] E Wright, *Mrs. Gaskell The Basis for Reassessment* (Oxford University Press, 1965) 85; B Crick, 'Mrs. Gaskell's *Ruth*: A Reconsideration' (1976) 9(2) *Mosaic: An Interdisciplinary Critical Journal* 85, 87.

stepmother and fairy godmother, she promises the girls that, as a reward, four 'of the most diligent' will go to the ball.[5] The apprentices are 'too sleepy to care', and that, as it turns out, is the best attitude to have. As Gaskell explains, sardonically:

> Mrs Mason was a very worthy woman, but, like many other worthy women, she had her foibles; and one (very natural to her calling) was to pay an extreme regard to appearances. Accordingly, she had already selected in her own mind the four girls who were most likely to do credit to the 'establishment'; and these were secretly determined upon, although it was very well to promise the reward to the most diligent. She was not really aware of the falseness of this conduct; being an adept in that species of sophistry with which people persuade themselves that what they wish to do is right.[6]

When, the next day, Mason announces her choices, 'One or two of the girls looked astonished, but the majority having anticipated the selection, and knowing from experience the unexpressed rule by which it was made, received it with the sullen indifference which had become their feeling with regard to most events'.[7] The majority, at least, have not been deceived.

The incident may seem trivial, but it is an important first statement of a theme that will be repeated, and varied – the theme of breach of faith. Crucially, Mason experiences no qualms, or hesitation – the pursuit of her own self-interest is so routine, the falsity so habitual as barely to register. In the repeated metaphor of the prettiest girls doing 'credit' to the house is a dangerous hint of what might be on offer in exchange for this commercial advantage.

It hardly comes as a surprise that Mason's duplicity about who will attend the ball is not her only, or her worst, breach of faith towards her apprentices. In addition to her exploitative demands, she systematically fails to perform her duties to provide heat and food for them. 'On Sundays [Mason] chose to conclude that all her apprentices had friends who would be glad to see them to dinner, and give them a welcome reception for the remainder of the day'.[8] Ruth is described as eating a 'fasting dinner' of a bun. To add hypocrisy to neglect, on her return Mason summons

> her 'young people' once more into the parlour, she read a prayer before dismissing them to bed. She … asked no questions as to their proceedings through the day; perhaps, because she dreaded to hear that one or two had occasionally nowhere to go, and that it would be sometimes necessary to order a Sunday's dinner, and leave a lighted fire on that day.[9]

Although the most obviously striking aspect of this account is the divorce between religious practice and moral conduct, the legal dimensions are also suggestive. Failure to provide adequate food and warmth for an apprentice of 'tender years'

[5] Gaskell, *Ruth* (n 1) 7.
[6] ibid 8.
[7] ibid 9.
[8] ibid 34.
[9] ibid 35.

was a crime at common law; but there is never any danger of Mrs Mason being dragged to the town's assizes.[10] Mason is also in breach of the standard contractual obligations governing apprenticeships, but here, again, the law seems to offer no real protection. The reality of the contractual situation is nicely illustrated by the experiences of Jenny, Ruth's fellow apprentice, and, momentarily, a potential mentor for her. Jenny knows she is ill:

> The tightness at her side was worse than usual. She almost thought she ought to mention it in her letters home; but then she remembered the premium her father had struggled hard to pay, and the large family, younger than herself, that had to be cared for, and she determined to bear on …[11]

Soon, unfortunately, Jenny's illness becomes unbearable, and her parents come to take her away from Mason's. Jenny's dilemma is, of course, partly a product of the classic legal structure of apprenticeships, in which the premium is paid in full at the start of the term – the incentive to complete performance is very much on the apprentice, and there is no opportunity for the apprentice to withhold payment until working and living conditions are ameliorated. As a matter of strict law, however, the apprentice's position is less vulnerable than it might at first seem: a master's obligation under the circumstances Jenny faces was to look after the ill apprentice. Such an obligation should, in turn, encourage a master to take care for an apprentice's wellbeing. As one legal writer put it, the master took the apprentice 'for better for worse, and is to provide for him in sickness and in health'.[12] Gaskell's depiction is rather less romanticised: there is never the slightest suggestion that Mason might either voluntarily honour such a commitment, or be compelled by law to do so.

If the conditions to which Ruth is subjected are due to ineffectual legal enforcement, how Ruth comes to be at Mason's in the first place is a story of law being followed to the letter. Ruth is an orphan; her guardian is a 'flourishing maltster', whom Ruth's father nominated in his will as 'the person of most consequence' among his acquaintance. The (unnamed) guardian's role is explained in a single tumultuous sentence:

> He was a sensible, hard-headed man of the world; having a very fair proportion of conscience as consciences go; indeed, perhaps more than many people; for he had some ideas of duty extending to the circle beyond his own family; and did not, as some would have done, decline acting altogether, but speedily summoned the creditors, examined into the accounts, sold up the farming-stock, and discharged all the debts; paid about £80 into the Skelton bank for a week, while he inquired for a situation or apprenticeship of some kind for poor broken-hearted Ruth; heard of Mrs Mason's, arranged all with her in two short conversations; drove over for Ruth in his gig; waited while she and the

[10] J Chitty, *A Practical Treatise on the Law Relative to Apprentices and Journeymen and to Exercising Trades* (W Clarke and Sons, 1812) 74–75; *R v Ridley* (1811) 2 Camp 650.
[11] Gaskell, *Ruth* (n 1) 9.
[12] Chitty (n 10) 75.

> old servant packed up her clothes, and grew very impatient while she ran, with her eyes streaming with tears, round the garden, tearing off in a passion of love whole boughs of favourite China and damask roses, late flowering against the casement-window of what had been her mother's room.[13]

No one, it is made clear, can have any complaints about the law not being followed; which rather highlights the law's priorities: property, creditors, debts. Ruth is disposed of in a brisk, businesslike settling of accounts; she receives as much consideration as the farm stock.[14] The guardian's reported anger when Ruth later asks him for the money to buy a winter shawl is perhaps not so much miserly (we are told that he is angry, not that he refuses) as an irritated response to an attempt to reopen a transaction that the guardian regarded as closed. Certainly he feels no ongoing obligation to guard Ruth against being taken advantage of.

When Ruth encounters the suave, aristocratic Bellingham at the ball, the scene is thus already set for her fall. Like the aristocratic house-owners of former days, Mrs Mason places Ruth in a spotlight, then leaves her to a waiting predator. Mason, indeed, brings the situation to a crisis when, seeing Ruth out walking with Bellingham she regards the appearance of possible impropriety as a sufficient ground to discharge Ruth on the spot.[15] All is, perhaps, still not lost: Ruth asks Bellingham to take her to her former family home, where two of the old servants still live. Bellingham, however, has other ideas: the carriage takes them to London. It is the last in a series of breaches of faith that culminates in Ruth's seduction.

III

When we rejoin the story, Ruth has been living with Bellingham for several months. They arrive, unannounced, at a Welsh inn where Bellingham has stayed before. There is no room at the inn, but Bellingham has a word with the landlady: 'Can't you persuade some one who is not an old friend to move across? Say, if you like, that I had written beforehand to bespeak the rooms ….'[16] Ruth is confused: they have been told that the inn is full. Bellingham sets her straight: 'I dare say [the inn is full]; but I shall pay her well; she can easily make excuses to some poor devil, and send him over to the other side ….'[17] Bellingham's prediction is correct, his breach of faith contagious:

> The remembrance of his former good payment prompted many little lies of which Mrs Morgan [the landlady] was guilty that afternoon, before she succeeded in turning

[13] Gaskell, *Ruth* (n 1) 37.

[14] A similarly impersonal and disorienting disposal occurs at the beginning of 'The Old Nurse's Tale' (in E Gaskell, *Gothic Tales* (L Kranzler (ed), Penguin, 2000) 11, 12).

[15] cf the legal position set out in Chitty (n 10) ch 4: discharge for misconduct by the apprentice requires a magistrates' order.

[16] Gaskell, *Ruth* (n 1) 63.

[17] ibid 64.

> out a gentleman and lady, who were only planning to remain till the ensuing Saturday at the outside, so, if they did fulfil their threat, and leave on the next day, she would be no very great loser.[18]

As with Mason's offer of a trip to the ball for the 'most diligent' apprentices, the incident may appear trivial, but it exemplifies the novel's most serious themes: Ruth is an uncomprehending innocent in a world of matter-of-fact duplicity, dishonesty, self-interest and manipulation, where personal integrity is a tradeable commodity. It is, of course, a world that cannot be honest with itself, it insists on the keeping up of appearances. Thus, when Ruth's 'faith' makes her so keen to attend on Bellingham when he is taken ill, the landlady complains that she shall 'lose the character of [her] inn' if Ruth is seen so much and talked about.[19] It is a perfect inversion of values. The landlady's cynical and manipulative breach of faith is covert – so the 'character' of the inn is not threatened; Ruth's public keeping of faith, her visible integrity, by contrast, is a potential social and financial embarrassment. We should also notice here that the law is no help. Even if the displaced guests were to take the trouble to sue the landlady for breach of contract, they would be unable to deprive her of the gain she had made from the breach, nor could they recover damages for their disappointment or annoyance. They could only recover a sum that would place them in the same financial position as if the contract had been honoured.[20] On the facts as we have them, the couple have been deprived of a couple of nights accommodation at the inn, but they will not have to pay for those nights – the net recoverable loss is, therefore, zero. The law's values, it turns out, are in perfect harmony with Bellingham's and the landlady's.

IV

After Bellingham has abandoned Ruth in Wales, she is saved from suicide by Thurstan Benson, a man who lives by a very different set of values. Thurstan summons his sister, Faith, to help him to look after Ruth. One of the first dilemmas the three of them face is what to do about a £50 note that Bellingham's mother has sent to Ruth enclosed in a short letter exhorting her to 'an honest life'.[21] Ruth decides to return the note:

> 'I have a strong feeling against taking it. While he,' said she, deeply blushing, and letting her large white lids drop down and veil her eyes, 'loved me, he gave me many things – my watch – oh, many things; and I took them from him gladly and thankfully because he loved me – for I would have given him anything – and I thought of them as signs

[18] ibid 64.
[19] ibid 87 ('faith') and 86.
[20] D Ibbetson, *An Historical Introduction to the Law of Obligations* (Oxford University Press, 1999) 229.
[21] Gaskell, *Ruth* (n 1) 91.

> of love. But this money pains my heart. He has left off loving me, and has gone away. The money seems – oh, Miss Benson – it seems as if he could comfort me, for being forsaken, by money.'[22]

Faith replies that she shall be 'glad' to send it back, 'They don't deserve to have the power of giving: they don't deserve that you should take it.'[23]

This is a critical moment.[24] Ruth's instinctive sensitivity to the meaning of the payment is unerring – the Bellinghams see themselves as closing the transaction, even as paying 'handsomely' for what they have taken: by their own lights they see themselves as behaving well.[25] Ruth, however, registers that the payment devalues and degrades her – it makes her, as she delicately puts it, the kind of person who can be comforted by money. Her reaction is partly an expression of a general sensitivity to being offered money after being treated badly: the assumption that money cures the hurt adds insult to injury.[26] That insight in itself casts an ironic and troubling light on the standard legal mechanisms of providing compensation for injury. More specifically, though, Ruth's response distinguishes her very emphatically from women 'comforted' by money in connection with sexual transgressions – ie sex workers. As Lansbury suggests, prostitution lurks in the background of this novel, despite the fact that – unlike, say, in *Mary Barton* – none of the characters are prostitutes.[27] Society, it seems, is incapable of distinguishing; it is certainly incapable of empathising, as Ruth will discover.

This will not be the last time that Bellingham tries, and fails, to buy Ruth. When he appears in her life several years later, having changed his name to secure an inheritance, he attempts to reclaim her. Having been initially rebuffed, he says, to himself, 'She thinks she has baffled me now. We will try something more, and bid a higher price.'[28] He offers marriage, which Ruth also refuses. As Freeland puts it, Ruth will be neither bought nor sold.[29] The episode is, of course, primarily a reflection of Ruth's integrity and sense of self-worth, but Bellingham's instinctive analysis of it as a transaction of sale and purchase tells us a lot about him, and the society in which he thrives. For it is not as if Bellingham himself cannot be bought for the right price – he changes his name to obtain an inheritance, for instance – nor as if he confines his mischaracterisation of relationships as sales to his dealings with Ruth: as a successful Parliamentary candidate he is involved in extensive bribery.

[22] ibid 126–27.

[23] ibid 127.

[24] P Parker, '"The Power of Giving": Elizabeth Gaskell's *Ruth* and the Politics of Benevolence' (1999) 13 *Gaskell Society Journal* 54.

[25] Gaskell, *Ruth* (n 1) 91. Bellingham 'knew that his mother, always liberal where money was concerned, would "do the thing [ie, pay off Ruth] handsomely"'.

[26] See similarly 'The Poor Clare' in Gaskell, *Gothic Tales* (n 14) 49, 59.

[27] C Lansbury, *Elizabeth Gaskell and the Novel of Social Crisis* (Elek Books, 1975) ch 3.

[28] Gaskell, *Ruth* (n 1) 302.

[29] N Freeland, '*Ruth*'s Perverse Economies: Women, Hoarding and Expenditure' (2003) 70/1 *ELH* 197 at 199.

Bellingham himself does not distribute the money. That is done by Mr Hickson, a barrister – and the only lawyer character to make an appearance in the novel. Hickson is 'briefless', ie, unsuccessful; in a move characteristic of him, he repackages this failure as a reflection of his own highly principled aversion to 'a 'great sham', which involved an immensity of underhand action, and truckling, and time-serving, and was perfectly encumbered by useless forms and ceremonies, and dead obsolete words.'[30] He professes to be fighting corruption in the law by securing the election of Liberal Members of Parliament, 'these certain members being pledged to effect a reform in the law, according to Mr Hickson.' The final clause here is hardly a guarantee of truthfulness. When it comes to the bribery, Hickson's position is straightforwardly that the end justifies the means:

> And, as he once observed confidentially, 'If you had to destroy a hydra-headed monster, would you measure swords with the demon as if he were a gentleman? Would you rather not seize the first weapon that came to hand? And so do I. My great object in life, sir, is to reform the law of England, sir. Once get a majority of Liberal members into the House, and the thing is done. And I consider myself justified, for so high – for, I may say, so holy – an end, in using men's weaknesses to work out my purpose. Of course, if men were angels, or even immaculate – men invulnerable to bribes, we would not bribe.'[31]

Even the apparent moderation of the final sentence is no more than a concession to pragmatism.

The situation Gaskell creates here, in which neither the candidate, nor his Parliamentary agent, distribute bribes, had baffled attempts at legal regulation. Clearly the person giving the bribe was liable, but what about the candidate? Even after the law had been reformed by statute in 1854 (a year after the publication of *Ruth*), the author of a treatise prompted by the new Act drew attention to the continuing difficulty, suggesting that although the candidate would not be guilty of a criminal offence, the election would be vulnerable to being voided by a Parliamentary committee.[32] This legally difficult case suits Gaskell's literary purposes perfectly. Rather like Mrs. Mason's deliberately turning a blind eye to her apprentices' care on Sundays, Bellingham and his parliamentary agent can fall back on deniability if they are challenged. Appearances are preserved, while corruption flourishes behind the façade. For Gaskell to have made the only lawyer character in her book the willing tool of carefully orchestrated criminality is eloquent: it is hopeless to look to the law to uphold the most basic values of decency and honesty. Ruth's judgement of

[30] Gaskell, *Ruth* (n 1) 254.

[31] ibid 254–55.

[32] Corrupt Practices Prevention Act 1854, 17 & 18 Vict c 102; for the full text of the Act, see J Clerk, *A Practical Treatise on the Law of Elections of the United Kingdom and 'The Corrupt Practices Prevention Act 1854'* (H Sweet, 1855) Appendix cii. For legal analysis of the 'by no means uncommon practice for a candidate to pay a large sum of money into the hands of two or three persons, … with permission to such persons to draw upon such sum of money', typically done 'where it is considered expedient that a candidate should know as little as possible of the means used to procure his return' see ibid 101–102. Two years later the question was still unresolved: J Clerk, *The Law and Practice of Elections and Election Committees with an appendix of statutes and forms* (H Sweet, London, 1857) 101–102.

Hickson is especially telling; after observing him in conversation with Bellingham and her employer, Mr Bradshaw, she notes that 'it was part of Mr Hickson's trade to assume an interest if he felt it not.'[33] Here again is Hickson's characteristic falsity, but with an added element of 'trade'. There is a sharp contrast with Hickson's ostensible status as a legal professional; most strikingly, though, Ruth sees that Hickson is in the business of selling himself. Her insightfulness may, perhaps, be prompted by the fact that this, implicitly, is the reproach that society unjustly directs at her.

V

Though Hickson distributes the bribes for Bellingham, the money is neither Hickson's, nor Bellingham's; it belongs to Mr Bradshaw, a wealthy manufacturer who regularly attends the chapel of which Thurstan Benson is minister, and who employs Ruth as governess to his children. In Bradshaw the struggle between law, duty, conscience, propriety and authority is painful, both for himself and for other characters. In our first glimpse of him, he has given unsolicited advice to Faith Benson (Thurstan's sister) about the Bensons' old servant, Sally, saying that they 'might get a far more efficient and younger servant for the money [they pay Sally].'[34] It later becomes clear that Sally is utterly devoted to the Bensons; indeed, she is one of the family, and the wages she earns, as we shall see, are treated by all parties in an eccentrically non-economic fashion. Bradshaw's intervention is, therefore, peculiarly jarring and intrusive in seeking to monetise, and depersonalise, a relationship that has moved far beyond its contractual legal origin.

Bradshaw is, at least, consistent. His eldest daughter, Jemima, is being wooed by Bradshaw's sensible middle-aged business partner, Mr Farquhar; Jemima is made to feel that 'she was to be transferred by [Bradshaw], and accepted by [Farquhar] as a kind of stock in trade.'[35] Here, again, is an uneasy echo of prostitution; at the very least, it is an alarming characterisation of an arrangement in which Jemima is merely inert. Jemima is painfully aware of the clash between what is happening to her and the classical, legal and romantic idea of marriage as an expression of the free choice of bride and groom: she feels that Farquhar is looking for a wife as he would look for a carpet, and, after a discussion between Bradshaw and Farquhar which has been staged (by Bradshaw) to show off Farquhar's best points, Jemima reflects that – 'She felt as if she would rather be bought openly, like an Oriental daughter, where no one is degraded in their own eyes by being parties to such a contract.'[36] Jemima's determination to feel that she is making her own choices almost destroys the match; indeed, as soon as she has accepted Farquhar

[33] Gaskell, *Ruth* (n 1) 277.
[34] ibid 125.
[35] ibid 228.
[36] ibid 240–41.

she forbids him from telling her father – 'She dreaded her father's consideration of the whole affair as a satisfactory disposal of his daughter to a worthy man, who, being his partner, would not require any abstraction of capital from the concern.'[37] Gaskell is very careful here to prevent Jemima from being degraded: Jemima's wishes happen to coincide with her father's, she makes her own choice. At the same time, any romance of the proposal scene is radically undercut by some plain speaking about power. Jemima says to Farquhar –

> 'You won't forbid my going to see Ruth, will you? Because if you do I give you notice I shall disobey you.' The arm around her waist clasped her yet more fondly at the idea suggested by this speech, of the control which he should have a right to exercise over her actions at some future day.
>
> 'Tell me,' said he, 'how much of your goodness to me, this last happy hour, has been owing to the desire of having more freedom as a wife than as a daughter?'
>
> She was almost glad that he should think she needed any additional motive to her love for him before she could have accepted him. She was afraid that she had betrayed the deep, passionate regard with which she had long looked upon him. She was lost in delight at her own happiness. She was silent for a time. At length she said:
>
> 'I don't think you know how faithful I have been to you ever since the days when you first brought me pistachio-candy from London – when I was quite a little girl.'
>
> 'Not more faithful than I have been to you,' for in truth, the recollection of his love for Ruth had utterly faded away, and he thought himself a model of constancy …[38]

The control Farquhar will be able to exercise in the future is, of course, the power conferred on him as a husband by the law. Jemima may have escaped classification as an object, but she can hardly look forward to a partnership of equals with a man who is so excited about being in charge. The final exchange complicates things further – it is not the idea of pistachio-candy that makes us a little queasy here; and perhaps we have to discount Farquhar's profession of equal faithfulness as a merely conventional response to Jemima; but the suggestion that he still sees her in some ways as a child-bride remains unresolved.

Bradshaw's attitude to his daughter is not, ultimately, destructive; the same cannot be said of his attitude to his son. Richard Bradshaw has been formed by the unremitting application of his father's rules. 'If another's son turned out wild or bad,' we are told, 'Mr Bradshaw had little sympathy; it might have been prevented by a stricter rule, or more religious life at home ….'[39] The immediate result of this strictness is hypocrisy – Richard attends the theatre in London, but joins in his father's sanctimonious condemnation of playgoers. Worse is to come: Mr Benson has been puzzled that dividends due to him on shares have not been paid; Bradshaw's firm holds the share certificates. It turns out the shares have been sold; but the signature on the document is not Benson's – it has been forged

[37] ibid 376.
[38] ibid 375.
[39] ibid 211.

by Richard Bradshaw. By this point in the novel we have come to expect falsity as standard – indeed, sale induced by fraud seems, as it were, to be the signature transaction of the society in which the novel is set. Gaskell's interest is not so much in Richard as in his father. Bradshaw senior's first instinct is to press Benson to prosecute:

> I have not one standard for myself and those I love – (and Mr Benson, I did love him) – and another for the rest of the world. If a stranger had forged my name, I should have known it was my duty to prosecute him. You must prosecute Richard.[40]

Benson refuses. Bradshaw's rejoinder is startling:

> He is no longer as my son to me. I have always resolved to disown any child of mine who was guilty of sin … Of course, you understand that I must feel shame at our connexion; it is that that is troubling me; that is but consistent with a man who has always prided himself on the integrity of his name;

Bradshaw here conveniently forgets his own complicity in election bribery, but it is also important to notice his attempt to be consistent ('I have always …'), for there to be continuity between his life prior to the revelation of his son's fraud and his life after. As Benson comments in a later scene, when declining a suggestion to accompany Farquhar on a visit to Bradshaw – 'he is reminded of things he has said to me formerly, and which he thinks he is bound to act up to.'[41] Bradshaw, in short, sees himself as an infallible law-giver by virtue of his position as head of the family; where other people have preferences, he gives commands; even topics of conversation are censored by his 'tacit prohibition.'[42] He can only be saved from committing himself to perversely misguided positions by family members pretending to be unaware of his earlier pronouncements.[43] Bradshaw becomes trapped by two kinds of law – the external, criminal law with its logic of retribution, and his own, self-appointed patriarchal pronouncements, which dictate the abandonment of his own son. Some happier relation with law must, surely, be possible.

VI

In the Benson household law figures very differently – most obviously in the Bensons' decision not to consign Ruth to the poor law system, as strict observance of the law would suggest.[44] But there are also more subtle, and more telling, differences. Elsewhere bargains – whether legitimate or illegitimate – structure the characters' lives and interactions. With the Bensons, bargains are suitable only for the most trivial arrangements – Thurstan promises to box Faith's ears when

[40] ibid 404.
[41] ibid 409.
[42] ibid 421.
[43] ibid 416.
[44] ibid 148 (Sally's instinct is different).

she annoys him, if Faith will promise to scold him rather than whistling when he annoys her; Faith promises to wear a new ribbon if Sally buys it for her.[45] Similarly, money – ubiquitous elsewhere – is marginal here; the giving of money is help 'of the lowest kind'.[46]

Even the composition of the household itself departs from the expected norms: Thurstan and Faith are brother and sister, and Sally is a servant who seems to be on equal terms with them, which makes her references to 'Master Thurstan' nicely ambiguous as between 'head of the household' and 'young man'. The informal ceremony when Ruth joins the household, involving changing her name and receiving a wedding ring (so that she can pass as a widow) achieves many of the practical consequences of marriage without meeting any of its legal requirements. Certainly the Bensons' commitment to Ruth far exceeds anything she could expect from Bellingham's belated, half-hearted offer of conventional matrimony.

At their most radical, the Bensons quietly reconfigure and revalue relationships. Thus, when Ruth proposes moving out of their house after her child is born, so as to spare them expense, Thurstan's reply reverses the burden and benefit:

> 'let me beg you, Ruth, as a favour to me – as a still greater favour to my sister, is it not, Faith?'
>
> 'Yes; you may put it so if you like.'
>
> 'To stay with us'.[47]

What matters most to the Bensons are not bargains, but gifts. At the crucial moment (discussed above[48]) when Ruth decides to return Bellingham's £50 note, Faith's comment that Bellingham does not deserve to have the power of giving, nor deserves that Ruth accepts the gift, articulates the key concept of her, and her brother's, philosophy. To give is a privilege, and to receive a gift is to confer (not receive) a favour. Gifts must, of course, be unconditional, pure. Ruth instinctively shares this philosophy: it is why, in her conversation with Faith, she distinguishes between the gifts Bellingham gave her as her lover and the money he now offers as compensation.

VII

The Bensons' attitude is, of course, admirable, but it generates complexities when they have to engage with systems – particularly the legal system – which do not share their values. In chapter XVIII Gaskell develops two examples, one comical the other more troubling, that highlight the difficulties.

[45] ibid 128; 436.
[46] ibid 136.
[47] ibid 172.
[48] See s IV.

The comical example is Sally's will. Sally has only needed to turn her mind to testamentary provision because of Thurstan and Faith's decision to impose an increase in Sally's wages. Sally initially resented this, but, as she explains to Ruth, she then changed her mind:

> 'a notion had come into my head … I thought I should like to be an heiress wi' money, and leave it all to Master and Miss Faith; and I thought if I'd six pounds a year I could, maybe, get to be an heiress; all I was feared on was that some chap or other might marry me for my money, but I've managed to keep the fellows off; so I looks mim and grateful, and I thanks Master Thurstan for his offer, and I takes the wages; and what do you think I've done?' asked Sally, with an exultant air.
>
> 'What have you done?' asked Ruth.
>
> 'Why', replied Sally, slowly and emphatically, 'I've saved thirty pound! But that's not it. I've getten a lawyer to make me a will …
>
> I was afeard the money might be thrown into Chancery, if I didn't make it all safe … At last, and at length, John Jackson, the grocer, had a nephew come to stay a week with him, as was 'prentice to a lawyer in Liverpool; so now was my time, and here was my lawyer.'[49]

Sally then produces a small piece of parchment:

> 'Now do you know what this is?' said she, holding it up. 'It's parchment, and it's the right stuff to make wills on. People gets into Chancery if they don't make them o'this stuff, and I reckon Tom Jackson thowt he'd have a fresh job on it if he could get it into Chancery; for the rascal went and wrote it on a piece of paper at first, and came and read it me out loud off a piece of paper no better than what one writes letters upon. I were up to him; and, thinks I, Come, come, my lad, I'm not a fool though you may think so; I know a paper will won't stand, but I'll let you run your rig. So I sits and listens. And would you belie' me, he read it out as if it were as clear a business as your giving me that thimble – no more ado, though it were thirty pound! I could understand it mysel' – that were no law for me. I wanted summat to consider about, and for th' meaning to be wrapped up as I wrap up my best gown. So says I, 'Tom! It's not on parchment. I mun have it on parchment.' 'This 'ill do as well', says he. 'We'll get it witnessed and it will stand good.' Well! I liked the notion of having it witnessed, and for a while that soothed me; but after a bit, I felt I should like it done according to law, and not plain out as anybody might ha' done it; I mysel', if I could have written. So says I, 'Tom! I mun have it on parchment.' 'Parchment costs money', says he, very grave. 'Oh, oh, my lad! are ye there?' thinks I. 'That's the reason I'm clipped of law.' So says I, 'Tom! I mun have it on parchment, and I'll tell thee what, lad! I'll gie ye sixpence for every good law-word you put in it, sounding like, and not to be caught up as a person runs. Your master had need to be ashamed of you as a 'prentice if you can't do a thing more tradesman-like than this!' Well! he laughed above a bit, but I were firm, and stood to it. So he made it out on parchment. Now, woman, try and read it!' said she, giving it Ruth.
>
> Ruth smiled, and began to read; Sally listening with rapt attention. When Ruth came to the word 'testatrix', Sally stopped her.

[49] ibid 193–94.

> 'That was the first sixpence', said she. 'I thowt he was going to fob me off again wi' plain language; but when that word came, I out wi' my sixpence, and gave it to him on the spot. Now go on.'
>
> Presently Ruth read, 'accruing'.
>
> 'That was the second sixpence. Four sixpences it were in all, besides six-and-eightpence as we bargained at first, and three-and-fourpence parchment. There! That's what I call a will; witnessed according to law, and all. Master Thurstan will be prettily taken in when I die, and he finds all his extra wage left back to him.'[50]

We later discover that Tom has been transported.[51]

The episode is worth quoting at length because it involves so many different law-related themes. That Tom is a lawyer's apprentice and future criminal eloquently reaffirms Gaskell's estimation of the innate moral qualities of legal professionals. She also shows law's inability to capture, or reflect, the nuance of the transaction as Sally imagines it: Sally never thinks of the money as her own, despite the fact that by law it is. At the same time that Sally imagines a transaction that the law cannot comprehend, she brings to the creation of the will some comical, clichéd misunderstandings about law. She is not an 'heiress' – heiresses inherit, rather than earning, then bequeathing. Nor, of course, is parchment necessary for legal effectiveness – although Sally's more general suspicion that inadequately formal wording might make a bequest miscarry is not misplaced. In the same spirit, for Sally the technical legal terms are merely decorative – a sign of 'tradesman-like' work. For her, what makes something a truly legal utterance is that it is incomprehensible; legal discourse is meaningless – that is the point of it;[52] the material it is written on matters more.

The second example in Chapter XVIII is Ruth's appointment as governess to Bradshaw's youngest daughters, as recounted by Faith to her brother. The process begins with Mr Bradshaw inviting Faith to tea 'because Mrs. Bradshaw wanted to speak to [her].'[53] Our immediate suspicion that Mrs. Bradshaw is no more than Bradshaw's mouthpiece is confirmed when Mrs. Bradshaw tells Faith that –

> Mr Bradshaw had told her, that he did not like Jemima being so much confined with the younger ones … and Mr Bradshaw (for, of course, I saw his thoughts and words constantly peeping out, though he had told her to speak to me) believed that our Ruth would be the very person.[54]

Thurstan's instinct is to inform Bradshaw about Ruth's past. But, as Faith explains matters have gone further:

> I was only too glad to accept the proposal, and so I told Mrs Bradshaw then; and I afterwards repeated it to Mr Bradshaw, when he asked me if his wife had mentioned

[50] ibid 194–96.
[51] ibid 380.
[52] Freeland (n 29) 209–10 sees the will as 'a pure symbol divorced from its use value.'
[53] Gaskell, *Ruth* (n 1) 197.
[54] ibid.

> their plans. They would understand that I must consult you and Ruth, before it could be considered finally settled.[55]

Ruth has already assented. Thurstan, hesitatingly, decides not to complicate matters.

The underlying legal transaction is a simple one: Bradshaw offers Ruth a post; Ruth accepts. But the way the transaction is concluded is anything but simple – Bradshaw and Ruth never exchange a word. The Bradshaws' marriage often seems like a dramatisation of the legal doctrine of coverture, under which a married woman's identity was subsumed in that of her husband.[56] Mrs. Bradshaw does not try to pretend that she is anything other than Bradshaw's messenger. Whether Faith can act for Ruth, by contrast, is far less clear; Faith seems to have accepted on Ruth's behalf without consulting her – there is a slightly awkward echo of the guardian's placement of Ruth with Mrs. Mason – and we cannot be sure whether the Bradshaws would, indeed, have 'understood' that Ruth was to be consulted. Bradshaw would probably have considered Ruth's acceptance a formality. Perhaps the most intriguing question, though, revolves around Thurstan Benson. As a matter of law he is, of course, irrelevant; but he senses the fleeting presence of an obligation on him to disclose Ruth's past. The obligation may possibly derive from the uneasy relationship of patronage and dependency which exists between the two men; there is also perhaps a sense which Benson is aware of – without necessarily sharing – that, like Jemima's marriage, this is a transaction between men concerning the transfer of a woman. The ostensible legal simplicity belies the social complexity. When, eventually, Ruth's past does come to light, Bradshaw, all too predictably, does not blame himself for failing to seek references, or remember his speeches in praise of 'the keenest, sharpest work, consistent with honesty' in trade.[57] If we regard Bradshaw's indignant reaction as anything more than merely self-serving, it looks very much like double standards. Bradshaw seems to feel that he is entitled to demand that others perform obligations far beyond strict legal requirements, while he himself need only comply with the letter of the law. Perhaps he might say 'trade' is one thing, hiring a governess another – although, as we have seen, he seems even to view his own daughter's marriage as essentially 'trade'. It is a moment that, satisfyingly, shows Bradshaw on the receiving end of his own law-bound moralising. It is also a moment which shows us, paradoxically, that Bradshaw, in spite of his apparent strength and power, is a weak man. He cannot trust his own judgement, or rely on what he and his family know about Ruth from their frequent interactions with her, but must defer to the indiscriminate social prejudice against unmarried mothers. In this situation the absence of any legal obligation on Thurstan Benson to inform Bradshaw about Ruth's past has

[55] ibid 199.
[56] W Cornish, S Banks, C Mitchell, P Mitchell and R Probert, *Law and Society in England 1750–1950*, 2nd edn (Hart Publishing, 2019) 347–50.
[57] Gaskell, *Ruth* (n 1) 239. Bradshaw discovers Ruth's past in ch XXVI (p 328).

offered Ruth a glimpse of a fresh start; but the possibility is promptly extinguished by a societal attitude more damning, and inexorable, than any legal requirement.

VIII

If Bradshaw epitomises weakness in his apparent strength, Ruth stands for the converse position. Despite her low social status and her straitened finances, her personal integrity and commitment to values of love and care, prevail over contrary societal expectations and legal assumptions. Her dealings with Bellingham exemplify the point. Judged by their own standards – and, we can infer, those of their peers – the Bellinghams behave well, indeed 'handsomely', in sending Ruth £50.[58] The law here remains neutral. When it comes to Ruth and Bellingham's child, the law is clear: Leonard is *filius nullius*, the child of no one. Bellingham can assert no rights over him.[59] However, it is only at the very end of the novel that Bellingham is told, in no uncertain terms, that this is the legal position. Prior to this Ruth has tormented herself with the possibility that Bellingham may seek to take Leonard away from her:

> 'He will take him away from me. He will take the child from me.'
>
> These words rang like a tolling bell through Ruth's head. It seemed to her that her doom was certain. Leonard would be taken from her! She had a firm conviction – not the less firm because she knew not on what it was based – that a child, whether legitimate or not, belonged of legal right to the father …[60]

Ruth's conviction is misplaced – she has, ironically, confused her position with that of a married woman, where a husband had very extensive rights in respect of the custody of children.[61] And taking responsibility is not really Bellingham's style. But the moment is affecting, all the same: Ruth's desperation and her instinctive sense that the law will be against her are hardly irrational responses to her previous experiences. Nor is the law here being compassionate: Leonard is, by law, *nobody*'s child – the maternal bond counts for nothing. Leonard cannot even claim a surname as of right, he can only acquire it by reputation.[62] Gaskell is surely ironising and subverting this legal rule when, towards the end of the novel, Leonard is proud to claim Ruth as his mother, and, especially, when the local surgeon wishes

[58] ibid 90 and 91. Later, at 187, the Bradshaws' tea service is described as being 'as handsome and as ugly as money could purchase.'

[59] B Leigh Smith Bodichon, *A Brief Summary in Plain Language of the Most Important Laws Concerning Women* (London, 1854) 11; Cornish and Banks (n 55) 353; A Easson, *Elizabeth Gaskell* (Routledge & Kegan Paul, 1979) 120.

[60] Gaskell, *Ruth* (n 1) 290.

[61] W Cornish et al, *Oxford History of the Laws of England: Volume XIII: 1820–1914 Fields of Development* (Oxford University Press, 2010) ch V, 'Children', s 3, 'Legitimate Children: The Governance of the Father'.

[62] Bodichon (n 58) 11–12.

to make Leonard his apprentice because of what he has witnessed of Ruth's nursing skills.[63] In this latter instance Ruth has only had the opportunity to show those skills because professional nurses could not be tempted to work in dangerous conditions, even for higher wages – the legal and economic market mechanism has failed, and in the vacuum Ruth's very different ethic is needed.

Perhaps the most striking clashes of values between Ruth and others relate to gifts. Indeed, one could say that in this novel a character's ability to make truly unconditional gifts defines their moral worth. The key example is Bradshaw, who persists in making gifts of expensive material and dresses to Ruth:

> [Bradshaw] resolved to buy Mrs Denbigh [Ruth's assumed name] a handsome silk gown the next day. He did not believe she had a silk gown, poor creature! He had noticed that dark grey stuff, this long long time, as her Sunday dress. He liked the colour; the silk one should be just the same tinge. Then he thought that it would, perhaps, be better to choose a lighter shade, one which might be noticed as different to the old gown. For he had no doubt she would like to have it remarked, and, perhaps would not object to tell people that it was a present from Mr Bradshaw – a token of his approbation.[64]

Bradshaw's expanding fantasy expresses a potentially sexual possessiveness, but it is also inspired by the desire to have the gift recognised by others as a gift. The gift, in other words, is being used to purchase social attention. Thurstan Benson realises that Bradshaw uses gifts in this instrumental way – to apologise for, or 'pay for' ungracious speeches. Benson's dependency on Bradshaw and his desire to keep the peace lead to him taking an accommodating position, in which he uneffusively accepts the gifts. But, for Ruth, such sophistry is unimaginable – she literally cannot understand Benson's advice to follow his example. As she says earlier, to Faith, 'I cannot see why a person whom I do not know should lay me under an obligation.'[65] The following passage of dialogue with Thurstan, prompted by a present of muslin, shows Ruth's position:

> 'You think [making a gift] is a right which must be earned?'
>
> 'Yes', said she, after a minute's pause. 'Don't you?'
>
> 'I understand what you mean. It is a delight to have gifts made to you by those whom you esteem and love, because then such gifts are merely to be considered as fringes to the garment – as inconsiderable additions to the mighty treasure of their affection, adding a grace, but no additional value, to what before was precious, and proceeding as naturally out of that as leaves burgeon out upon the trees; but you feel it to be different when there is no regard for the giver to idealise the gift – when it simply takes its stand among your property as so much money's value. Is this it, Ruth?'
>
> 'I think it is. I never reasoned why I felt as I did; I only knew that Mr Bradshaw's giving me a present hurt me, instead of making me glad.'[66]

[63] Gaskell, *Ruth* (n 1) 429 and 439.
[64] ibid 234.
[65] ibid 156.
[66] ibid 157.

The immediate context here makes Ruth's alarm all the more vivid. She is still hoping that Bellingham might be trying to find her; she hopes that the parcel is from him. When it turns out to be from Bradshaw there is an immediate inference – which is not immediately dispelled – that Bradshaw is a would-be lover. Ruth's declaration that Bradshaw's gift hurts her demonstrates her extraordinary instinctive perceptiveness and sensitivity – she is quite right to fear that Bradshaw is laying claim to her, and is creating an obligation far more burdensome and oppressive than any contractual duty precisely because that obligation is unspecified. The dissonance between Ruth's own conception of gifts and what she correctly intuits about Bradshaw's is, literally, painful; the fact that, as a matter of legal analysis, Ruth's gifts and Bradshaw's gifts are the same kinds of transactions is a further reminder of how much legal rules fail to register.

IX

As the law seems incapable of discriminating between good and bad, right and wrong, where can we find rules and values worth paying attention to? The novel's potentially cryptic answer is 'the law', but 'the law' understood in a broader, more expansive way than the rules recognised by a legal system. When, for instance, Jemima is tormented by jealousy of Ruth, 'she laid her head on her arms, which rested on the window-sill, and grew dizzy with the sick weary notion that the earth was wandering lawless and aimless through the heavens.'[67] This is law in the sense of the proper order of things, a sense in which the word was also used by, among others, Wordsworth, as we shall see. But how was a person to know what 'the law' in this sense was? One very important indication can be seen in the account of Leonard's development after the shock of the revelation of his mother's past:

> The hopeful parts of his character were the determination evident in him to be a 'law unto himself,' and the serious thought which he gave to the formation of this law. There was an inclination in him to reason, especially and principally with Mr Benson, on the great questions of ethics which the majority of the world have settled long ago.[68]

There is a very noticeable contrast here with Bradshaw's slavish adherence to conventional views. The central concept is that Leonard is becoming 'a law unto himself'. It is an expression which calls for a little explanation as it has come to have a certain ambivalence. In the *OED*, for instance, the phrase is glossed as meaning: 'to behave according to his or her own impulses, beliefs, conscience.' The phrase in effect covers a range of behaviours – acting impulsively being morally very

[67] ibid 333.

[68] Gaskell, *Ruth* (n 1) 383. See further A Wilson, 'Elizabeth Gaskell's subversive icon: motherhood and childhood in *Ruth*' (2002) 16 *Gaskell Society Journal* 85 and P Stoneman, 'Gaskell, gender and the family' in J Matus (ed), *The Cambridge Companion to Elizabeth Gaskell* (Cambridge University Press, 2007) 131.

different to obeying one's conscience.[69] It is, therefore, important to understand that Gaskell would surely have intended the phrase as a wholly positive scriptural allusion to St Paul's epistle to the Romans:

> But glory, honour, and peace, to every man that worketh good, to the Jew first, and also to the Gentile. For there is no respect of persons with God. For as many as have sinned without law shall also perish without law: and as many as have sinned in the law shall be judged by the law. (For not the hearers of the law are just before God, but the doers of the law shall be justified. For when the Gentiles, which have not the law, do by nature the things contained in the law, these, having not the law, are a law unto themselves. Which shew the work of the law written in their hearts, their conscience also bearing witness, and their thoughts the mean while accusing or else excusing one another.)[70]

Compliance with the law of God, on this account, does not require any prior knowledge of rules or texts – it can be achieved 'by nature'. But this is not a mere question of acting as you please: conscience and reasoning, of the kind Leonard is seen engaging in with Mr Benson, are crucial. The novel also suggests that, having once learned to be 'a law unto oneself', the sense of right and wrong becomes instinctive:

> The gentle, blessed mother, who had made her [ie Ruth's] childhood home holy ground, was in her very nature so far removed from any of earth's stains and temptations, that she seemed truly one of those
>
> Who ask not if Thine eye
>
> Be on them; who In love and truth,
>
> Where no misgiving is, rely
>
> Upon the genial sense of youth.
>
> In the Bensons' house there was the same unconsciousness of individual merit, the same absence of introspection and analysis of motive, as there had been in her mother; but it seemed that their lives were pure and good, not merely from a lovely and beautiful nature, but from some law, the obedience to which was, of itself, harmonious peace, and which governed them almost implicitly, and with as little questioning on their part, as the glorious stars which haste not, rest not, in their eternal obedience. This household had many failings: they were but human, and, with all their loving desire to bring their lives into harmony with the will of God, they often erred and fell short; but, somehow, the very errors and faults of one individual served to call out higher excellences in another, and so they re-acted upon each other, and the result of short discords was exceeding harmony and peace. But they had themselves no idea of the real state of things; they did not trouble themselves with marking their progress by self-examination.[71]

The narrator's perspective here betrays a certain lack of confidence, a hesitation. Ruth's mother and the Bensons are in some ways to be envied because, in addition

[69] *Oxford English Dictionary* (online ed) 'law', P.3.a.
[70] Romans 2.10-15.
[71] *Ruth* (n 1) 141–42.

to their lovely natures they obey the law like the stars 'obey' the laws of physics – it seems that no intervening mental process or conscious choice is required. In Wordsworth's 'Ode to Duty', from which the quotation in the passage is taken, the poet makes clear that he is not one of those 'Who do thy work, and know it not.'[72] The poet has a far more difficult relationship with Duty, which he addresses as a 'Stern Lawgiver'; but in the poem, as in Gaskell, there is a deliberate equivocation about whether duty requires a conscious awareness – duty is praised for preserving 'the Stars from wrong.' The concluding stanza, in which the poet commends himself to the 'guidance' of duty and asks for 'the confidence of reason' leaves the matter unresolved, and Gaskell's narrator shares that dilemma. It is as if there are two very different routes to 'the law' – the dogged, hard won, questioning analysis epitomised by Leonard, and the serene, unquestioning acceptance of everything epitomised by Ruth's mother and the Bensons.

The latter route is, perhaps, happier; it is certainly less strenuous; but the narrator's comment that the Bensons 'had no idea of the real state of things' strikes a troubling note. Is such blissful ignorance really the best way? And the full implications of the Bensons' approach comes through very shortly after Leonard has found out about Ruth's past:

> When his bedtime came, Mr Benson told him of the hour, although he feared that Leonard would have but another sorrowful crying of himself to sleep; but he was anxious to accustom the boy to cheerful movement within the limits of domestic law, and by no disobedience to it to weaken the power of glad submission to the Supreme; to begin the new life that lay before him, where strength to look up to God as the Lawgiver and Ruler of events would be pre-eminently required.[73]

The importance of a regular routine for young children, particularly after a disruptive event, needs no justification. But the justification offered – in which children's bedtimes are somehow interwoven with 'glad submission to the Supreme' links together mundane household rules with all world events as instances of following 'law'. There is something troubling about a world-view that does not distinguish between the two. It is, perhaps, even hinted at in Benson's own thoughts – namely, that in the same way that a child has to accept a parent's instruction to go to bed, people have to accept whatever happens to them as being determined by the 'Ruler of events'. The keyword here is 'submission'; submission is, perforce, unconditional, the subject has no power or agency. It is the attitude which Ruth brings to the many harshnesses and prejudices to which she is exposed, and which she teaches, by example, to Leonard. But here, again, the language of the narrative betrays that all is not well:

> Leonard was regaining some of his lost tenderness towards his mother; when they were alone he would throw himself on her neck and smother her with kisses, without any apparent cause for such a passionate impulse. If anyone was by, his manner was cold

[72] 'Ode to Duty' in W Wordsworth, *Selected Poems* (S Gill (ed), Penguin, 2004) 155.
[73] Gaskell, *Ruth* (n 1) 359.

> and reserved. The hopeful parts of his character were the determination evident in him to be a 'law unto himself,' and the serious thought which he gave to the formation of this law. There was an inclination in him to reason, especially and principally with Mr Benson, on the great questions of ethics which the majority of the world have settled long ago. But I do not think he ever so argued with his mother. Her lovely patience, and her humility, was earning its reward; and from her quiet piety, bearing sweetly the denial of her wishes – the refusal of her begging – the disgrace in which she lay, while others, less worthy, were employed – this, which perplexed him, and almost angered him at first, called out his reverence at last, and what she said he took for his law with proud humility; and thus softly, she was leading him up to God.[74]

Leonard seems to be being pulled apart. With Mr Benson he challenges everything; with Ruth, eventually, nothing. There is obviously a personal preference behind this, which belies the narrator's assurance that Leonard is simply working at developing his own law. It is also difficult to share the narrator's sense of progress: the condition of 'proud humility' which Leonard attains in relation to Ruth sounds more like a permanent state of instability and conflict than any kind of resolution. The narrator's insistently reassuring conclusion is not entirely credible.[75]

As if this were not problematic enough, there is Leonard's excessively passionate physical affection. The passage above suggests that such moments are initiated by Leonard, but a few pages earlier it has been Ruth who takes the lead:

> 'Kiss me, Leonard!' said she – 'kiss me, my darling, once more in the old way!' Leonard threw himself into her arms, and hugged her with all his force, and their lips clung together as in the kiss given to the dying.[76]

Nor is Leonard the only character in whom Ruth inspires such passionate feelings. Bellingham is captivated by her physicality;[77] we suspect that there is more to Bradshaw's gift-giving than mere respectful admiration; and in Bradshaw's daughter, Jemima, the feelings can be expressed without restraint. Here is the description of Ruth and Jemima's reconciliation:

> As Ruth sat, suddenly she was aware of a figure by her; she started up, and in the gloom of the apartment she recognized Jemima. In an instant they were in each other's arms – a long, fast embrace.
>
> 'Can you forgive me?' whispered Jemima in Ruth's ear.[78]

As Lansbury has observed, there is far more intensity and passion in this moment than in any of Jemima's dealings with her fiancé, Farquhar.[79] Ruth's irrepressible physical desirability exercises its own powerful magnetism in a way that the

[74] ibid 383–84.
[75] cf the comments by Lansbury (n 27) on the narrator in *Mary Barton*: 9, 25.
[76] Gaskell, *Ruth* (n 1) 343. See also B Crick, 'Mrs. Gaskell's *Ruth*: A Reconsideration' (1976) 9(2) *Mosaic: An Interdisciplinary Critical Journal* 85 at 101.
[77] Crick (n 75) at 95–96 makes a persuasive comparison with DH Lawrence.
[78] Gaskell, *Ruth* (n 1) 384–85.
[79] Lansbury (n 27) 76–77.

narrator can record, but not fully register; the characters who fall under its sway are submitting to another kind of inevitable law.

X

What makes *Ruth* such an interesting, and challenging, novel, is the sense of so many kinds of laws, ranging from the domestic to the divine, being in play at once. Law in the lawyer's sense of the word is merely one among many varieties; it can claim no presumptive authority or obedience, and its powers are relatively weak. Thus, the criminal law provides no deterrence of robbery, bribery or forgery; the law of contract is routinely breached with scarcely a second thought; the law on children born outside of marriage is obtuse. In purely legal terms, justice is systematically not done: Bellingham's bribery goes undetected, and he advances up the political ladder to become a member of government; Richard Bradshaw is never prosecuted for forgery, he escapes to a comfortable position in Glasgow; Mason is never threatened with criminal or civil proceedings for the treatment of her apprentices.

At the same time – and this is what makes the conclusion of *Ruth* so notoriously problematic[80] – it remains painfully unclear that *any* laws have been vindicated. Ruth dies after catching fever from Bellingham, whom she has insisted on nursing. Bellingham makes a full recovery, and is last seen walking away from the house where Ruth's corpse has been laid out – he is both unscathed and unrepentant. Benson has refused Bellingham's offer to pay for Leonard's upbringing, but we know by now that Benson and Bellingham have very different ideas about who is doing whom a favour in gift-giving transactions. Even Benson's faith that there is a 'Ruler of events' is challenged – at Ruth's funeral, on the spur of the moment, he puts aside his prepared sermon and reads, instead, from the Book of Revelations. We never learn what the sermon said, but it seems safe to assume that it would have touched on Ruth's life and virtues. Putting aside the sermon suggests that Benson cannot make sense of her life, cannot explain it by reference to a divine plan: the governing law cannot be understood, it can only be presupposed as an act of faith. In a book replete with so many laws this is a profoundly unsettling note to end on.

[80] See eg N Auerbach, 'The Rise of the Fallen Woman' (1980) 35(1) *Nineteenth Century Fiction* 29, 40: 'the ending's abrupt reversal'; P Parker, '"The Power of Giving": Elizabeth Gaskell's *Ruth* and the Politics of Benevolence' (1999) 13 *Gaskell Society Journal* 54, 66 – 'difficult to interpret the novel's ending'; E Wright, *Mrs. Gaskell The Basis for Reassessment* (Oxford University Press, 1965) 71, n 40: 'The death of Ruth is an uneasy gesture – the melodrama and style reveal it – to public and social convention.' Contrast SA Malton, 'Illicit Inscriptions: Reframing Forgery in Elizabeth Gaskell's *Ruth*' (2005) 33(1) *Victorian Literature and Culture* 187 at 198, who interprets Ruth's death as 'Gaskell's telling re-assignment of the forger's sentence of death.'

4

North and South

the real true law business

I

As its title immediately announces, *North and South* is a novel about opposites. Its central narrative arc follows Margaret Hale as, with her parents, she is uprooted from her home in the New Forest and moves to 'Milton-Northern, in Darkshire', Gaskell's thinly-disguised Manchester. The shock of the change, and Margaret's struggles with her new environment, generate much of the novel's drama and development of character. It would be possible to see the novel as being, simply, about the contrast between the ways of life in the north and south of England; and to see the happy ending – where Margaret accepts a marriage proposal from a Milton cotton manufacturer – as a symbolic resolution of those contrasts.

That this simplistic interpretation is inadequate almost goes without saying: *North and South* is far richer, and more complex. What is, perhaps, less obvious, is that the novel resists such an interpretation right from the start.[1] The story begins not with Margaret in the New Forest, but with Margaret in London, at the home of her aunt Shaw and cousin Edith. Edith is about to marry an army officer, who is stationed on Corfu, and some of the conversation revolves around the differences between life in England and life in the Mediterranean. For a moment Gaskell allows us to wonder whether her 'South' might be Greece. The introduction of Indian shawls, a gift from aunt Shaw's late husband, who was a general, widens the geographical frame further south and eastwards, only for it to narrow as Margaret returns to her parents' home in Helstone, in the New Forest. We still do not know which South, if any of these, is the South of the title.

The North is only slightly more defined. Margaret's father's abrupt decision that he must leave Helstone, and his impulse to go somewhere that will not remind him of the New Forest, takes the family to Milton. But not immediately. First they stay at Heston, a charming seaside town twenty miles from Milton. The town is characterised by 'a Scotch word … "purposelike"', and contrasted with similar places on 'the

[1] A Shelston, 'Preface' in E Gaskell, *North and South* (A Shelston (ed), Norton, 2005) xi – 'a much wider and thus more suggestive frame of geographical reference than its title implies.'

continent'.[2] There is a delightful playfulness about this. Mr. Hale is trying to forget Helstone by escaping to a place with almost the same name. Is Heston dramatically different to the south? Is it, even, 'the North'? Gaskell's geographical markers place it between Scotland and France. We seem to be reading *Middle and Middle*.

For geography to offer so little elucidation of *North and South* seems puzzling, at least initially. As the novel unfolds it becomes clearer that 'North' and 'South' are to be sharply contrasted; indeed, that that is the point of those terms.[3] They are not so much opposites as oppositions, with 'the North' defining itself against 'the South', and vice versa. It is not a matter of geography, but of attitudes and values, in which characters identify themselves against what they, usually ignorantly, imagine to be the properties of the unfavoured term. *You* are either North or South. That is the dominant distinction with which the characters have to grapple, but by no means the only one. Examples of distinctions closely related to North and South include those between urban and rural, manufacturing and agricultural (seen not merely as descriptions, but as endorsements of a way of life). Then there are more socially nuanced demarcations, the centrality of which Gaskell highlights by making them titles of chapters: 'Masters and Men', 'Men and Gentlemen', etc.

II

In this world of stark oppositions and choices, law is central. Indeed, it is law that sets the entire plot in motion, since it is Mr. Hale's inability to bring himself to subscribe to the Thirty-Nine Articles of the Church of England that drives him to renounce his parish living in Helstone. This requirement to subscribe had been introduced by the Act of Uniformity 1662. Hale's 'doubts', the details of which are never given, but which relate only to the Church of England – his Christian faith remains intact – prevent him from being able to sign conscientiously when offered a better position; this crisis of conscience makes him feel that his current position within the Church (in respect of which he had subscribed, conscientiously, decades earlier) has now become untenable. Hale accepts the consequences, distressing as those consequences are; and to the end of his life, he remains convinced that he has acted rightly. But this straightforward, uncompromising and uncompromised interaction with the law stands out in the novel as exceptional.

The reactions to Hale's decision indicate that his interpretation of what the law demanded of him was not inevitable. Mrs Hale's indignant declaration that she would have 'nipped [his doubts] in the bud' is not a boast about her theological expertise, but an appeal to allow more personal duties and obligations to prevail.[4]

[2] Gaskell, *North and South* (n 1) 54.
[3] Shelston (n 1) xi. P Ingham, 'Introduction' to E Gaskell, *North and South* (P Ingham (ed), Penguin, 2009) xiii.
[4] *North and South* (n 1) 43.

It is perhaps no more than we might expect from a rather weak and self-centred character, whose judgement may also be distorted by serious illness. That said, far stronger and more powerful characters are seen bending the law for reasons of personal loyalty, as we shall see later.

The response of Henry Lennox is particularly interesting, for Henry Lennox is an archetypical Gaskellian lawyer: clear-sighted, analytical, intelligent and worldly. His view of Hale's decision is not given until long after the event, in a conversation with Hale's old friend, Mr. Bell:[5]

> Perhaps I have been wrongly informed. But I have been told, by his successor in the living – a clever, sensible man, and a thoroughly active clergyman – that there was no call upon Mr. Hale to do what he did, relinquish the living, and throw himself and his family on the tender mercies of private teaching in a manufacturing town; the bishop had offered him another living, it is true, but if he had come to entertain certain doubts, he could have remained where he was, and so had no occasion to resign. But the truth is, these country clergymen live such isolated lives – isolated, I mean, from all intercourse with men of equal cultivation with themselves, by whose minds they might regulate their own, and discover when they were going either too fast or too slow – that they are very apt to disturb themselves with imaginary doubts as to the articles of faith, and throw up certain opportunities of doing good for very uncertain fancies of their own.

Bell takes this badly, and Lennox initially makes matters worse by describing Hale as having a 'morbid state of conscience'. Once Lennox realises that Bell is annoyed, and with a characteristically lawyerly indifference to a point on which nothing (for Lennox) turns, he makes amends with the following speech:[6]

> To be sure, there is something fine in a man of Mr. Hale's age leaving his home of twenty years, and giving up all settled habits, for an idea which was probably erroneous – but that does not matter – an intangible thought. One cannot help admiring him, with a mixture of pity in one's admiration, something like what one feels for Don Quixote.

But for the narrator's assurance that Bell was mollified, we would surely doubt whether the comparison of Mr Hale with Don Quixote could be a flattering one; and the fact that Bell is mollified is quite revealing of Bell's view of his friend's actions.

For Lennox, where Mr. Hale has gone wrong has been to confuse legal formality with moral substance. Lennox's view of the case is simple. On taking up his post in Helstone, Hale had duly signed the Articles; it was irrelevant to the continued validity of that first appointment that he had later felt unable to subscribe anew, in relation to a different post. Lennox's position, we should notice, is not a purely technical or legalistic one. The determination of what the law requires is not a relatively straightforward question of ascertaining the meaning of a written rule, or following a process of logical reasoning – that has been precisely Mr Hale's mistake. The literal meaning, and its obvious implications, should, on Lennox's approach,

[5] ibid 345–46.
[6] ibid 346.

give way if they are contrary to the consensus of like-minded people about what is appropriate in the circumstances; there should also be some assessment of the inevitable costs of interpreting the rule literally, so as to prioritise doing good. It is striking that these essentially non-legal arguments about the importance of the law yielding, and allowing accommodations in its application, should be given to the novel's only lawyer character, whom we might have expected to say that the law simply has to be observed.

It is also important to register that, in adopting the position that he does, Lennox cannot be dismissed as a different kind of lawyer stereotype – the kind of legal practitioner with no integrity, and an endless readiness to manipulate the law in the most self-serving way for his clients. Gaskell refuses us that easy way out: Lennox is not arguing, and never will argue, Mr Hale's case. Perhaps more importantly, Lennox presents himself as echoing the analysis of the current vicar of Helstone, a man whom, we later discover, is in many ways unlikeably zealous. For this man to feel that Mr Hale's conduct in resigning the living was excessive perhaps hints at an ability on the new vicar's part to compartmentalise and be selective about the requirements of conscience; at the very least, it shows Mr. Hale to have been acting very much by his own standards.

Convicting and punishing oneself by one's own standards is emphatically presented as nothing to be admired. Mr Bell's finding consolation in the thought that his friend was Quixotic is almost more damning than Lennox's earlier critique, for it gives us the sense of Mr Hale as a fundamentally deluded idealist, hopelessly lost in his own world of unattainable and anachronistic values. This, for Bell, is the *best* that can now be said of him. We almost need to remind ourselves of what Hale has done: he has regarded his subscription to the Thirty-Nine Articles as a continuing public profession of his acceptance of those Articles. Was this really so naïve? It tells us much about the world of *North and South* that the resounding answer is 'Yes'.

III

Lennox's attitude is not personal to Hale, or specific to Hale's situation. As his conversation with Margaret in the very first chapter of the novel makes clear, it is a worldview. Margaret has been musing on whether all the frenetic preparations for Edith's wedding were really necessary, and whether 'there might not rather be a calm and peaceful time before [a wedding]'. Lennox may well have been involved in the legal preparations (his brother is the bridegroom): he has arrived late, and remarks, when he finds the ladies looking at Edith's Indian shawls, that 'I suppose you are all in the depths of business – ladies' business, I mean. Very different to my business, which is the real true law business. Playing with shawls is very different to drawing up settlements.'[7] His reply to Margaret's observations about wedding

[7] ibid 12.

preparations is that 'There are forms and ceremonies to be gone through, not so much to satisfy oneself, as to stop the world's mouth, without which stoppage there would be very little satisfaction in life.'[8]

These two short speeches say so much. As it happens, Lennox has stumbled upon a scene in which the women are in fact engaging in the law's 'true business', for Mrs Shaw is busy handing down these very valuable shawls to her daughter, under the envious gaze of the guests. Whether the 'true business' of the law is to assure the transmission of inherited wealth hangs over the novel almost mockingly. Certainly the law's one unqualified success in the plot is to effect such a transmission when Margaret inherits from Mr Bell. At other, crucial moments the law is impotent, absent, intrusive or damaging.

Lennox's second speech is the key to his character. He is ready to conform, to comply with forms, but with a clear understanding that he does so only so as to neutralise unwanted social consequences. There is both a deference to, and condescending contempt for, the prosaic judgments of others; these conflicting attitudes can co-exist only by divorcing form from content. Complying with requirements of form is, of course, a classically lawyerly approach, and an entirely appropriate attitude to bring to the drafting of legal documents like settlements. But Lennox's speech shows the dangers of applying the same attitude to life: the radical splitting of form and content generates falsity. The empty formalities of Edith and her aunt's circle, with its 'neighbours whom Mrs. Shaw called friends, because she happened to dine with them more frequently than with other people'[9] show where Lennox's worldview logically leads.

IV

When Margaret reaches Milton there is an immediate contrast with London and Helstone: for the first time, she sees factories puffing out thick smoke. She registers the visual and environmental change immediately. But the smoking chimneys also exemplify a dramatically different attitude to law, for this is '"unparliamentary" smoke'. Although our first glimpse of Milton is focalised through Margaret, she cannot possibly know that the smoke is being emitted in breach of a statutory provision – she does not even know that there *is* smoke in Milton, having initially assumed that the cloud she could see meant it might rain. 'Unparliamentary', she will later learn, is Milton's slighting usage; the proleptic use of the term signals its importance – we are to appreciate what kind of smoke this is before Margaret can realise it.

'Unparliamentary' is an extraordinarily resonant adjective. Its most common usage is in relation to speech in Parliament: 'unparliamentary language' is the use

[8] ibid 12–13.
[9] ibid 8.

of words which breach Parliamentary conventions of dignity and respect. In this sense, the smoke might be seen as ill-mannered and crass. Conversely, the rules on unparliamentary language can be seen as requiring those subject to them to suppress the truth and to speak in euphemisms. Taken in this sense, the unparliamentary smoke seems forthright and unpretentious. There is no place here, it seems, for the purely formal compliance with inconvenient rules that we associate with Henry Lennox. Bearing in mind Mr Hale's recent, painful inability to subscribe to the Articles imposed by Act of Parliament, the unparliamentary smoke strikes a contrast between Hale's embarrassed retreat and the Milton manufacturers' unapologetic flouting of the law. Gaskell may, here, have had in the back of her mind Joseph Priestley's famous rebuke that the post-1662 Church of England was a 'Parliamentary religion.'[10] But most forcefully, 'unparliamentary' is a direct, mocking challenge to authority. Parliament may have said that this smoke should not be emitted; what of it? The word rejects not just the specific statutory provision, but all statutes; to say that the smoke is 'unparliamentary' rather than 'illegal' is to deny *all* Parliamentary sovereignty. These are the conditions for civil war – and a further sense of 'unparliamentary' casts the cotton-lords as Royalists confronting the Parliamentarians in the English Civil War. Glancing references to the 'Rump' Parliament, and to Cromwell elsewhere in the novel suggest that the War was not far from Gaskell's thoughts.[11]

In the later chapter where Thornton visits the Hales and expounds the Milton manufacturers' attitudes, there are echoes of these different senses of 'unparliamentary'.[12] To Mrs Hale, and perhaps also to Margaret, the smoke is a pollutant, which soils their clean muslin blinds. Thornton himself feels that it needs to apology; indeed, he takes pride in it as a symbol of Milton's disobedience of Parliament. As the dialogue continues, Thornton relates anecdotes about the early cotton-lords' sense of entitlement and abuse of their power. Thornton intends these anecdotes to illustrate that Milton is progressing towards more equal relations between masters, workers, and buyers, and we have no reason to doubt Thornton's word when he says that he would never refuse to see a customer in the way that earlier cotton-lords apparently did. But it is hardly a stark contrast: power, assertiveness and disdain for perceived social inferiors are as much hallmarks of the current generation of Milton manufacturers as they were of their predecessors. It is ironic that Thornton expresses contempt for the 'aristocratic' ways of the south – an attitude he seems to have derived not from personal experience but from his mother; for 'aristocratic' perfectly describes both the mindset and actions of the Milton manufacturers.[13]

[10] A Easson, 'Mr Hale's Doubts in *North and South*' (1980) 31 *Review of English Studies, New Series* 30, 33.

[11] Gaskell, *North and South* (n 1) 43, 113–14. S Markovits, '*North and South*, East and West: Elizabeth Gaskell, the Crimean War, and the Condition of England' (2005) 59(4) *Nineteenth Century Literature* 463, 475.

[12] Gaskell, *North and South* (n 1) Vol 1, Ch X.

[13] ibid 72.

The dialogue in this chapter also begins to sketch out how legal rules interact with other norms, values and priorities in Milton. Thornton strikes the keynote when he says 'we are bidden by parliament to burn our own smoke; so I suppose, like good little children, we shall do as we are bid – some time.'[14] 'Good little children' would, of course, obey immediately. Gaskell tells us that Thornton is smiling as he speaks – 'some time' is a little joke, and 'little children' a light-hearted description. But as the discussion progresses, the underlying seriousness and resentment of Thornton's position becomes clearer. He speaks of 'parliament' (with a lower-case 'p') having 'meddled' with the smoke, and makes the same imputation about its involvement in labour relations: 'a meddler with only a smattering of the knowledge of the real facts of the case, even though that meddler be called the High Court of Parliament.'[15] We do not know which statutory provisions Thornton has in mind here, and the point is never returned to. The most plausible candidates would be the Factories Acts of 1833 and 1844, which limited factory working hours and imposed obligations on mill-owners to fence machinery.[16] It is worth pausing here for a moment to register the significance of Thornton's dismissal of these statutes as ill-informed, impertinent interference. If Parliamentary intervention is illegitimate when it aims to protect life and health, there simply is no place for statute law here at all.

Thornton presents himself as speaking for Milton manufacturers in general. But it becomes clear that he is exceptional. His chimneys do not breach the law because he has had them altered, prior – he is at pains to explain – to 'the act' being passed. He gives as the reason that the altered chimneys save money by consuming less coal; that might well be true, although it is noticeable that other manufacturers have not made the same calculation. If he had not already made the changes, Thornton tells us that he would have hesitated to do so, despite the economic incentive:[17]

> I'm not sure whether I should have done it, if I had waited until the act was passed. At any rate, I should have waited to be legally informed against and fined, and given all the trouble in yielding I legally could. But all laws which depend for their enforcement upon informers and fines, become inert from the odiousness of the machinery. I doubt there has been a chimney in Milton informed against for five years past, although some are constantly sending out one-third of their coal in what is here called unparliamentary smoke.

This is a remarkable statement: he would rather forego the financial benefits of alteration than submit to a statutory requirement. The only thing that counts here is mastery; and exploiting the law's ineffectiveness and dilatoriness is part of that struggle for supremacy. Law is, on principle, to be resisted.

[14] ibid 76.
[15] ibid 78.
[16] W Cornish et al, *Law and Society in England 1750–1950*, 2nd edn (Hart Publishing, 2019) 295.
[17] Gaskell, *North and South* (n 1) 76.

Thornton's confident dismissal of law for its lack of effective machinery will be borne out by the novel's events. There are two would-be informants, Boucher and Leonards. After the failure of the strike, for which Boucher is culpable, he offers the mill-owners any information he has about the workers' organisation. Boucher's offer is spurned, and he commits suicide after failing to find work.[18] Leonards is the least attractive character in the book – a drunkard and all-round disgrace, he recognises Frederick Hale and tries to apprehend him in order to claim the reward offered by the authorities for his capture. Frederick shakes Leonards off, causing him to fall; the fall may, or may not, contribute to Leonards' death shortly afterwards, but no one really cares. Thornton has the inquest called off to save Margaret from public embarrassment, and when Mr. Bell is told, later, that Frederick may have accidentally killed a would-be informant, he comments 'How awkward.'[19] Mr Bell's valuation of Leonards' life is also the novel's.

V

The dialogue concludes with Thornton explaining how people should be left to get on without Parliamentary 'meddling'. His view, essentially, is that the 'battle' should be left to play itself out between masters and workers. 'Every one who rules himself to decency and sobriety of conduct, and attention to his duties, comes over to our ranks', he says, while sensual, self-indulgent people remain antagonists. If there are any rules to be obeyed by the combatants, Thornton does not mention them – he seems to envisage, and relish, the prospect of direct, unmediated conflict. Nor is this idea of war out of place for its time – it would not be until 1864 that the first Geneva Convention, which made provision for the wounded and non-combatants, was agreed.[20]

Margaret does not realise it, but she has already glimpsed a tell-tale sign of the war of attrition between masters and workers in Heston. There she notices that fashions are different to the South. 'There were no smock-frocks, even among the country-folk; they retarded motion, and were apt to catch on machinery, and so the habit of wearing them had died out.'[21] It is a nice touch to have Margaret, as someone new to the area, relegate the aptness to catch on machinery to second place, for the tendency of women's loose garments to become entangled in machinery, dragging their wearers to serious injury and death was one of the most notorious dangers of factory work. The first factory safety legislation required the fencing of machinery in an attempt to reduce the risks, but systematic enforcement was

[18] ibid vol II, ch XI.
[19] ibid 360.
[20] Convention for the Amelioration of the Condition of the Wounded in Armies in the Field. Geneva, 22 August 1864. Available at ihl-databases.icrc.org/en/ihl-treaties/gc-1864?activeTab=.
[21] Gaskell, *North and South* (n 1) 54.

impracticable given the factory inspectorate's limited resources.[22] To say, then, that machinery has caused the wearing of smock-frocks to 'die out' is rather more than the flat, clichéd metaphor it might first appear; it is, unhappily, gruesomely accurate.

When Margaret happens to meet Bessy Higgins shortly after her arrival in Milton, there is no need for a subtle interpretation of signs. The stark truth of Bessy's situation is that she is only 19 years old and terminally ill with a lung disease she has contracted through working in the carding-room of a cotton mill. Shortly before her death she gives Margaret an account of her working life, from which it emerges that her chances of avoiding illness would have been boosted by the installation of a large ventilation wheel. Some factories had these wheels, but, Bessy explains, 'father was afeard of letting me go to a strange place, for though yo' would not think it now, many a one then used to call me a gradely lass enough.'[23] This is a disturbing detail, hinting at dangers of assault or worse; because of this risk, Bessy chooses to remain at her unventilated workplace. Bessy's explanation of why no ventilation was installed makes depressing reading. Employers were reluctant to incur the expense. Workers complained that, without the cotton particles to inhale, they felt hungry – and demanded a higher wage than their colleagues in unventilated mills. 'Between masters and men', as Bessy puts it, 'th' wheels fall through.'[24]

Gaskell refrains from giving judgement in Bessy's case,[25] but the facts speak for themselves. Within the structure of *North and South* the most immediate significance of Bessy's story is that it falsifies Thornton's complacent vision of a world without meddlers, in which people of prudence and ability naturally rise to the top, while those lacking self-discipline deservedly suffer. Bessy's suffering is patently undeserved. At a broader level, Bessy's case is an indictment of the law itself. The criminal law seems to offer no real deterrent to the men who might be tempted to molest a pretty young woman like Bessy; it is that knowledge which forces her to continue working in the differently dangerous environment of the unventilated mill. Effective safety legislation seems to be notable by its absence, and even tort liability would be doubtful. The duty of care only requires 'reasonable care'; it does not mandate that the highest standards of protection are offered; nor can there be a successful negligence claim where the claimant has consented to the risk of injury.[26] Bessy's potential claim might fail for any of these reasons, which, in itself, challenges and problematises these legal platitudes. But perhaps the most eloquent criticism here is the silence. In a novel preoccupied with law-breaking,

[22] Factories Act 1844, discussed in Cornish et al (n 16) 488–89.

[23] Gaskell, *North and South* (n 1) 94.

[24] ibid.

[25] M Debrabant, 'Smoke or no Smoke? Questions of Perspective in *North and South*' (2010) 71 *Printemps, Cahiers victoriens et édouardiens* 75, para 20 – 'There is no schematic denunciation of negligence …'.

[26] For the classic definition of the standard of care in negligence, laid down shortly after the publication of *North and South*, see *Blyth v The Company of Proprietors of the Birmingham Waterworks* (1856) 11 Exch 781, 784. For consent to risk see W Cornish et al, *Law and Society* (n 16) 472–73, particularly the comments of Bramwell B in *Dynen v Leach* (1857) 26 LJ Ex 221 quoted at 473.

no-one suggests that Bessy can, should, or even ought to, have a claim. Nor, despite Bessy being the daughter of a union official, is there ever the slightest suggestion that the union should take this question up and campaign to have the law changed – there is only ever one question for the union, which is the level of wages. What happens to Bessy, it seems, is none of the law's business.

VI

Thornton has put himself forward, slightly reluctantly, it is true, as an exemplar of successful prudence, and it is to Thornton's dealings with the law that we now turn. Though we do not realise it at the time, Thornton's account of his early life provides an illustration of his peculiar attitude to law. For, though Thornton rejects all Parliamentary intervention as illegitimate, he is not an anarchist. He chooses what to be bound by – his submission to his mother's household 'laws' being a comical example.[27] In his early life he worked as a draper's assistant, and, regulated by his mother, practiced strict economy so as to be able to save money despite providing for himself, his mother and his sister. This is as much as Thornton tells us. But we soon find out that the aim of this financial prudence, in which Thornton succeeded, was to settle in full debts owed by his late father.[28] There was no legal obligation on Thornton whatsoever – actions for debt lay only against the deceased's personal representatives (ie, his executors or administrators) and extended only to the deceased's assets.[29] Thornton here has chosen to go far beyond the law in assuming responsibility for another's liabilities.

The same thought-processes can be seen at the end of the novel, though the precise details of the transaction are different. Thornton's business is on the verge of failure; he is offered the chance to take part in a risky speculation, the profits from which would extricate him from his difficulties. Thornton, however, refuses. His explanation is that 'As I stand now, my creditors' money is safe – every farthing of it; but I don't know where to find my own – it may be all gone, and I am penniless at the moment. Therefore it is my creditors' money that I should risk.'[30] In saying this, Thornton is diverging from the legal position: it is not (yet) the creditors' money, it is merely a debt owed to those creditors. But, of course, Thornton is not making an elementary mistake in his legal analysis. On his own way of looking at things – which, so often with him, is the only way that counts – the money *is* the creditors', because he has the sum on hand and no genuine prospect of receiving its equivalent in the near future. Thornton would commit no legal wrong if he invested the money in the speculation; but he would do wrong by his own lights, which he cannot accept.

[27] See eg *North and South* (n 1) 73.
[28] ibid 80.
[29] J Chitty, *A Practical Treatise on the Law of Contracts Not Under Seal*, 5th edn by J Russell (Sweet, 1853) 7, 95, 245.
[30] ibid 384.

It is difficult to imagine that Henry Lennox would feel similar qualms, much less act on them, and the contrast suggests something striking and paradoxical about Gaskell's use of law. Thornton, the denier of Parliamentary sovereignty, is constrained far more inflexibly by his own personal code than by any legal rule; while for the lawyer the law is an externally imposed inconvenience requiring no more than apparent compliance for the sake of form. It is the lawyer who is the less rule-bound.

Thornton's personal code of financial responsibility is not, of course, the only instance of him laying down his own law. His position as master of a large mill brings with it the necessity of determining the terms on which he offers work to the operatives. In particular, he decides what conduct is punishable by fines (ie a deduction from wages), and in what amount. He seems to perform this role well: the small number of offences for which he legislates, and the transparent way in which he enforces them, earn the grudging respect of the workers, and are contrasted with the devious methods of other masters.[31]

More troubling situations arise when Thornton's own sense of what is right and his habit of making his own rules come into conflict with the law. A suggestion of the difficulties can be seen in the proceedings against the rioters in the aftermath of the strike. Our first account of these, focalised through Thornton, is brisk and businesslike:[32]

> Mr Thornton went straight and clear into all the interests of the following day. There was a slight demand for finished goods; and as it affected his branch of the trade, he took advantage of it, and drove hard bargains. He was sharp to the hour at the meeting of his brother magistrates, – giving them the best assistance of his strong sense, and his power of seeing consequences at a glance, and so coming to a rapid decision … The evidence against Boucher, and against other ring-leaders of the riot, was taken before him; that against the three others, for conspiracy, failed. But he sternly charged the police to be on the watch; for the swift right arm of the law should be in readiness to strike, as soon as they could prove a fault.

It is only if we pay very careful attention here that we realise that there has been a preliminary meeting of the magistrates followed by a court sitting, at which Thornton has presided. In the next chapter we discover that the brief account of the proceedings was significantly incomplete. Nicholas Higgins provides Margaret (and us) with the missing information:[33]

> now, when th'Union would ha' thanked [Thornton] for following up th' chase after Boucher, and them chaps as went right again our commands, it's Thornton who steps forrard and coolly says that, as strike's at an end, he, as party injured, doesn't want to press the charge again the rioters. I thought he'd had more pluck. I thought he'd ha' carried his

[31] ibid 124. For an example of an early, and exceptionally detailed, system of factory discipline (including fines) see N McKendrick, 'Josiah Wedgwood and Factory Discipline' (1961) 4 *Historical Journal* 30.

[32] *North and South* (n 1) 195–96.

[33] ibid 212–13.

> point and had his revenge in an open way; but says he (one in court telled me his very words) 'they are well known; they will find the natural punishment of their conduct, in the difficulty they will meet wi' in getting employment. That will be severe enough.'

What unites these two passages is that, for Thornton, his role as judge requires no adjustment to his everyday attitudes and actions. There is an alarming seamlessness to his dealing with his own business and the legal business, a sense that the enforcement of the criminal law is a matter of his own person discretion – he controls the machinery of justice as he does the machinery of his mill. Where this will lead us is his suppression of the inquest into Leonards' death.

VII

For Thornton, the circumstances of Leonards' death involve a collision of the painfully personal with his judicial responsibilities. Mrs. Hale is dying; she longs to see her son Frederick, who has lived in exile ever since his involvement in a mutiny. If Frederick is apprehended in England he will be court-martialled and almost certainly sentenced to death. Nonetheless, Frederick runs the risk and all goes well until he is about to leave Milton. He and Margaret decide that it is safer for him to travel from a remote station; while they are waiting for the train, Thornton rides past on horseback. He recognises Margaret, but not, of course, her brother; Thornton jumps to the conclusion that Frederick must be Margaret's lover. After Thornton has gone, Frederick and Margaret move to the station platform, where Leonards, a railway porter, recognises Frederick, and attempts to apprehend him. A struggle ensues, Leonards falls just as the train arrives, and Frederick escapes. Leonards consoles himself at a nearby public-house, where he has the idea of sending a telegraph to alert the authorities to Frederick's whereabouts. It is as he is hurrying to the telegraph office that he suffers the stroke from which he will die shortly afterwards. Thornton is the magistrate who is summoned to hear Leonards' death-bed statement. This is Thornton's summary: 'I went and heard some kind of rambling statement, which the clerk said was of no great use. I'm afraid he was a drunken fellow, though there is no doubt he came to his death by violence at last.'[34]

Thornton is speaking to a police inspector, Watson, who has been tasked with investigating Leonards' death. Watson has a good lead: witnesses of the scuffle between Leonards and Frederick have identified Margaret as the woman with them on the platform. Watson comes to question Margaret, and explains the reason for his call:[35]

> A man has died at the Infirmary, in consequence of a fall, received at Outwood station, between the hours of five and six on Thursday evening, the twenty-sixth instant. At the

[34] ibid 254.
[35] ibid 249.

> time, this fall did not seem of much consequence; but it was rendered fatal, the doctors say, by the presence of some internal complaint, and the man's own habit of drinking … It is supposed that an inquest will have to be held.

Margaret, desperate to baffle possible pursuit of Frederick, lies: 'I was not there', she says.

Her denial makes Watson uneasy, and somewhat nonplussed. Fortunately, it seems, for him, as he is leaving the Hales' house he meets Thornton. He explains his difficulty, seeking Thornton's guidance 'both as the magistrate who saw Leonards on his death-bed, and as the gentleman who got me my berth in the force.'[36] Thornton immediately realises that Margaret's denial was a lie.

His response is extraordinary:[37]

> There should be no inquest. He would save Margaret. He would take the responsibility of preventing the inquest, the issue of which, from the uncertainty of the medical testimony (which he had vaguely heard the night before, from the surgeon in attendance), could be but doubtful; the doctors had discovered an internal disease far advanced, and sure to prove fatal; they had stated that death might have been accelerated by the fall, or by the subsequent drinking and exposure to cold. If he had but known how Margaret would have become involved in the affair – if he had but foreseen that she would have stained her whiteness by a falsehood, he could have saved her by a word; for the question, of inquest or no inquest, had hung trembling in the balance only the night before.

Thornton instructs Watson to take no further steps, and to meet him that afternoon at Thornton's warehouse. In the event Thornton is unable (or, perhaps, unwilling – a vague, but pressing, appointment suddenly materialises) to meet Watson, but he leaves him the following note: 'There will be no inquest. Medical evidence not sufficient to justify it. Take no further steps. I have not seen the coroner; but I will take the responsibility.'[38] The episode draws to a close with Watson's reflections:[39]

> 'Well', thought Watson, 'it relieves me from an awkward job. None of my witnesses seemed certain of anything except the young woman. She was clear and distinct enough; the porter at the railroad had seen a scuffle; or when he found it was likely to bring him in as a witness, then it might not have been a scuffle, only a little larking; and Leonards might have jumped off the station platform himself.'

It is not only the porter who has reconsidered what he saw. Another witness had recognised Margaret from her being a customer at the shop where he worked. Of him, Watson observes to Margaret, 'At first the young man was so positive; and now he says that he doubted all along, and hopes that his mistake won't have occasioned you such annoyance as to lose their shop your custom.'[40]

[36] ibid 254.
[37] ibid 255.
[38] ibid 256.
[39] ibid.
[40] ibid.

The function of a coroner was, precisely, to investigate deaths where there was a reasonable suspicion that the deceased had met a violent end.[41] Quite plainly, Leonards' death meets this threshold. Gaskell's depiction of the law's failure here is as restrained as her treatment of Bessy Higgins, and as compelling. What makes it so powerful is her delicate delineation of a whole cluster of humdrum factors which combine to enable Thornton to accomplish his end.

To begin with the inspector. He is a diligent and attentive man, and pretty much knows that Margaret is lying to him, but he hesitates to say so. Margaret's regal demeanour and her vaguely genteel status make an allegation of lying inappropriate – the equivalent of unparliamentary language. All Watson can do is to raise the prospect of her having to repeat the denial at an inquest (where she would be under oath). When Thornton becomes involved, Watson owes him respect as a magistrate, and a sense of obligation for past assistance in his profession. Both aspects restrict Watson's freedom of investigative action. It is important here that Gaskell never (rudely) characterises Watson's actions as 'returning a favour'; the patronage and influence of Thornton is more insidious, pervasive and structuring than a simple *quid pro quo*. Nor has Watson been bribed; it is, in a way, worse than that – he does not need to be.

The way in which the witnesses' evidence melts away would be purely comical if it did not also soberingly show how little fidelity the law can count on. The railway porter who now thinks that Leonards may have jumped off the platform for fun at least seems to have no motive beyond wanting to avoid the inconvenience of having to give evidence at the inquest. For the grocer's assistant, Margaret's modest continuing custom is more important than telling the truth about how a person came by his death. The sheer pettiness of the financial gain, and the fact that it will only indirectly benefit an employee of the shop, illustrates precisely how highly the assistant values his legal obligations. If this is how ordinary people view the legal system, the outlook for it is bleak.

When, at the apex of that system, judges behave as Thornton does, and do not suffer for it, the picture of the legal system becomes profoundly disturbing. Whatever Thornton's view of the state of the evidence, he is suppressing a judicial investigation specifically designed for such cases; he also arrogates to himself a power that is the coroner's alone. When, in his note to Watson, he says 'I will take the responsibility', he of course means that the decision to stay the police investigation is being made on his authority, and that he, rather than Watson, will bear any consequences of that decision. But, the phrase can also be read a third way. If the emphasis is placed on 'will take', the phrase becomes an assertion of power, and 'take' can be read as 'take away': he will seize the power, which is rightfully the coroner's, to make the decision.

At the moment he makes his decision Thornton may genuinely believe that the medical evidence is conclusive, and that the fall played no part in Leonards' death

[41] P Polden, 'Coroners and their Courts' in W Cornish et al, *The Oxford History of the Laws of England Volume XI: 1820–1914 English Legal System* (Oxford University Press, 2010) 934, 944.

Gaskell's brilliant depiction of his psychological processes, however, leaves open – at the very least – the possibility that he is deliberately deceiving himself. Both Watson and Thornton (prior to his awareness of Margaret's involvement) are clear that the fall did contribute to the death. Watson, whose word we have no reason to doubt, tells Margaret that this is what 'the doctors say'.[42] Once Thornton realises that Margaret is implicated, he discovers doubts where none existed before. The 'medical testimony (which he had vaguely heard the night before, from the surgeon in attendance)' was now 'uncertain', the issue 'doubtful'. Gaskell's detail that he had only heard the medical evidence 'vaguely' is beautifully incriminating: there is no question here of Thornton carefully revisiting the medical evidence and discovering that it does not quite hang together as well as he had first thought. What he has seized on is the possibility of asserting that the medical evidence is doubtful, in order to force through his desired result. His regret that he had not known of Margaret's involvement earlier, for then he could have quashed all possibility of an inquest the night before, shows us what is really driving his decision-making.

We later learn that Thornton has been to see the surgeon before writing his note to Watson. The surgeon reportedly tells Thornton that 'there was an internal disease of long standing, caused by Leonards' habit of drinking to excess; that the fact of his becoming rapidly worse while in a state of intoxication, settled the question as to whether the last fatal attack was caused by excess drinking, or the fall.'[43] At first glance, the surgeon's statement seems to go some way towards vindicating Thornton's actions. On closer examination, however, the position is more troubling. Assuming that this report is completely accurate, it is very curious indeed that the surgeon is now prepared to be so categorical in his exclusion of the fall as a causal factor when, the previous evening, he had expressed the opposite view. He seems to have been replying to 'the question' of whether it was the drinking *or* the fall which caused the death; this was, of course, a question put to him by Thornton. The form of that question assumes a binary, mutual exclusivity of the fall and the drinking as causal factors; but everything we had heard up to this point suggested that both factors contributed in combination. In framing the question as he does, and forcing the surgeon to choose, Thornton extracts precisely the answer he was determined to obtain.

The theme that runs through Thornton's activities as a magistrate is that he recognises no boundaries between his public and private selves. It is impossible to describe him as 'performing' a 'role' as a judge – no adjustments are made, no care taken to exclude from his considerations factors which are legally irrelevant. While Henry Lennox is a little too much the lawyer, Thornton is no lawyer at all. What is truly remarkable is that Thornton sees no difficulty with this. When his business is on the verge of failure, he explains to his mother why he will not risk money he has allocated to paying his creditors: 'my peace of conscience should be gone!'.[44]

[42] ibid 249.
[43] ibid 283.
[44] ibid 384.

Yet there is never the slightest hint that Thornton's conscience is troubled by his activities as a magistrate. That can only be because he sees nothing wrong in what he has done; and that, in turn, shows us Thornton as someone who acknowledges no external limits of his power, no rule of law other than his own law.

VIII

On the face of it, Thornton's attitude to law contrasts sharply with his workers' attitude, especially during the strike. From the outset, the workers are mindful of their legal obligations – Thornton tells his mother that they are carrying out their existing contractual duties in full, it being (at that time) a criminal offence to refuse to perform a contract of labour.[45] The union is also insistent that, in observing the strike, the workers comply with the law. As Bessy Higgins explains to Margaret:[46]

> above all there was to be no going again the law of land. Folk would go with them if they saw them striving and starving wi' dumb patience; but if there was once any noise o'fighting and struggling – even wi' knobsticks [strike-breakers] – all was up, as they knew by th' experience of many, and many a time before.[47] They would try and get speech o' th' knobsticks, and coax 'em, and reason wi' em, and m'appen warn 'em off; but whatever came, the Committee charged all members o'th' Union to lie down and die, if need were, without striking a blow; and then they reckoned they were carrying th' public with them. And beside all that, Committee knew they were right in their demand, and they didn't want to have right all mixed up wi'wrong, till folk can't separate it, no more nor I can th' physic-powder from th' jelly yo' gave me to mix it in; jelly is much the biggest, but powder tastes it all through …

Bessy is speaking regretfully, when the strike has failed following the riot at Thornton's mill.

In considering the importance of law in the strike it is, of course, important not to confuse respect for the law with subjection to the power that lies behind it. Thornton's workers probably knew that he would prosecute them for breaking their contracts, and we are told that workers at other mills, where the owners are unlikely to bother with the expense of prosecutions, are already on strike.[48] Trade union activities were also significantly curtailed by statute, and the very restrained technique of furthering the strike reflects that.

[45] ibid 132. Masters and Servants Act 1823, discussed in Cornish et al (n 16) 282.
[46] Gaskell, *North and South* (n 1) 181–82.
[47] Although A Shelston's Norton Critical Edition (n 1) ends this sentence 'many; and many a time before', the semi-colon seems to be a mistake: it should be a comma. See E Gaskell, *North and South* (Chapman and Hall, 1855) vol I, 310, which is followed in the Penguin Classics edition by P Ingham (Penguin, 1995) 198, and the Oxford World's Classics edition by A Easson (Oxford University Press, 1998) 200.
[48] Gaskell, *North and South* (n 1) 132.

Bessy's image of the physic-powder in the jelly, however, seems to take us beyond mere compliance with the law for fear of the consequences of breach. She seems to be saying that illegality taints noble actions. It is a strikingly different view to anything we see elsewhere in the novel; the contrast with Frederick Hale, for instance, whose significance we will examine in the next section, is especially acute. It is also a somewhat problematic and unconvincing view – the strikers' chief 'weapons', it seems, are persuasion and a readiness to starve themselves and their families in the hope that their employers will succumb to financial pressure.[49] It is impossible to avoid the feeling that the strikers have more to lose. Even Bessy's simile seems unstable: the physic-powder is, after all, the medicine; if you want to be cured, you have to endure the nasty taste. The starving strikers' tactics seem to be being compared with eating jelly in the hope that it will cure an ailment. It seems futile. But Bessy's account is more subtle than this. The union is not relying on these tactics as having a direct impact upon employers; rather, they are hoping to carry 'th' public with them'. We are never told who this influential public might be. Later on, Nicholas Higgins refers to his dashed hopes that 'strangers far away' might help the workers and this is, perhaps, to be understood as a reference to Parliament.[50] But whoever this 'public' is, it makes us see Bessy's position in a different light. In an uncanny echo of Henry Lennox, she is saying that law is to be obeyed not for its own sake, but to make the right impression on others. The strike is a performance, and successful performances need to please the public. It is, surely, to satisfy the taste of this public that there must be no physic-powder in the jelly.

IX

There is one character in *North and South* who has made his choice not to comply with the law, and lives with the consequences. This is Frederick Hale – former naval officer and mutineer. Frederick has been prompted to mutiny by the tyrannical cruelty of a naval ship's captain, whose arbitrary and completely unnecessary mistreatment of the crew has caused a sailor's death. Frederick is a wanted man, and must live abroad, under an assumed name. As we have seen, his daring return to Milton provides one of the dramatic cruces of the novel, but he is not a mere melodramatic plot detail[51] – his conduct, and the law's response to it, occupies the thoughts of the Hale family and of Henry Lennox, providing yet another variation on the theme of law and legality.

Characteristically, it is Mr Hale who follows through the painful logic of Frederick's transgression when he says to Margaret that:[52]

[49] G Carnall, 'Dickens, Mrs. Gaskell and the Preston Strike' (1964) 8(1) *Victorian Studies* 31, 48.
[50] Gaskell, *North and South* (n 1) 210.
[51] cf E Wright, *Mrs Gaskell The Basis for Reassessment* (Oxford University Press, 1965) 143–44.
[52] Gaskell, *North and South* (n 1) 186.

> it is necessary, of course, for government to take very stringent measures for the repression of offences against authority, more particularly in the navy, where a commanding officer needs to be surrounded in his men's eyes with a vivid consciousness of all the power there is at home to back him, and take up his cause, and avenge any injuries offered to him, if need be. Ah! It is no matter to them how far their authorities have tyrannised, – galled hasty tempers to madness – or, if that can be any excuse afterwards, it is never allowed in the first instance; they spare no expense, they send out ships, – they scour the seas to lay hold of the offenders, – the lapse of years does not wash out the memory of the offence, – it is a fresh and vivid crime on the Admiralty books till it is blotted out by blood.

The other characters strive to escape from this inexorable logic. At first Mrs. Hale and Margaret can do little more than assure each other that they are 'prouder of Frederick standing up against injustice, than if he had simply been a good officer.'[53] They are all too aware that a court-martial of others involved in the mutiny has seen things very differently. During Frederick's visit to Milton, however, Margaret begins to explore whether Frederick's conviction by a court-martial would really be as inevitable as it appears. Frederick's immediate response is not encouraging:[54]

> In the first place, Margaret, who is to hunt up my witnesses? All of them are sailors, drafted off to other ships, except those whose evidence would go for very little, as they took part, or sympathised in the affair. In the next place, allow me to tell you, you don't know what a court-martial is, and consider it as an assembly where justice is administered, instead of what it really is – a court where authority weighs nine-tenths in the balance, and evidence forms only the other tenth. In such cases, evidence itself can hardly escape being influenced by the prestige of authority.

He is, however, persuaded to consult Henry Lennox – despite misgivings that 'Many a briefless barrister might twist his conscience into thinking, that he could earn a hundred pounds very easily by doing a good action – in giving me, a criminal, up to justice.'[55] Lennox is cautiously optimistic: 'there might be some chance of his acquittal, if he could but prove his statements by credible witnesses – that in such a case it might be worth while to stand his trial.'[56] Unfortunately, it transpires that the witnesses cannot be located, and Frederick ends the novel, as he began it, in exile.

As a matter of legal analysis it is difficult to pinpoint the legal basis on which Frederick's hopes rest. He was not defending himself, nor was he protecting others from an imminent threat. The hope, it seems, is that once the court-martial hears all the circumstances, it will exercise a residual discretion, and grant Frederick a merciful acquittal. This gives an additional echo to Frederick's characterisation of a court-martial as a place where 'authority' weighs so heavily: it is not only the

[53] ibid 100.
[54] ibid 237.
[55] ibid 237.
[56] ibid 260.

seniority of the officers sitting in judgment, but also the weight of legal precedent that is against him.

For a court-martial to act in the way that Margaret and Frederick hope for would be exceptional, not least because it would undermine the policy reasons explained so well by Mr. Hale for the rigorous punishment of mutiny. We are never told of any other such acquittals. Moreover, the Hales' hopes are juxtaposed (in the same chapters) with the fiasco of the Leonards inquest; the readiness of witnesses to evade appearing at that inquest hardly makes us optimistic about people coming forward to act as witnesses at a court-martial where they risk incriminating themselves. Indeed, had Gaskell brought about a fairy-tale acquittal for Frederick, it would surely have compromised her commitment to realism. For, notwithstanding Lennox's 'some chance', the prospect of a merciful acquittal was little more than a fantasy; perhaps Lennox imagines himself making his name by brilliant advocacy in defence of the brother of the woman he loves. But the stark reality of it is that here, for once, the law will not be put to one side or subverted.

How Frederick himself responds to this setback is illuminating. He writes Margaret an angry letter denouncing England and wishing that he could 'unnative' himself; but he is not devastated for long. He is living in Cadiz, in love, newly-married, wealthy and developing a taste for sherry. Little Spanish turns of phrase in his letters hint that he is adapting to his new home. He is very clearly not a tragic victim – his situation prompts Lennox to reflect (to himself) that he 'wished that he were as rich and prosperous as he believed he should be some day.'[57] Like many of Gaskell's sailor characters, Frederick has an admirable resilience, energy, adaptability and readiness to make the best of things. It says a lot about the role of law in *North and South* that the fugitive from justice has such an idyllically happy life to look forward to, and is envied by his lawyer. And ultimately Frederick seems to offer a key to many of the novel's puzzles, in which the characters are constantly being trapped into taking sides – whether it be between north and south, city and country, tradition and change. Frederick does not experience the world in this way – he travels the globe, feels at home 'wherever there is water under a plank', acclimatises.[58] He refuses to be made to choose, or to live other than by his own values; when other values are sought to be imposed upon him, he escapes. Of all the characters, he seems to offer the most attractive model of how to navigate between north and south.

[57] ibid 348.

[58] ibid 238. CA Martin, 'Gaskell, Darwin, and *North and South*' (1983) 15(2) *Studies in the Novel* 91, 99. J Sun-Joo Lee, 'The Return of the "Unnative": The Transnational Politics of Elizabeth Gaskell's *North and South*' (2007) 61(4) *Nineteenth Century Literature* 449.

5

Six Weeks at Heppenheim

A strange kind of paternal law

I

Six Weeks at Heppenheim is a delightful example of Gaskell's witty, ironical titles. The narrator, a young English traveller, does indeed spend six weeks in the German village of Heppenheim. But for at least half of that time he is unconscious, having collapsed on the day of his arrival with a serious illness.[1] He spends the second half of his stay recuperating, gradually regaining his strength and awareness of what is going on around him. The key dramatic events in the story unfold between characters at the inn over the course of the final fortnight of the narrator's stay; although, as with so much of Gaskell's shorter fiction, the events' significance and impact depend on far longer-term formative experiences.[2] 'Six Weeks', then, is not an entirely inappropriate time period to have chosen for a title, but it subtly asserts the narrator's control and importance in a work where the narrator goes to some effort to be self-effacing, and to assure us that he is a mere spectator of events. As we shall see, this equivocation about whether the narrator is also a subject structures the entire story.

'Heppenheim' is, at least, accurate. But, as with 'Six Weeks', its significance is rather less than we might infer from its prominence in the title. It is only at the very end of the story that the narrator is well enough to set foot outside the inn. Before that, the full extent of his engagement with his surroundings has been his enjoyment of a view of the inn's garden from an armchair. Heppenheim remains a rural setting, rather than an element of narrative centrality. Whatever else it is, this is definitely not a story about an exotic adventure.

If the title offers little by way of direction, the story itself seems littered with misleading and mistaken clues. On first arriving at the inn, as he is starting to fall ill, the narrator has supper brought to him by Thekla, a 'servant'. He later recalls (or, at least, *thinks* he recalls) a very vivid, attractive image of her by candle-light from that first evening. Is this, we wonder, a romance? Or, perhaps, a love

[1] E Gaskell, 'Six Weeks at Heppenheim' in E Gaskell, *A Dark Night's Work and Other Stories* (S Lewis (ed), Oxford University Press, 1992) 195 at 199.

[2] E Duthie, *The Themes of Elizabeth Gaskell* (Macmillan, 1980) 193.

triangle in which another lover is preferred to the narrator, since he has already told us he is a bystander? The narrator then falls into a long deep sleep, from which he is brought back to life by Thekla's patient nursing; we hardly need to remind ourselves of Gaskell's interest in fairytales to wonder if this might be a (parodic) variation of Sleeping Beauty.[3] As he is recovering, the narrator's conversations with Thekla involve the regular misapplication of narrative tropes. He wrongly presumes that her step-mother is wicked, that she has been seduced and abandoned, and incorrectly assumes that Thekla will be able to live happily ever after with her childhood sweetheart, when the fact is that the family business is bankrupt.[4] The narrator even casts himself as a kind of fairy godmother, imagining himself advancing money to Thekla to allow her to re-establish the business; but this never happens. We can, perhaps, flatter ourselves that we are less obtuse than the narrator, but the fact remains that this is a story which is revelling in subverting the rules.

II

As the story unfolds, we discover that *Six Weeks at Heppenheim* is, indeed, a romance, but an utterly unconventional one. Thekla has grown up in nearby Altenahr, and is the daughter of an innkeeper. Her family was on friendly terms with the Webers, who owned a neighbouring inn, and with whose son, Franz, Thekla has an affectionate childhood friendship which develops into love. She believes her love to be reciprocated, but Franz travels to gain experience in the hotel trade, and his letters to her become less encouraging, and more concerned with borrowing money to pay off his gambling debts. It is Thekla's habit of re-reading these troubling letters while she is watching the narrator during his illness that prompt the narrator's curiosity and involvement in the story. While Franz flits from inn to inn, Thekla becomes indispensable at the Half Moon in Heppenheim. She is, effectively, in charge, being constantly appealed to for information, help, or to mediate between the other servants and the innkeeper's irritable sister, Fraülein Müller. Thekla is also the main carer for the widowed innkeeper's children, particularly his two-year-old son, Max.

The first dramatic crisis in the story comes when Franz arrives unexpectedly in Heppenheim, offering to take Thekla back to Altenahr and marry her. The narrator decides to help Thekla financially, but only if he is satisfied that Franz is not 'an absolute good-for-nothing'.[5] As he is still convalescing, the narrator enlists the help of Fritz Müller, the inn's landlord, to investigate. Müller's report is damning: Franz

[3] See the openings of *North and South* and *Wives and Daughters* for examples of Gaskell's deliberate use of the sleeping beauty motif.

[4] Gaskell, 'Six Weeks at Heppenheim' (n 1) 205, 205–206, 213.

[5] ibid 214.

drinks too much, has no money, and boasts about his successes with women. Later the same day, Müller revisits the narrator. Now his tone has changed:

> One has perhaps no right to rule for another person's happiness. To have such a … woman as Thekla to love him ought to raise any man. Besides, I am no judge for him or for her. I have found out this morning that I love her myself, and so the end of it is, that if you, sir, who are so kind as to interest yourself in the matter, and if you think it is really her heart's desire to marry this man … I shall be very glad to go halves with you in any place for setting them up in the inn at Altenahr; only allow me to see that whatever money we advance is well and legally tied up, so it is secured to her.[6]

In the meantime, we then learn, Thekla has been to see the narrator too. She wants to know whether it is her duty to accept Franz, as she sees that she can help him. The narrator assures, and persuades, her that she has no such duty – indeed, he tells her that it would be sinful to marry Franz, as it would be 'doing evil that possible good may come.'[7]

Müller is quick to act. He finds Thekla hard at work in the kitchen, under the disapproving supervision of his sister, who has seen Thekla with the disreputable-looking Franz the day before. Müller seizes Thekla's hand and declares his love for her. Thekla manages to twist her hand free, but has to endure the sister's humiliating comments. 'And then [Thekla] went up, close to the angry Fräulein, and had said quite quietly, but with a manner of final determination which had evidently sunk deep into her suitor's heart, and depressed him into hopelessness, that the Fräulein had no need to disturb herself; that on this very day she had been thinking of marrying another man, and that her heart was not like a room to let, into which as one tenant went out another might enter.'[8]

Thekla decides to leave Heppenheim for good. It is only a sudden crisis in Max's health, where her care is crucial, that brings about a change of heart, and her acceptance of Müller's second proposal.

III

One of the most striking, and unusual, features of this unconventional romance is Gaskell's repeated – almost insistent – reference to law. It begins in the opening paragraph:

> After I left Oxford, I determined to spend some months in travel before settling down in life. My father had left me a few thousands, the income arising from which would be enough to provide for all the necessary requirements of a lawyer's education; such as lodgings in a quiet part of London, fees and payment to the distinguished barrister with whom I was to read; but there would be small surplus left for luxuries or amusements;

[6] ibid 216.
[7] ibid 217.
[8] ibid 219.

> and as I was rather in debt on leaving college, since I had forestalled my income, and the expenses of my travelling would have to be defrayed out of my capital, I determined that they should not exceed fifty pounds. As long as that sum would last me I would remain abroad; when it was spent my holiday would be over, and I would return and settle down somewhere in the neighbourhood of Russell Square, in order to be near Mr _'s chambers in Lincoln's Inn.[9]

Our narrator is destined to become a lawyer, although he hardly seems to be relishing the prospect. It is, perhaps, his looming legal career, along with his illness, that makes him unusually sensitive to legal restrictions, in particular when he is deprived of grapes:

> I asked [the Fräulein] if I could have some grapes, which had been provided for me on every day but this, and were especially grateful to my feverish palate. She was a good, kind woman, although, perhaps, her temper was not the best in the world; and she expressed the sincerest regret as she told me that there were no more in the house. Like an invalid I fretted at my wish not being granted, and spoke out.
>
> 'But Thekla told me the vintage was not till the fourteenth; and you have a vineyard close beyond the garden on the slope of the hill out there, have you not?'
>
> 'Yes; and grapes for the gathering. But perhaps the gentleman does not know our laws. Until the vintage – (the day of beginning the vintage is fixed by the Grand Duke, and advertised in the public papers) – until the vintage, all owners of vineyards may only go on two appointed days in every week to gather their grapes; on those two days (Tuesdays and Fridays this year) they must gather enough for the wants of their families; and if they do not reckon rightly, and gather short measure, why they have to go without. And these last two days the Half-Moon has been besieged with visitors, all of whom have asked for grapes. But tomorrow the gentleman can have as many as he will; it is the day for gathering them.'
>
> 'What a strange kind of paternal law', I grumbled out. 'Why is it so ordained? Is it to secure the owners against pilfering from their unfenced vineyards?'
>
> 'I am sure I cannot tell,' she replied. 'Country people in these villages have strange customs in many ways, as I daresay the English gentleman has perceived. If he would come to Worms he would see a different kind of life.'
>
> 'But not a view like this,' I replied, caught by a sudden change of light – some cloud passing away from the sun, or something. Right outside of the windows was, as I have so often said, the garden. Trained plum-trees with golden leaves, great bushes of purple Michaelmas daisy, late flowering roses, apple-trees partly stripped of their rosy fruit, but still with enough left on their boughs to require the props set to support the luxuriant burden; to the left an arbour covered over with honeysuckle and other sweet-smelling creepers – all bounded by a low grey stone wall which opened out upon the steep vineyard, that stretched up the hill beyond, one hill of a series rising higher and higher into the purple distance. 'Why is there a rope with a bunch of straw tied in it stretched across the opening of the garden into the vineyard?' I inquired, as my eye suddenly caught upon the object.

[9] ibid 195.

> 'It is the country way of showing that no one must pass along that path. Tomorrow the gentleman will see it removed; and then he shall have the grapes.[10]

A little later, in a conversation between the narrator and Fritz Müller, the subject is revisited:

> When is the vintage?' asked I. 'I hope it will take place soon, for I am growing so well and strong I fear I must leave you shortly; but I should like to see the vintage first.'
>
> 'Oh, never fear! you must not travel yet awhile; and Government has fixed the grape-gathering to begin on the fourteenth.'
>
> 'What a paternal Government! How does it know when the grapes will be ripe? Why cannot every man fix his own time for gathering his own grapes?'
>
> 'That has never been our way in Germany. There are people employed by the Government to examine the vines, and report when the grapes are ripe. It is necessary to make laws about it; for, as you must have seen, there is nothing but the fear of the law to protect our vineyards and fruit-trees; there are no enclosures along the Berg-Strasse, as you tell me you have in England; but, as people are only allowed to go into the vineyards on stated days, no one, under pretence of gathering his own produce, can stray into his neighbour's grounds and help himself, without some of the Duke's foresters seeing him.'
>
> 'Well,' said I, 'to each country its own laws.'[11]

This is the first and last time that we hear about a discussion of enclosure, but it seems safe to infer that the narrator was drawing a contrast between the open, German vineyards, and the fenced fields of an English enclosed system. The contrast depends, of course, upon the legal facilitation of enclosure, law shaping the English countryside just as it has done the view from the inn at Heppenheim. It seems almost cruel of Gaskell to have her aspiring lawyer be so slow to recognise the physical manifestations of a simple legal rule that has been explained to him seconds earlier; but the moment, as well as serving to remind us how far our narrator falls short of omniscience, marks a felt, somewhat jarring, intrusion of law into an otherwise idyllic, natural scene.

Gaskell never spells out why she gives such prominence to the German vintage laws. One obvious reason is dramatic: the climax of the story takes place against the backdrop of the festivities of the vintage, and the legal rules contribute to building the tension by explaining why all the grapes are being gathered on the same day. A further reason might be to add veracity and local colour.[12] Early nineteenth century German viticulture was increasingly focused on quality control, and from the 1830s wine ordinances stipulated for the separate harvesting of grapes of different ripenesses. Ripeness was scientifically determined by measuring must

[10] ibid 210–11.

[11] ibid 222.

[12] S Lewis, 'Introduction' in E Gaskell, *A Dark Night's Work and Other Stories* (S Lewis (ed), Oxford University Press, 1992) xiv. C Skrine (ed & tr), '*Six Weeks at Heppenheim* seen from Heppenheim' (1998) 12 *Gaskell Society Journal* 55.

weight – which is, essentially, the density of the grapes' juice.[13] Heppenheim was subject to these rules – a newspaper report of a wine-tasting at the 'Halber Mond' in 1835, for instance, observes that 'in our locality the vineyards will close on 24 October even in the case of those growers who would prefer to leave their grapes to hang rather longer. Any grower who acts contrary to this order issued by our 'vineyard police' will incur the appropriate penalty.'[14]

But dramatic impact and local colour fail to capture the sheer suggestiveness of the German laws, and the narrator's condemnation of them as 'strange' and 'paternal', in relation to Thekla's story. The sense that Gaskell is using these laws for more ambitious literary purposes is perhaps hinted at by the way she depicts their effects: while the newspaper report quoted above anticipated that growers might fail to comply with the law by leaving their grapes hanging, Gaskell emphasises the converse problem – perfect grapes which the law insists remain unharvested. The fixing by law of a date of ripeness, before which the grapes may not be gathered, seems to be in ironic counterpoint with the development of Thekla's feelings as, within the space of two tumultuous weeks, her long-standing love for Franz Weber is destroyed, and a new love takes its place. One can read the juxtaposition of the vintage laws and Thekla's experience as showing, wittily, that whatever the success of attempts to legislate for the ripeness of grapes, the course of love follows no such predictable trajectory – there, all metaphors of growth, maturity and ripeness are out of place.

The idea of 'strange' and 'paternal' law, however, also has a resonance in the story as a whole, which goes beyond its immediate application to Thekla's experiences, for all of the main characters are either subject to, or baffled by, such laws and rules. At the very beginning of the story, for instance, the narrator finds himself dismayed and repelled when he visits the area of London in which he has decided to live while reading for the Bar:

> I went to examine the streets in which I purposed to live; I had picked them out, from studying a map, as desirable; and so they were, if judged entirely by my reason; but their aspect was very depressing to one country-bred, and just fresh from the beautiful street-architecture of Oxford. The thought of living in such a monotonous grey district for years made me all the more anxious to prolong my holiday …[15]

The clash here between reason and desire is reproduced when the narrator tries to make sense of Thekla's being attracted to Franz Weber:

> From time to time I thought of Thekla and Franz Weber. She was the strong, good, helpful character, he the weak and vain; how strange it seemed that she should have cared for one so dissimilar; and then I remembered the various happy marriages when to an

[13] J Robinson (ed), *The Oxford Companion to Wine*, 4th edn (Oxford University Press, 2015) 318 (the entry on 'must weight' is at 489).

[14] Skrine (n 12) 56.

[15] Gaskell, 'Six Weeks at Heppenheim' (n 1) 195.

> outsider it seemed as if one was so inferior to the other that their union would have appeared a subject for despair if it had been looked at prospectively.[16]

The same vain appeal to reason as the governing law of attraction can be heard in Müller's complaint to the narrator (after Thekla has rejected his first proposal): 'Why cannot she like an honest man who likes her?'[17]

In all these instances the strangeness of a rational rule is felt, and rejected with little difficulty. More specifically paternal laws, however, are less easily resisted. We should begin with the story's opening paragraph (quoted above at pp 65–66). On a first reading it sounds as if our narrator is in control of his destiny, planning out his career and treating himself to a little holiday too. But his repulsion over the streets where he is to live, and his desire to avoid beginning his legal training for as long as possible, suggest a different interpretation. It is, surely, his father who has made these decisions about career and expenditure – a dead father who can never be persuaded to change his mind. The narrator's decision to spend £50 of his capital on the holiday is an act of rebellion against this paternal law. Indeed, it is tempting to regard the narrator's sudden collapse on his arrival at Heppenheim on his way 'home'[18] as, at least in part, a psychosomatic reaction to a future he dreads.

Thekla, too, feels the force of paternal expectation. Virtually the only thing we know about her father, apart from his occupation, is that he and Franz Weber's father have looked forward to Thekla and Franz marrying. When she asks the narrator if it is her duty to marry Franz, the narrator believes that she is driven by a sense of self-sacrifice; that is, of course, possible, but other senses of family duty are surely in play for Thekla. More importantly than her father's expectation, however, a strange paternal law controls Thekla's ability to respond to her feelings for Müller. The point comes through in two places. The first time is in Thekla's dignified response to Müller's first proposal: 'her heart was not like a room to let, into which as one tenant went out, another might enter.'[19] The second time is in the following exchange with the narrator:

> 'I know that your master wanted to marry you, and that you refused him. Do not deceive yourself. You are sorry for that refusal now?'
>
> She kept her serious look fixed upon me; but her face and throat reddened all over.
>
> 'No,' said she, at length; 'I am not sorry. What can you think I am made of; having loved one man ever since I was a little child until a fortnight ago, and now just as ready to love another? I know you do not rightly consider what you say, or I should take it as an insult.'

[16] ibid 208–209.
[17] ibid 221.
[18] ibid 196.
[19] ibid 219.

> 'You loved an ideal man; he disappointed you, and you clung to your remembrance of him. He came, and the reality dispelled all illusions.'
>
> 'I do not understand philosophy,' said she.[20]

Here Thekla is judging herself, as she knows the world will judge her, by standards of female propriety in love. The impassioned witticism about her heart not being like a room to let – with the hint of prostitution that such an arrangement would imply – invites the question: what, then, are the rules? Her dialogue with the narrator answers it: the requirements are of development, maturity, ripeness, constancy. Tellingly, she does not say to the narrator that she rejects Müller because she does not care for him; the problem is that she cannot (yet) be seen to care for him. Only once she and Müller have been (apparently) brought together by their love for Max in his life-threatening illness, is marriage to Müller legitimate.

These rules of propriety, by which Thekla is bound, are perhaps not explicitly identifiable as 'paternal' in the story, but they are very clearly gendered. Müller seems never to have thought of Thekla romantically until the day when the narrator sends him to check up on Franz Weber. Indeed, it seems to be Weber's suit that mimetically sparks off Müller's own desire for Thekla.[21] Müller allows his feelings to ripen and mature for all of a couple of hours before forcefully declaring his love. We never doubt Müller's sincerity – his is the passion of the sudden revelation of what has been in front of him all along; but the point is that this kind of demonstrative emotional spontaneity is forbidden to Thekla, and she knows it.

IV

If *Six Weeks at Heppenheim* revolves around its characters' struggles to come to terms with strange, paternal and unsatisfactory laws, what alternative rules does it propose? Thekla embodies an ethic of familial, maternal law – but in a special, and unusual sense. We see her acting like a family member or mother towards people with whom, as a matter of law, she has no family or blood relationship. She is technically a stranger to them. At times it can seem as if Gaskell is underlining the point that no language exists which is adequate to register this ethic. One of the unusual stylistic features of the story is that it occasionally reads like a very literal translation of a German original: thus, for example, we are told that the inn has an 'eating-room' (*Eßzimmer*),[22] that everyone was busy 'about the poor little Max' (*um den armen kleinen Max*),[23] and, in an attempt to render the familiar 'you' (*du*), 'Hast thou told our good friend?' which unintentionally transports

[20] ibid 223.
[21] On mimetic desire see R Girard, *Deceit, Desire and the Novel: Self and Other in Literary Structure* trans Y Freccero (Johns Hopkins University Press, 1966).
[22] ibid 196.
[23] ibid 229.

us to Yorkshire.[24] These moments can, perhaps, be simply explained away as the narrator gauchely showing off the knowledge of German of which he has boasted on the first page of the story. But the designations of Thekla are different. She is 'the maiden' or 'the house maiden',[25] which work as a literal translations of *Mädchen*, *Hausmädchen*, but also have other properties. Thekla is, of course, a maid, but she is also a 'maiden', with all that that meant for Gaskell – she is independent-minded, dignified, courageous, chaste.[26] Yet she is, in all but name, a mother – she hears little Max crying 'as quickly as if she was his mother'.[27] In the same way she is a 'servant' who manages relationships between Müller's sister and the staff; everyone seeks her help; she is even expected to remember where the sister has left her keys (!).[28] Mother-maiden, manager-maid – these apparently self-contradictory roles, which she performs completely naturally, and in which she is needed, wanted and loved, quietly defy orthodox categories, and are completely at odds with legal classifications, in which one half of each composite term would, necessarily, mutually exclude the other.

Thekla has found the kind of role that the narrator yearns for for himself. We learn at the very start of the story that his father has left him an inheritance, and a couple of pages later, after he wakes from his fever, he breaks down at the recollection that his mother and sister are also dead.[29] One of the first things he notices after waking from the fever is that his recovery gives Müller 'the truest pleasure … [and he] shook the hand of the doctor, in a pantomime expressive of as much thankfulness as if I had been his brother.'[30] He describes Thekla as caring for him like a sister; and tries to encourage Thekla to regard him as either a brother or, more desperately, a kind of mother.[31] His plan to help her financially seems to owe something to the fairy godmother, which is, of course, the quintessential quasi-familial relationship. Perhaps most strikingly, at the dramatic climax of the story, the narrator physically exerts himself to the full, saying 'this good family had treated me too much like one of their own for me not to do what I could in such a case as this.'[32] It is this journey to being accepted, to being part of a new family, that is the high point of the narrator's own story – and explains his wanting to write, not of his travels in Europe, but of (his own) six weeks at Heppenheim.

[24] ibid 231.
[25] ibid 196; 201.
[26] See, for instance, the attribution to Margaret Hale in *North and South* (A Shelston (ed), WW Norton & Company, 2005) of 'quiet maiden freedom' (59) and 'maiden pride' (173).
[27] Gaskell, 'Six Weeks at Heppenheim' (n 1) 220.
[28] See eg ibid 202, 220.
[29] ibid 199.
[30] ibid 198.
[31] ibid 204, 205, 206.
[32] ibid 228.

6

Tenancies: Flitting and 'The Squire's Story'

I

Relationships between landlords and tenants, and the ideas associated with such relationships, are a frequent and significant theme in Gaskell. We have already seen, in the previous chapter, how the idea of a tenancy of the heart brings to a climax the confrontation between Thekla and Fräulein Müller. This skilful integration of a legal concept for dramatic and literary effect is characteristic, as this chapter aims to show. We shall begin by looking at Gaskell's deployment of the idea of 'flitting' – ie, absconding to avoid paying rent due – and then move on to 'The Squire's Story', in which tenancy is a fundamental theme.

II

Two particularly striking uses of the idea of 'flitting' deserve attention. The first is in the chapter title of *North and South*, volume II, chapter XVIII: 'Margaret's Flittin''. The chapter deals with Margaret's departure from Milton after the death of her father, and Shelston comments that 'The term was usually used for working-class people who left their accommodations while still owing rent; Gaskell's application of it to Margaret here is thus jocular.'[1]

It is certainly true that there is nothing covert or hurried about Margaret's departure and, in that sense, hers is not a classic flitting. However, her father having died intestate, Margaret is his heir and executor. The tenancy of the house in Milton is not terminated by Hale's death – it continues, with the corresponding liability to pay rent, until its term expires, or the heir gives notice to end it.[2] The terms of the lease Hale has signed seem not to allow for early termination – hence Mr Bell's comment to Margaret that her 'Milton landlord has … defeated me after all.

[1] E Gaskell, *North and South* (A Shelston (ed), WW Norton & Company, 2005) 330.

[2] See eg JF Archbold, *The Law of Landlord and Tenant* (Shaw and Sons, 1846) 78. The point is made more emphatically in the later JM Lely (ed), *Woodfall's Law of Landlord and Tenant*, 14th edn (Sweet & Maxwell, 1889) vol 1, 379. It is still good law: *Youngmin v Heath* [1974] 1 WLR 135; Lord Justice Lewison et al, *Woodfall: Landlord and Tenant* (Sweet & Maxwell, 2024, looseleaf) vol 1 at 9.229.

He won't take the house off our hands till next June twelvemonth. Luckily, Mr. Thornton found a tenant for it.'[3] The legal sense of 'flitting' is not inapt here after all. But flitting also carries other overtones – of embarrassment, disappointed expectations, unfinished business, being in another's debt (as she is to Thornton for his suppression of the Leonards' inquest), which harmonise with the events in the story.

Gaskell had already exploited some of the possibilities of 'flitting' in 'Libbie Marsh's Three Eras', the opening section of which is subtitled 'Valentine's Day', and begins with this paragraph:

> Last November but one, there was a flitting in our neighbourhood; hardly a flitting, after all, for it was only a single person changing her place of abode from one lodging to another; and instead of a cartload of drawers and baskets, dressers and beds, with old king clock at the top of all, it was only one large wooden chest to be carried after the girl, who moved slowly and heavily along the streets, listless and depressed, more from the state of her mind than of her body. It was Libbie Marsh, who had been obliged to quit her room in Dean Street, because the acquaintances whom she had been living with were leaving Manchester.[4]

Much of the dramatic force here comes from the blunt allegation of wrongdoing being only partly erased by its retraction. Even though we know that Libbie is up to date with her rent, her removal still has the feel of a flitting. The implied comparison with a family's or wealthy person's possessions suggests material embarrassment, but the true source of pain, and shame, hinted at, mockingly, in the subtitle, is the absence of love. Libbie is not moving to join her family, or to start one – the hint of a sneer in 'single' reinforces the point. She has no one to love, or be loved by; nor is this some sudden crisis, for we are told that the removal has been necessitated by the choices of mere 'acquaintances'. Lacking these essential emotional connections, she has become a kind of shadow, a flitting ghost. Happily, as the story unfolds, her final removal results in her joining a kind of family.

III

One tenant who never gives his landlord the slightest cause for concern is Robinson Higgins in 'The Squire's Story'. Indeed, the landlord, like the inhabitants of the small town in which 'The White House' is situated, is only too pleased to welcome such an open-handed gentleman to take up residence. Higgins lives happily in Barford for many years, maintains a respectable establishment, marries the daughter of a local squire and funds his genteel, leisured lifestyle from the rents of his southern estates. But Higgins is also a murderer and a highwayman, whose crimes eventually catch up with him.

[3] Gaskell, *North and South* (n 1) 341.

[4] E Gaskell, 'Libbie Marsh's Three Eras' in *A Dark Night's Work and Other Stories* (S Lewis (ed), Oxford University Press, 1992) 167.

Gaskell's narrative perspective in this story is a subtle and complex one. The title, as so often in her shorter fiction, gives us little direction. There are only two squires in the story – Higgins' father-in-law and brother-in-law (who succeeds as squire at the end of the story), but neither is identified as the narrator. The story was first published in the Christmas edition of *Household Words* for 1853, under the general heading of 'Another Round of Stories by the Christmas Fire', and alongside other stories where the narrator is obviously named in the title (including Gaskell's 'The Scholar's Story', which begins with the scholar assuring the assembled company that he will not bore them with pedantic learning). Perhaps, then, as we know that the story takes place in the 1770s, we have to assume that the narrator of 'The Squire's Story' is a descendant of the squires mentioned in it. But, taken out of its *Household Words* context, 'The Squire's Story' is suggestive in a different way, as being the story of a man who played the part of a squire so well that everyone believed in him. It is the readiness to believe in Higgins as a squire that is the focus of Gaskell's interest.

In choosing to approach her subject-matter in this way, Gaskell was surely defining herself against two predecessors – Shakespeare and de Quincey. She quotes from *Macbeth* – without acknowledgement – when, having sketched the community of Barford, she adds 'to make the mixture thick and slab, you must add for yourselves the bustle, the mystery and importance which every little event either causes or assumes in a small town.'[5] De Quincey is not directly quoted, but an awareness of his work would have been almost unavoidable. Higgins is based on a real person who had lived at Knutsford, where Gaskell grew up. De Quincey had used Higgins' story in 'On Murder Considered as One of the Fine Arts', where he is 'the celebrated Lancashire highwayman, who concealed his profession for some time from his neighbours, by drawing woollen stockings over his horse's legs, and in that way muffling the clatter which he must else have made in riding up a flagged alley that led to his stable.'[6] The speaker delivering this lecture is disposed to attribute the notorious Ruscombe murder to the highwayman, which, by the inverted values of the Society of Connoisseurs of Murder (which he is addressing), is high praise indeed:

> however praiseworthy the case of Sir Edmondbury Godfrey may be [the lecturer has just called it 'the finest work of the 17th century'] … still I cannot consent to place it on a level with that of Mrs Ruscombe of Bristol, either as to originality of design, or boldness and breadth of style. This good lady's murder took place early in the reign of George III – a reign which was notoriously favourable to the arts generally. She lived in College Green, with a single maid-servant, neither of them having any pretension to the notice of history but what they derived from the great artist whose worksmanship I am recording. One fine morning, when all Bristol was alive and in motion, some suspicion

[5] E Gaskell, 'The Squire's Story' in E Gaskell, *Gothic Tales* (L Kranzler (ed) Penguin, 2000) 33 at 34. The quotation is from W Shakespeare, *Macbeth* IV, i, 32.

[6] T de Quincey, 'On Murder Considered as One of the Fine Arts' in T de Quincey, *On Murder* (R Morrison (ed), Oxford University Press, 2006) 8 at 25.

> arising, the neighbours forced an entrance into the house, and found Mrs Ruscombe murdered in her bed-room, and the servant murdered on the stairs; this was at noon; and, not more than two hours before, both mistress and servant had been seen alive. To the best of my remembrance, this was in 1764; upwards of sixty years, therefore, have now elapsed, and yet the artist is still undiscovered … no unpractised artist could have conceived so bold an idea as that of a noon-day murder in the heart of a great city.[7]

De Quincey's essay was published in *Blackwood's Magazine* in 1829. This was a periodical for which Gaskell had great (though not unconditional) affection, her father having been one of its first contributors, and it also being the location of her first published work.[8] De Quincey was a Manchester author, writing on a very local subject. Gaskell was also probably familiar with De Quincey's famous essay 'On the Knocking at the Gate in Macbeth'. There, in seeking to account for the powerful effect that the knocking at the castle gate has immediately after Macbeth has murdered Duncan, de Quincey observes that:

> Murder in ordinary cases, where the sympathy is wholly directed to the case of the murdered person, is an incident of coarse and vulgar horror; and for this reason – that it flings the interest exclusively upon the natural but ignoble instinct by which we cleave to life …; this instinct … because it annihilates all distinctions, and degrades the greatest of men to the level of 'the poor beetle we tread on,' exhibits human nature in its most abject and humiliating attitude. Such an attitude would little suit the purposes of the poet. What then must he do? He must throw the interest on the murderer: our sympathy must be with *him*; (of course I mean a sympathy of comprehension, sympathy by which we enter into his feelings, and are made to understand them, – not a sympathy of pity or approbation:) … in the murderer, such a murderer as the poet will condescend to, there must be raging some great storm of passion, – jealousy, ambition, vengeance, hatred, – which will create a hell within him; and into this hell we are to look.[9]

'The Squire's Story' can be read as a reaction to these ideas – it is the story of a murderer, yet it has no interest in the murder victim (who is, merely, a miserly old woman) and, unlike *Macbeth*, pays only the most cursory attention to the murderer's state of mind (he is rather careless in leaving behind an incriminating clue, and shaken in the crime's immediate aftermath). Nor does it dwell on the way that the crime is carried out, or detected. It is as if Gaskell responds to the claim about a poet's (and dramatist's) requirements by asserting the perspective of the novelist, in particular the novelist of social observation. It may, indeed, be that we can see the germ of her approach in a comment made by de Quincey's lecturer, who recounts a conversation with 'a Lancashire lady',

> who thereupon informed me, that she had herself lived in the neighbourhood of that highwayman, and well remembered two circumstances, which combined in the opinion of all his neighbours, to fix upon him the credit of Mrs Ruscombe's affair. One was, the

[7] ibid 24–25.

[8] E Gaskell, *The Letters of Mrs Gaskell* (JAV Chapple and A Pollard (eds), Manchester University Press, 1966) no 415 at 531–32.

[9] T de Quincey, 'On the Knocking at the Gate in Macbeth' in *On Murder* (n 6) 1 at 4–5.

> fact of his absence for a whole fortnight at the period of that murder: the other, that, within a very little time after, the neighbourhood of this highwayman was deluged with dollars: now Mrs Ruscombe was known to have hoarded about two thousand of that coin. Be the artist, however, who he might, the affair remains a durable monument of his genius; for such was the impression of awe, and the sense of power left behind, by the strength of conception manifested in this murder, that no tenant (as I was told in 1810) had been found up to that time for Mrs Ruscombe's house.[10]

Here are the two key elements that Gaskell imaginatively recombined in 'The Squire's Story' – the fact that there were no suspicions about Higgins before the 'deluge of dollars', and the difficulty of finding tenants.

IV

From the very first sentence of 'The Squire's Story' Gaskell highlights that to be a tenant of the White House is not merely to have certain legal rights and obligations as against the owner, it is to occupy a prestigious social position: 'the little town of Barford was thrown into a state of great excitement by the intelligence that a gentleman (and "quite the gentleman," said the landlord of the George Inn) had been looking at Mr Clavering's old house.'[11] Of Higgins' predecessor as tenant, it is said that he was 'a Northumberland gentleman of good family – who had come to live in Barford while he was but a younger son; but when some elder branches of the family died, he had returned to take possession of the family estate.' 'The house of which I speak', continues the narrator, 'was called the White House, from its being covered with a greyish kind of stucco.'[12] The juxtaposition of these two sentences is eloquent: the people of Barford see what they want to see – the grey house is white; the new tenant is a gentleman like the old one. The Barfordites' readiness to see the newcomer as a respectable gentleman is compounded by their almost desperate desire to have some resumption of the kinds of dinners which Mr Clavering gave, at which town and county families mixed. As Gaskell observes, 'I mention these things that you may have an idea of the desirability of the letting of the White House in the Barfordites' imagination; and to make the mixture thick and slab, you must add for yourselves the bustle, the mystery and the importance which every little event either causes or assumes in a small town.'[13] 'Thick and slab' here, on a first reading, suggests something like realism, or depth; but the fact that the phrase is used in Macbeth by one of the witches, in relation to ingredients being added to their cauldron, creates a feeling of unease. The combination of the legal status of tenant with the overheated expectations of the townspeople is unhealthy and potentially toxic.

[10] 'On Murder Considered as One of the Fine Arts' in *On Murder* (n 6) 8 at 25–26.
[11] Gaskell, 'The Squire's Story' (n 5) 33.
[12] ibid.
[13] ibid 34.

Our first sight of the new tenant, in the company of Mr Jones, the lawyer's clerk, does little to dispel the sense of unease. Jones has just been showing Higgins over the house, an event which has attracted the curiosity of a crowd of 'ragged little urchins':

> Presently, out came the 'gentleman' and the lawyer's clerk … The gentleman was tall, well-dressed, handsome; but there was a sinister cold look in his quick-glancing, light blue eye, which a keen observer might not have liked. There were no keen observers among the boys, and ill-conditioned gaping girls. But they stood too near; inconveniently close; and the gentleman, lifting up his right hand, in which he carried a short riding-whip, dealt one or two sharp blows to the nearest, with a look of savage enjoyment on his face as they moved away whimpering and crying. An instant after, his expression of countenance had changed.
>
> 'Here!' said he, drawing out a handful of money, partly silver, partly copper, and throwing it into the midst of them. 'Scramble for it! fight it out, my lads! come this afternoon, at three, to the George, and I'll throw you out some more.' So the boys hurrahed for him as he walked off with the agent's clerk. He chuckled to himself, as over a pleasant thought. 'I'll have some fun with those lads,' he said; 'I'll teach 'em to come prowling and prying about me. I'll tell you what I'll do. I'll make the money so hot in the fire-shovel that it shall burn their fingers. You come and see the faces and the howling. I shall be very glad if you will dine with me at two; and by that time I may have made up my mind respecting the house.'
>
> Mr Jones, the agent's clerk, agreed to come to the George at two, but, somehow, he had a distaste for his entertainer. Mr Jones would not like to have said, even to himself, that a man with a purse full of money, who kept many horses, and spoke familiarly of noblemen – above all, who thought of taking the White House – could be anything but a gentleman; but still the uneasy wonder as to who this Mr Robinson Higgins could be, filled the clerk's mind long after Mr Higgins, Mr Higgins' servants and Mr Higgins' stud had taken possession of the White House.[14]

In this short sequence, Gaskell gives us the psychological key to the story. Anyone who throws money around is well-liked in Barford – it is not just the boys, but also his later dinner-guests, who enjoy his largesse. More importantly, the lawyer's clerk, who registers that something is not right about Higgins, is almost unable to process it, so strong is the presumption in favour of a White House tenant. 'Somehow' in that final paragraph is perfect. Jones has witnessed Higgins' instinctive cruelty, and heard his premediated sadistic plan of putting coins in the fire shovel, but he still struggles to disapprove. Perhaps his experience as a lawyer's clerk has trained him not to be fastidious about clients. But there is surely something more here – the White House is acting as a kind of guarantor of respectability and good character, to which the lawyer's clerk defers.

Once Higgins has taken possession of the White House, it is his entry into county society. On meeting Sir Harry Manly, the leader of the local hunt, for the first time, Higgins says 'I am only lately come to occupy the White House at Barford, and I have

[14] ibid 34–35.

not as yet presented my letters of introduction.' There is a sense that the White House is offered as a substitute for the letters vouching for him. Sir Harry replies that 'a man with a seat like yours, and that good brush in your hand [Higgins is a very good fox-hunter] might ride up to any door in the county … and be a welcome guest.'[15] Whether the 'seat' refers to Higgins' country house, or his posture on the horse, does not perhaps matter so much as the outcome: unquestioned social acceptance.

V

Higgins' social acceptance enables him to meet the daughter of a local squire. Catherine is wealthy – she will have 'ten thousand pounds down, the day she's married, by her mother's will.'[16] Her father is anxious, but is reassured by his old friend Harry Manly's approval of Higgins. Things then take an unexpected turn:

> With every encouragement … from the old squire [Catherine's father], it took everybody rather by surprise when, one morning, it was discovered that Miss Catherine Hearn was missing; and when, according to the usual fashion in such cases, a note was found, saying that she had eloped with 'the man of her heart', and gone to Gretna Green, no one could imagine why she could not quietly have stopped at home, and been married in the parish church. She had always been a romantic, sentimental girl; very pretty and very affectionate, and very much spoiled, and very much wanting in common sense. Her indulgent father was deeply hurt at this want of confidence in his never-varying affection; but when his son came, hot with indignation from the baronet's (his future father-in-law's house, where every form of law and of ceremony was to accompany his own impending marriage), Squire Hearn pleaded the cause of the young couple with imploring cogency, and protested that it was a piece of spirit in his daughter, which he admired and was proud of.[17]

His son, Nathaniel, however, is not persuaded. 'Who is this man – this fellow?' he insists. 'Where does he come from? What are his means? Who are his family?'[18]

The legal background here is the Clandestine Marriages Act 1753, which laid down that minors (under the age of 21) could not enter valid marriages without parental consent. The Act did not apply in Scotland, and Scots law was notably less insistent on formalities for valid marriages, with the position being that declarations made before two witnesses were sufficient, and the wedding ceremony need not be conducted by a clergyman. In the 1770s one of the easiest Scottish villages to reach from England was Gretna Green, where a thriving wedding industry quickly sprang up, led by the village's entrepreneurial blacksmiths.[19]

[15] ibid 37.
[16] ibid 37.
[17] ibid 38.
[18] ibid 39.
[19] A Francis Steuart, 'Gretna Green' (1929) 41 *Juridical Review* 144 gives a good overview of the subject.

The obvious reason for couples to elope to Gretna Green was to avoid the need for parental consent where the bride or groom was underage. There is no suggestion of Catherine's father refusing his consent, which makes the elopement with Higgins baffling and potentially suspicious. Gaskell never spells it out, but the initiative must surely have come from Higgins.[20] A traditional wedding would almost certainly have exposed him to precisely the questions that Nathaniel Hearn is asking. Given the bride's wealth, some kinds of legal arrangements about Higgins' property would also have been expected, and the very last thing that Higgins wants to do is to disclose the nature of the estates from which he raises his 'rents'.

Gaskell's real interest in this situation, however, is not Higgins, but the social systems and values that allow him to flourish. The Gretna Green wedding is not a cause for suspicion in Barford, because it is easily explicable by resorting to cliché – there even seems to be a standard form of elopement note, which Catherine's has followed. The cliché was, of course, that Gretna Green marriages were spontaneous, romantic fulfilments of true love. It was a cliché that endured, despite the very questionable motives that often drove evasions of the Act.[21] In this context Higgins becomes an indulgent fiancé, charmingly gratifying the whims of his sentimental bride. Such is the aura of romance that Nathaniel Hearn – asking all the right questions – comes across as a pompous, self-important pedant. Higgins succeeds because he exploits the ambivalent attitudes that had grown up around the 1753 Act, and capitalises on Barfordites' readiness to see only what they want to see.

VI

Higgins' most audacious mockeries of the law arise from his dealings with Mr Dudgeon, the local attorney. The hunt has pursued the fox to an area of the common where 'a few of the most wealthy townspeople' have begun enclosing the land.

> Among these, the principal was a Mr Dudgeon, the attorney of Barford, and the agent for all the county families about. The firm of Dudgeon had managed the leases, the marriage settlements and the wills, of the neighbourhood for generations. Mr Dudgeon's father had the responsibility for collecting the land-owners' rents just as the present Mr Dudgeon had at the time of which I speak; and as his son and his son's son have done since. Their business was an hereditary estate to them; and with something of the old feudal feeling, was mixed a kind of proud humility at their position towards the

[20] See note 16 by C Mitchell in E Gaskell, *The Works of Elizabeth Gaskell Volume 3 Novellas and Shorter Fiction II* (C Mitchell (ed), Routledge, 2016) 451.

[21] For example the notorious case of Edward Gibbon Wakefield, summarised by Steuart (n 19) at 150. Gaskell was well aware of it – see her letter of 31 August/1 September 1831 to Harriet Carr, where, commenting on a pamphlet written by Gibbon Wakefield, she asks 'Can any good thing come from such a polluted source.' The letter also contains a quotation from *Macbeth*. See J Chapple and A Shelston (ed), *Further Letters of Mrs Gaskell* (Manchester University Press, 2015) 10 (quotation from *Macbeth* at 11). See also J Uglow, *Elizabeth Gaskell A Habit of Stories* (Faber, 1993) 43.

> squires whose family secrets they had mastered, and the mysteries of whose fortunes and estates were better known to the Messrs Dudgeon than to themselves.[22]

Although Dudgeon calls the house 'a mere cottage', it is extensive and expensively furnished; the gardens, too, are exquisite.

> It must have been somewhat of a mortification to the owner of this dainty place when, on the day of which I speak, the fox after a long race, during which he had described a circle of many miles, took refuge in the garden; but Mr Dudgeon put a good face on the matter when a gentleman hunter, with the careless insolence of the squires of those days and that place, rode across the velvet lawn, and tapping at the window of the dining-room with his whip handle asked permission – no! that is not it – rather, informed Mr Dudgeon of their intention – to enter his garden in a body, and have the fox unearthed. Mr Dudgeon compelled himself to smile assent, with the grace of a masculine Griselda; and then he hastily gave orders to have all that the house afforded of provision set out for luncheon, guessing rightly enough that a six hours' run would give even homely fare an acceptable welcome. He bore without wincing the entrance of the dirty boots into his exquisitely clean rooms; he only felt grateful for the care with which Mr Higgins strode about, laboriously and noiselessly moving on the tip of his toes, as he reconnoitred the rooms with a curious eye.[23]

Higgins compliments Dudgeon on his house, and Dudgeon offers to show him around. Dudgeon's pride and joy is his 'sanctum':

> Mr Dudgeon's sanctum was the centre room, over the porch, which formed a balcony, and which was carefully filled with choice flowers in pots. Inside, there were all kinds of elegant contrivances for hiding the real strength of all the boxes and chests required by the particular nature of Mr Dudgeon's business; for although his office was in Barford, he kept (as he informed Mr Higgins) what was the most valuable here, as being safer than an office which was locked up and left every night. But, as Mr Higgins reminded him with a sly poke in the side, when next they met, his own house was not over secure. A fortnight after the gentlemen of the Barford hunt lunched there, Mr Dudgeon's strong box, – in his sanctum upstairs, with the mysterious spring-bolt to the window invented by himself, and the secret of which was only known to the inventor and a few of his most intimate friends, to whom he had proudly shown it; – this strong-box, containing the collected Christmas rents of half-a-dozen landlords (there was then no bank nearer than Derby,) was rifled; and the secretly rich Mr Dudgeon had to stop his agent in his purchases of paintings by Flemish artists, because the money was required to make good the missing rents.[24]

The perpetrator(s) are never found:

> The Dogberries and Verges of those days were quite incapable of obtaining any clue to the robber or robbers; and though one or two vagrants were taken up and brought before Mr Dunover and Mr Higgins, the magistrates who usually attended in the

[22] Gaskell, 'The Squire's Story' (n 5) 41.
[23] ibid.
[24] ibid 42.

> court-room at Barford, there was no evidence brought against them, and after a couple of nights' durance in the lock-ups they were set at liberty. But it became a standing joke with Mr Higgins to ask Mr Dudgeon, from time to time, whether he could recommend him a place of safety for his valuables; or, if he had made any more inventions lately for securing houses from robbers.[25]

The broad black comedy of this episode is rich in legal aspects. First, there is the apparently irrelevant detail about enclosure. This works in at least two ways. One is that it makes an ironic contrast with the Dudgeons' 'feudal feeling' – that feeling is evidently directed at people, not land; there is no hankering on Dudgeon's part for a return to an actual feudal *system*. The allusion to enclosure also subversively suggests a kind of moral equivalence between the highwayman and the lawyer's rapacious acquisition of common land.[26] The lawyer, it seems, has been the first to exploit the law's machinery for his own benefit, which makes him a rather less sympathetic character than he otherwise might be. This sense that we do not need to feel too sorry for Dudgeon is reinforced by the information that, although he has to make good the loss of rents, this only inconveniences him to the extent of having to divert plentiful resources from elsewhere.

A second eye-catching feature is the laughable ineffectiveness of law enforcement. The ineptitude of the local constables is one thing; but Higgins as magistrate, alongside a man whose name gives little confidence in his integrity (to be 'done over' is to be tricked) starts to go beyond a joke. Gaskell maintains the comic tone by stopping short of having someone wrongly convicted, but it is difficult not to wonder about the (never described) appointment process in which Higgins becomes a justice of the peace. It is easy enough to imagine his neighbours putting his name forward, but the Justices Qualification Act 1731 imposed the property qualification of an annual income of £100; how has Higgins managed to finesse this??[27]

Undoubtedly the most powerful legal dimension, however, is Gaskell's portrayal of the country lawyer. Dudgeon's name is almost comically at odds with his manner, which is obsequious to the point of servility. Behind this position of apparent inferiority, however, lies real power and wealth in the county business that is 'an hereditary estate to them'. This metaphor already hints at a certain defensiveness and insecurity – the Dudgeons are compensating for the fact that they do not have an actual hereditary estate by regarding their business as their estate; 'to them' perhaps also implies 'that was how they saw it, but others, such as the squire who is telling the story, would disagree'. They are, as we are told at the start of the episode, busy acquiring an actual estate through enclosure, but seem to feel that this is not something to boast about – estates should be inherited, not created 'Proud humility' is a nicely ambiguous way to suggest some of the complexities

[25] ibid 42–43.
[26] cf K Marx, *Capital Volume 1* (B Fowkes (tr), Penguin, 1990) ch 27 'Expropriation of the Agricultural Population from the Land'.
[27] W Cornish et al, *Law and Society in England 1750–1950*, 2nd edn (Hart Publishing, 2019) 36.

and contradictions of their position – are they genuinely proud of being humble, ostentatiously (and, therefore, perhaps not sincerely) humble, or perhaps self-deceiving in thinking themselves humble when they are in fact proud?[28]

Whichever it is, Higgins is quick to take advantage of Dudgeon's vulnerabilities. When he makes his entrance, he looks like 'a gentleman hunter, with the careless insolence of the squires of those days'; Dudgeon's immediate instinct is to be deferential to a squire. The lunch arrangements take Dudgeon from humility to humiliation as he becomes 'a masculine Griselda'. Here is another contradiction, and a sharply pointed comparison. In the story of Griselda, told by Chaucer and Boccacio among others, Griselda suffers appalling abuse, manipulation and humiliation from her sadistic aristocratic husband, which she meekly accepts.[29] The husband's real reason for his actions is to 'test' her, but he often gives as his pretext and justification that she is a peasant's daughter. Griselda's attitude so impresses her husband that he eventually reinstates her as his wife. For Dudgeon to submit unprotestingly, as he does, to the invasion of his property, and then to set about making lunch for the invaders, might make him a good 'wife' by some criteria, but 'masculine' is exactly what he is not. Just as Griselda is made to feel that her inferior social origins and wifely duty require her to consent with equanimity to all of her husband's mistreatment, so Dudgeon seems to feel that his insecure social position and role as the county families' lawyer requires him to act with 'grace' in the face of insolence and arrogance.

The short scene in the 'sanctum' seals Dudgeon's fate. Partly, of course, Dudgeon only has his own foolish vanity to blame; but Gaskell also hints at the social matrix that encourages his rashness. He simply cannot imagine that a squire could also be a criminal – his 'old feudal feeling' blinds him to the possibility. And the ill-judged attempt to make an 'intimate friend' of a man who has treated him with contempt leaves us with an almost painful sense of the lawyer's position in this society – despite his wealth and influence, he is not treated as an equal, and is desperately eager to change that. It is a nice touch that, with his refined tastes in horticulture and art, Dudgeon is evidently superior to those from whom he craves acceptance.[30]

VII

'The Squire's Story' is a remarkable demonstration of Gaskell's ability to integrate thought-provoking ideas about law and lawyers into a short, ostensibly simple, narrative. She depicts a world in which law enforcement is inept, judges are

[28] Gaskell makes use of the same expression in *Ruth* – see ch 3 s IX.

[29] For Boccaccio's version, see G Boccaccio, *The Decameron* (WA Rebhorn tr, Norton, 2015) 331.

[30] Gaskell would return to explore the contradictions and sensitivities inherent in the position of such attorneys in *A Dark Night's Work* (1863): see ch 8.

criminals, and lawyers' chief concern is their anxiety about social status. Such systematic institutional failure creates the conditions in which highwaymen and murderers thrive. But it is in relation to the population at large that Gaskell makes her most telling points, as people are seen unquestioningly accepting the conventional excuses for evading the law even where those excuses do not apply, and, most significantly, treating a contractual relationship as conferring a kind of genteel, unchallengeable status. It is worth making the point that the population at large here is a rural population – there is no suggestion in Gaskell's urban fictions like *North and South* and 'Libbie Marsh's Three Eras' that a tenancy is anything other than a contractual arrangement. What is influencing the rural population is, surely, 'the old feudal feeling' of the Dudgeons, and in many ways the story can be read as a reflection on what happens when legal relationships become imperfectly detached from the social roles with which they have traditionally been associated. It is, as it were, a cautionary tale about the social implications of the shifting nature of tenancy, as it flits between status and contract.

7

Attorneys I: *The Moorland Cottage*

I

At the very start of her biography of Charlotte Brontë, as she is surveying the town of Keighley, Gaskell wonders where 'the necessary lawyer' must live.[1] As a declaration of her own interests, 'the necessary lawyer' could hardly be improved on, for her rural fiction, from *The Moorland Cottage* to *Wives and Daughters*, is populated by a rich and varied cast of attorneys. She evidently regarded their inclusion as essential for her depictions of social life outside the city; but the number, the variety, and the centrality of the attorney characters suggest that their role is not merely to start a scene. This chapter, and the next one, will explain why Gaskell found so much in her attorneys. By way of partial anticipation of the specific, detailed analyses offered in these two chapters, two key themes, which are intimately linked to the attorney profession in the nineteenth century, can be identified.

The first is the question, indeed the anxiety, about social status. As the leading modern treatment of the subject puts it, in its opening sentence, 'Attorneys and solicitors had a deep concern, sometimes almost amounting to an obsession with establishing a "respectable" or "liberal" profession.'[2] Such was the profession's desire to reinvent itself that even the title 'attorney' became undesirable: by the Judicature Act 1873 all members of the profession were 'solicitors'.

The second theme is the division of the profession between the metropolis and the provinces.[3] The division was reflected in, and perhaps exacerbated by, the existence of distinct professional bodies. For our purposes, the crucial point is that the introduction of 'a London lawyer' into a provincial setting immediately threatens cosy conventions and understandings. Gaskell makes the point explicitly in her early short story, 'Morton Hall'. The Hall has been inherited by a distant relative of its previous occupant – the new owner is a general in India, and dispatches a 'great London lawyer' to rural Morton in Lancashire, to put the house in order.[4] The lawyer promptly engages builders from Drumble (one of Gaskell's pseudonyms for

[1] E Gaskell, *The Life of Charlotte Brontë* (Angus Easson (ed), Oxford University Press, 1996) 9.

[2] P Polden, 'Solicitors' in W Cornish et al, *The Oxford History of the Laws of England Volume XI 1820–1914, English Legal System* (Oxford University Press, 2010) 1108.

[3] W Cornish, S Banks, C Mitchell, P Mitchell and R Probert, *Law and Society in England 1750–1950*, 2nd edn (Hart Publishing, 2019) 63.

[4] E Gaskell, 'Morton Hall' in E Gaskell, *Cousin Phillis and Other Stories* (H Glen (ed), Oxford University Press, 2010) 32, 54.

Manchester), and the shock registers immediately. As the narrator, whose family have a long history of service to the Morton family, explains:

> the lawyer sent for a Drumble builder, and gave him directions. We thought it would have been prettier if he had hired John Cobb, the Morton builder and joiner, he that had made the squire's coffin, and the squire's father's before that. Instead, came a troop of Drumble men, knocking and tumbling about in the Hall, and making their jests up and down all those stately rooms. Ethelinda and I never went near the place till they were gone, bag and baggage. And then what a change![5]

The threefold sense of alien invasion – from the empire, the south, the city – and, with it, the destruction of a rural economic ecosystem, is personified by the lawyer.

It is also, at the outset, worth making a further, general, point about attorneys, that made them particularly suitable for Gaskell's fiction. During the eighteenth century attorneys, particularly country attorneys, moved away from litigation and sought, instead, to offer 'the services landowners needed; they drew wills and settlements; were stewards to manorial courts; chased rents and arranged repairs; audited accounts; and collected debts.'[6] Although there is a lot of law, and a lot of lawyers, in Gaskell, there is hardly any litigation. Her satirical account of Jem Wilson's trial in *Mary Barton* perhaps hints at how little of any value she thought litigation yielded.[7] In any case, her interests as a novelist focused on the nuances and subtleties of social interaction – she was concerned with how people behaved in the world at large, not with the pathologies of lawsuits. Attorneys were, therefore, beautifully suited to her fictional purposes: they were very much of society, and operated within it, even if they were not entirely confident of where they belonged, and had the potential to bring in external, disruptive elements.

II

The depth of Gaskell's interest in attorneys can perhaps be gauged by the circumstances surrounding the writing of *The Moorland Cottage*. Her publisher had commissioned a Christmas book. Gaskell accepted, while virtually simultaneously expressing in private a revulsion against writing about 'virtue to order'. The work she delivered has only the most slight, and incidental allusions to Christmas; but it is preoccupied with legal rights, duties, obligations and professionals, with two of its central characters being attorneys.[8]

[5] ibid 54.
[6] Polden (n 2) 1131.
[7] See above, ch 2, s V.
[8] On the circumstances surrounding the commissioning of *The Moorland Cottage* see E Wright, *Mrs Gaskell The Basis for Reassessment* (Oxford University Press, 1965) 116; JG Sharps, *Mrs Gaskell's Observation and Invention* (Linden Press, 1970) 101–102; J Uglow, *Elizabeth Gaskell* (Faber and Faber, 1993) 251–52, quoting, at 251, Gaskell's letter describing her acceptance of the commission as 'a *very foolish* engagement'.

Even in the opening chapter, which introduces Mrs Browne, a clergyman's widow, and her two children, Edward and Maggie, who all live at the moorland cottage, there is an anticipatory hint of the role that law will play in the story. Maggie's love of the moors extends to a favourite rock, where she sits:

> Such a rock was Maggie's seat. I believe she considered it her own, and loved it accordingly; although its real owner was a great lord, who lived far away, and had never seen the moor, much less the piece of grey rock, in his life.[9]

At first glance this seems little more than an affectionate, perhaps slightly patronising, depiction of a child's charmingly innocent view of the world. But it repays closer reading. The rock as Maggie's 'seat' puts her on the same level as the lord whose seat is far away. We are told that Maggie, believing the rock to be hers, 'loved it accordingly'; but the lord who does own it does not correspondingly love it – on the contrary, he cares nothing about it. It is only Maggie who loves what she takes to be hers. We are invited to feel that, paradoxically, the non-owner's love gives her the superior claim, and that the law is missing the point when it prioritises the lord. As it transpires, nothing turns on this – we never hear of the 'great lord' again – but the theme of the law competing with other sources of rules and obligations, conflicting with love, and of law not deserving the priority it is accorded, will be developed with some eloquence.

Hints of the difficulties in which the characters will become embroiled appear quite quickly. Mrs Browne and her children are taken up by the local squire, Mr Buxton, and his family. In the course of a conversation with Mrs Browne, Buxton tells her that he gets an accountant to 'do up' his books every two or three years, but the books soon get out of order again.[10]

> 'Those quarries, Mrs Browne', says Buxton, 'which every one says are so valuable, and of the stone out of which I receive orders amounting to hundreds of pounds, what d'ye think was the profit I made last year, according to my books?'
>
> ''I'm sure I don't know sir; something very great, I've no doubt.'
>
> 'Just seven-pence three farthings!' said he, bursting into a fit of merry laughter.[11]

Why is this funny? It seems to be another instance of the 'perverse economies' we have encountered in *Ruth*, where normal economic values are subjugated to the characters' own, eccentric systems.[12] It is possible to read Buxton's merriment as a kind of boast that he has so much money that he can afford to make a joke of this otherwise alarming fact. It might, alternatively, be read as an indifference to money – and as demonstrating, for him, the overriding importance of domestic

[9] E Gaskell, *The Moorland Cottage* in E Gaskell, *The Moorland Cottage and other stories* (S Lewis (ed), Oxford University Press, 1995) 1, 7.

[10] ibid 28.

[11] ibid.

[12] See ch III, ss VI and VII. The expression 'perverse economies' was coined by N Freeland, '*Ruth*'s Perverse Economies: Women, Hoarding, and Expenditure' (2003) 70(1) *ELH* 197.

happiness, say. A later conversation with his son, Frank, however, reveals a more complicated picture. Mr Buxton is planning to go up to London:

> 'I think I shall go up myself some day soon. I can't understand all these lawyers' letters, about the purchase of the Newbridge estate; and I fancy I could make more sense out of it all, if I saw Mr. Hodgson.'
>
> 'I wish you would adopt my plan, of having an agent, sir. You affairs are really so complicated now, that they would take up the time of an expert man of business. I am sure all those tenants at Dumford ought to be seen after.'
>
> 'I do see after them. There's never a one that dares cheat me, or that would cheat me if they could. Most of them have lived under the Buxtons for generations. They know that if they dared to take advantage of me, I should come down upon them pretty smartly.'
>
> 'Do you rely upon their attachment to your family – or on their idea of your severity?'
>
> 'On both. They stand me instead of much trouble in account-keeping, and those eternal lawyers' letters some people are always dispatching to their tenants. When I'm cheated, Frank, I give you leave to make me have an agent, but not till then.'[13]

This is a rich, suggestive passage of dialogue. Gaskell delicately hints at the increasing juridification of relations between landlord and tenant, with Buxton proud of his own, more informal, approach. That approach rests on the Buxton family's social position, which, Mr Buxton confidently assumes, guarantees the deference and trustworthiness of the tenantry. It is an indication of how deeply Buxton holds this view that the sevenpence profit from the quarry does not make him hesitate. Gaskell associates the new, lawyerly approach with London – and surely invites us to notice that the recent purchase is of 'Newbridge', while the way from the moorland cottage to the local town is over an old 'wooden bridge'.[14] Under the London lawyers' influence, things are moving in new directions.

Buxton's attitudes and values will put him on a collision course with legal rules, and it is worth pausing for a moment to reflect on how his character – with its associated values and attitudes – has been formed. We can usefully borrow here a comment Gaskell makes on Buxton's niece, Erminia: 'Her life was a shattered mirror; every part dazzling and brilliant, but wanting the coherency and perfection of a whole.'[15] The shattered mirror image is extraordinary – powerful, disturbing, violent – despite Gaskell's softening emphasis on its gentler aspects. In Erminia's case a troubled childhood seems to blame (which makes the violence of the shattering so arresting); Mr Buxton has been subjected to nothing so traumatic, but his confident – and, as it will turn out, complacent – sense of his family's position, and the deference that automatically is due to it, has given him a fatally distorted view of the world around him. His image of that world is precariously partial; if it is coherent, it is only so by force of will, by choosing to ignore the obvious signs that he has got things wrong. He would, quite literally, rather believe that the quarries

[13] Gaskell, *The Moorland Cottage* (n 9) 33.
[14] ibid 1.
[15] ibid 26.

only yield seven pence in profit than wonder whether he (and, by association, his family), might be being disrespected by social inferiors.

III

While the London attorneys hover in the background, Gaskell introduces their provincial colleagues. Edward (and Maggie) grow up, and Edward announces that he will not be following his father into the Church:

> 'It's such slow work,' he said to his mother. 'One toils away for four or five years, and then one gets a curacy of seventy pounds a-year, and no end of work to do for the money. Now the work is not much harder in a lawyer's office, and if one has one's wits about one, there are hundreds and thousands a-year to be picked up with mightly little trouble.'
>
> Mrs. Browne was very sorry for this determination. She had a great desire to see her son a clergyman, like his father. She did not consider whether his character was fitted for so sacred an office; she rather thought that the profession itself, when once assumed, would purify the character; but, in fact, his fitness or unfitness for holy orders entered little into her mind. She had a respect for the profession, and his father had belonged to it.
>
> 'I had rather see you a curate at seventy pounds a-year, than an attorney with seven hundred,' replied she. 'And you know your father was always asked to dine everywhere – to places where I know they would not have had Mr. Bish, of Woodchester, and he makes his thousand a-year.'[16]

In the earlier chapters of the novella we have seen Edward's character develop. Although he is clever, he is also selfish, petulant and bullies his younger sister; their mother indulges him. In his schooling, we are told, 'his moral training had been little attended to.'[17] Edward, of course, gets his way – '[Mrs Browne] had long acknowledged her son's will as her law' comments the narrator, acidly, thus encapsulating the inversion of authority and respect that has occurred.[18] Edward's change of career is also revealing of the perception of attorneys. Mrs Browne has 'a respect for the profession' of the clergy;[19] implicitly she has no respect for attorneys; they are not respectable. Maggie perceives, as Mrs Browne does not, that Edward's character – 'a selfish, vain and impatient boy' – makes him unsuitable for the Church.[20] But no one suggests that it might hinder his legal career.

[16] ibid 30.
[17] ibid 28.
[18] ibid 32.
[19] ibid 30.
[20] ibid 32.

When we next see Edward, a few months into his articles, it is clear that he is relishing the work. He regales Mr Buxton and Frank with stories from legal practice:

> Worldly success was his standard of merit. The end seemed with him to justify the means; if a man prospered, it was not necessary to scrutinize his conduct too closely. The law was viewed in its lowest aspect; and yet with a certain cleverness, which preserved Edward from being intellectually contemptible. Frank had entertained some idea of studying for a barrister himself: not so much as a means of livelihood as to gain some idea of the code which makes and shows a nation's conscience: but Edward's details of the ways in which the letter so often baffles the spirit, made him recoil. With some anger against himself, for viewing the profession with disgust, because it was degraded by those who embraced it, instead of looking upon it as what might be ennobled and purified into a vast intelligence by high and pure-minded men, he got up abruptly and left the room.[21]

Mr Buxton, however, responds very differently:

> Mr. Buxton, in the dining-room, was really getting to take an interest in Edward's puzzling cases. They were like tricks at cards. A quick motion, and out of the unpromising heap, all confused together, presto! the right card turned up. Edward stated his case, so that there did not seem a loophole for the desired verdict; but through some conjuration, it always came uppermost at last. He had a graphic way of relating things; and, as he did not spare epithets in his designation of the opposing party, Mr. Buxton took it upon trust that the defendant or the prosecutor (as it might happen) was a 'pettifogging knave', or a 'miserly curmudgeon', and rejoiced accordingly in the triumph over him gained by the ready wit of 'our governor', Mr. Bish. At last he became so deeply impressed with Edward's knowledge of law, as to consult him about some cottage property he had in Woodchester.[22]

Despite their contrasts, both passages present equally unedifying accounts of attorneys at work: flashy cleverness and a rather suspect moral elasticity are the keys to success. Edward's admiring anecdotes about 'the governor' are also important for what they show us about Edward. He obviously has unpleasant, selfish character traits, but the novella consistently suggests that, in the right environment, these could be minimised, perhaps, even, eliminated altogether. The story of Edward's upbringing and education is, in this sense, a story of missed opportunities. His father's positive moral influence was curtailed by death; his mother indulges and spoils him precisely when his character is being formed. His school gives him excellent skills in Latin, but neglects his 'moral training'.[23] Gaskell contrasts the moral vacuity of this formal education with Mrs Buxton's invaluable, but informal and unstructured, lessons with Maggie.[24] Perhaps by the time Edward begins his articles it is already too late, but Mr Bish has the potential to be a positive role model, even a surrogate father figure, as Gaskell may be suggesting

[21] ibid 38.
[22] ibid 39.
[23] ibid 28.
[24] ibid 25–27.

by having Edward serve his articles alongside Mr Bish's son, and Edward's friend, Harry.[25] There is the potential here for one of Gaskell's most distinctive fictional strategies – the creation of a nuturing, supportive, quasi-familial relationship.[26] Mr Bish, however, seems to affirm, and to validate by example, Edward's worst characteristics; certainly, there is not the slightest suggestion that Edward's professional training will instil any moral values.

Frank's aversion is in part personal, but it is also rooted in social distinctions and hierarchies. He has previously expressed a dislike of 'boys brought up at those private schools'; Frank has been at Eton.[27] His plan to become a non-practising barrister makes him, socially, the polar opposite of a practising, provincial attorney. Whereas to be an attorney was not respectable, to be a barrister very emphatically was; and to be a non-practising barrister was to add gentlemanly leisure to respectability. Frank is a sympathetic, ultimately a heroic, character, but, at least on this occasion, his valuations conform to stereotype.

In Frank's reasons for wanting to become a barrister we are tempted to wonder whether Gaskell is not enjoying a little mockery. One would have to have had very little contact with the law indeed to be able to regard it as 'the code which makes and shows a nation's conscience.' Frank's position is almost absurdly idealistic, and his physical reaction of rushing out of the room almost comically violent; yet it is not entirely out of character. Later on in the novella he impulsively proposes to Maggie that they should elope to Australia: 'it would be the best thing we could do. My heart aches about the mysterious corruptions and evils of an old state of society such as we have in England.'[28] Similarly, when it seems that they are about to emigrate to the United States, Frank tells Maggie, 'I thought how happy you and I would be, striving together as poor people 'in that new world which is the old."[29] The passionate commitment to principles, the impulsive desire for adventure and the urge to be someone different – these all recall *Don Quixote*, a novel directly alluded to in earlier dialogue between Edward and Maggie. Maggie has just refused to do Edward's bidding, in response to which Edward has told her to 'be obedient'.

> 'I could be obedient to some people, without knowing their reasons, even though they told me to do silly things,' said Maggie, half to herself.
>
> 'I should like to know whom' said Edward, scornfully.
>
> 'To Don Quixote,' answered she, seriously; for, indeed, he was present in her mind just then, and his noble, tender, melancholy character had made a strong impression there.[30]

[25] ibid 31.

[26] See eg 'The Three Eras of Libbie Marsh', 'Lizzie Leigh', 'The Grey Woman', discussed in ch 12, s IV below. There is a particularly striking contrast with 'The Poor Clare', where the narrator, Preston, is effectively adopted by his uncle, 'an eminent attorney in London', and 'treated and esteemed as his son.' (E Gaskell, *Gothic Tales* (L Kranzler (ed), Penguin, 2000) at 61.)

[27] Gaskell, *The Moorland Cottage* (n 9) 29, 40.

[28] ibid 60–61.

[29] ibid 97. The quotation is from Alfred, Lord Tennyson, 'The Day-Dream': S Lewis, notes to *The Moorland Cottage* (n 1) 294.

[30] ibid 29.

It has been suggested that Maggie, in her many acts of self-sacrifice, is quixotic, 'although … not a Don Quixote in the strict sense.'[31] But surely the novella invites us to see Frank as Quixote, with Maggie his devoted, loving companion. In any case, with Frank's romantic idealism about law, it is as if, between him and Edward, Gaskell has split the ideal lawyer in two; as we shall see in the next section, she was about to introduce a powerful new lawyer character, who formidably fused clear-eyed principle with steely pragmatism.

IV

The first we hear of Mr Henry, shortly before his arrival at the Buxtons', is from Frank. Frank has heard that he is 'a very hard sort of man. He is what is called scrupulously honest and honourable; but I fear a little too much inclined to drive hard bargains for his client.'[32] Evidently Mr Henry is not a local man; where exactly he is from is never made clear – although Mr Buxton has mentioned going to London to consult 'Mr Hodgson', and Mr Henry's appointment may well have been a result of that consultation. What is made very clear is that Mr Henry is bringing with him priorities and values that threaten the social equilibrium. Being 'scrupulously honest and honourable' is effectively placed in sceptical quotation marks, made a code for hardness, or, at the very least, given a surprising ambivalence. It adds to the effect that Frank is an aspiring barrister – we might, perhaps, catch a glimpse here of the Bar's condescending attitudes to attorneys' pretensions to belong to an honourable profession. In any case, the criticism of Mr Henry that he drives hard bargains for his clients sounds like a point about not acting like a gentleman. We might perhaps feel that the criticisms tell us more about Frank's naïve ideals of legal practice than they tell us about Mr Henry's shortcomings, but what is very clear is that, if the reports are true, Mr Henry personifies values of professionalism and rigour that cannot be cosily accommodated in the Buxtons' social world.

Mr Henry does not disappoint. He is 'a quiet, stern-looking man, of considerable intelligence and refinement, and so much taste for music as to charm Erminia, who had rather dreaded his visit.'[33] This last point is an important clue to Mr Henry's character: he is refined, sensitive and sympathetic – when it is appropriate. 'But', Gaskell continues, 'all the amenities of life were put aside when he entered Mr Buxton's sanctum – his 'office', as he called the room where he received his tenants and business-people.' It is immediately apparent that, while Mr Henry is in the 'office', he does not regard himself as an office-holder under the Buxtons:

> Frank thought Mr. Henry was scare commonly civil in the open evidence of his surprise and contempt for the habits, of which the disorderly books and ledgers were but too

[31] B Puchol Vázquez, 'Gaskell and Spanish Culture: Quixotic Traces in *Cranford* and *The Moorland Cottage*' (2021) 35 *Gaskell Journal* 19 at 27–37; quotation at 37.
[32] Gaskell, *The Moorland Cottage* (n 9) 57.
[33] ibid 58.

> visible signs. Mr. Buxton himself felt more like a school-boy, bringing up an imperfect lesson, than he had ever done since he was thirteen.
>
> 'The only wonder, my good sir, is that you have any property left; that you have not been cheated out of every farthing.'
>
> 'I'll answer for it, said Mr. Buxton, in reply 'that you'll not find any cheating has been going on. They dared not, sir; they know I should make an example of the first rogue I found out.'
>
> Mr. Henry lifted up his eyebrows, but did not speak.
>
> 'Besides, sir, most of these men have lived for generations under the Buxtons. I'd give you my life, they would not cheat me.'
>
> Mr. Henry coldly said:
>
> 'I imagine a close examination of these books by some accountant will be the best proof of the honesty of these said tenants. If you will allow me, I will write to a clever fellow I know, and desire him to come down and try and regulate this mass of papers.'
>
> 'Anything – anything you like', said Mr. Buxton, only too glad to escape from the lawyer's cold, contemptuous way of treating the subject.[34]

This exercise in forensic accountancy lasts several days, during which 'Mr Buxton was bewildered by the questions [Mr Henry and the accountant] asked him. Mr Henry examined him in the worrying way in which an unwilling witness is made to give evidence.'[35]

Before we consider Mr Henry's findings, it is worth pausing for a moment to notice how Gaskell constructs the relationship between lawyer and client. Mr Buxton is made to feel, first, like a delinquent schoolboy being questioned by a master, then like a witness being subjected to hostile examination in court. The presumed professional power relationship whereby it is the lawyer who does the client's bidding, is inverted and with it, also, the social relationship. Evidently Mr Buxton has never experienced this kind of thing before. The accountants who have previously worked on his books must, we assume, have been deferential; but Mr Henry regards himself as being of at least equal social status to his client. How does he achieve this? Partly because he is an outsider – he is not dependent on the Buxtons' patronage – and partly through confidence in his own forensic expertise, which enables him to lay claim to significant social capital.

When Mr Henry and the accountant have completed their work, the results are all too predictable. Mr Henry sets out 'the defalcations, nay more, the impositions of those [Buxton] had trusted.'[36] Buxton's response is to become 'passionately angry':

> 'I'll prosecute them, sir. Not a man shall escape. I'll make them pay back every farthing, I will. And damages, too. Crayston, did you say, sir? Was that one of the names? Why, that is the very Crayston who was bailiff under my father for years. The scoundrel! And I set him up in my best farm when he married. And he's been swindling me, has he?'

[34] ibid 58.
[35] ibid.
[36] ibid 59.

> Mr. Henry ran over the items of the account – '42*l*, 13*s*. 4 ¾ d. Part of this I fear we cannot recover' –
>
> He was going on, but Mr. Buxton broke in:
>
> 'But I will recover it. I'll have every farthing of it. I'll go to law with the viper. I don't care for money, but I hate ingratitude.'
>
> 'If you like, I will take counsel's opinion on the case,' said Mr. Henry, coolly.
>
> 'Take anything you please, sir. Why this Crayston was the first man that set me on a horse – and to think of his cheating me.'[37]

This is a crucial passage of dialogue. Although it is not spelled out here, it must be implicit that, among those whom Mr Buxton trusted were the accountants who previously set his books in order – they, we must take it, were either completely incompetent, or effectively made themselves complicit in the cheating by telling Mr Buxton what he wanted to hear. Buxton's excessively emotional response continues, rather than correcting, his earlier misvaluations. Mr Henry, by contrast, eschews emotion, and, given that he will later be accused of vindictiveness, and of encouraging lawsuits, it is important to notice that he does not advise litigation – it is Buxton who insists on legal proceedings.

As the story builds to a dramatic climax, only one further, relatively minor, incident involving Mr Henry is directly narrated. That is his response to Frank's remonstrating that the tenantry should be given an opportunity to pay what they owe, without being subjected to lawsuits. 'Mr Henry', we are told,

> only raised his eyebrows and made answer:
>
> 'I like to see these notions in a young man, sir. I had them myself at your age. I believe I had great ideas then, on the subject of temptation and the force of circumstances; and was as Quixotic as any one about reforming rogues. But my experience has convinced me that roguery is innate. Nothing but outward force can control it, and keep it within bounds. The terrors of the law must be that outward force. I admire your kindness of heart; and in three-and-twenty we do not look for the wisdom and experience of forty or fifty.'[38]

Despite this small number of direct appearances, however, Mr Henry is credited with an almost uncanny influence over events and characters. He haunts the second half of the book, seeming to be everywhere, knowing everything – including his exposure of Edward's having forged Mr Buxton's signature on legal documents. Mr Buxton, in particular, seems both to depend upon him, and to be terrified of incurring his displeasure. Mr Henry even seems to be involved in Mr Buxton's attempts to persuade Maggie that Edward's fraud would justify Frank in breaking off his engagement to Maggie: 'Mr Henry says, even in a court of law what has come out about Edward would be excuse enough for a breach of promise of marriage.'[39]

[37] ibid 59.
[38] ibid 63.
[39] ibid 69.

This is a crucial moment, for it shows how far Mr Henry has penetrated into the family and, revealingly, when Maggie objects to Mr Henry's involvement, Mr Buxton replies that 'Mr Henry is a good friend of mine, who has my interest at heart.'[40] Not only is Mr Henry felt to be everywhere, controlling events, his influence, though derived from his expertise, is now unconstrained by the boundaries of his professional role.

Mr Henry's opinion that Frank would have a defence to any action for breach of promise is also legally very interesting, for the law was not quite as clear as his reported statement suggests. Although it seems that there was no closed list of the grounds on which a breach of promise of marriage could be justified, to judge by the legal texts, it never seems to have been sufficient to show misconduct (or criminality) by a family member of one of the parties.[41] A material misrepresentation, or a wilful suppression of the 'real position' of the claimant's family might perhaps have been enough – but in the story Maggie proposes that everything should be put before Frank, and that his decision will be final.[42] Parental disapproval of an engagement only went to mitigation of damages, it did not justify the breach.[43] Has Mr Henry made an uncharacteristic mistake here? It is, of course, possible, although there is nothing to suggest that it is deliberate, and that Mr Henry is guilty of telling his client what he knows the client wants to hear. But there is another, more interesting, reading. There was very little authority laying down the defences to breach of promise of marriage, and the differing accounts in the legal treatises derived from little more than their authors' impressions. The general sense is of a very open-textured cause of action, shaped by social standards and expectations as recognised by a jury. Is a legal treatise writer presumptively better placed than a novelist to register such standards and expectations? It is tempting to suggest exactly the opposite. Certainly there is no reason to regard the treatise writer's position as definitive – we are surely at a point where any such writer's claim to speak authoritatively is precariously weak. At the very least, by voicing Mr Henry's view of the law through a brilliantly acute lawyer, Gaskell persuasively suggests that the justifications for breaking an engagement need not be exclusively tied up with the individual parties' moral purity, they were potentially more wide-ranging, and extended to the idea of marriage as a union not just of individuals, but of families.[44] There is also a further important point here about legal uncertainty: no one knows exactly what the defences to breach of promise are, and when the law is radically uncertain in this way it is not merely inert and indecisive,

[40] ibid 69.

[41] Contrast the different lists of defences given in J Chitty, *A Practical Treatise on the Law of Contracts* (Sweet & Maxwell, 1826) 159–60; Anon, *A Familiar Compendium of the Law of Husband and Wife* (London, 1831) 213; JJS Wharton, *An Exposition of the Laws Relating to the Women of England* (Longman, Brown, Green and Longmans, 1853) 213.

[42] Wharton (n 41) 213 (no authority cited).

[43] Anon (n 41) 177.

[44] cf the emphasis on a fiancée's conformity to ideals of femininity in S Lettmaier, *Broken Engagements: The Action for Breach of Promise of Marriage and the Feminine Ideal 1800–1940* (Oxford University Press, 2010).

its uncertainty can be exploited to conjure up the most intimidating and humiliating possibilities. The hesitancy and tentativeness of the law in the books becomes the untrammelled menace of the law in action. It is a testament to Maggie's moral courage and strength of character that she is not cowed.[45]

In the end, the fear of Mr Henry's thoroughness leads to a plan for Edward to flee to the United States. 'If Ned is in England, Mr Henry will ferret him out' observes Mr Buxton, who now actively frustrates Mr Henry's efforts to bring Edward to justice.[46] The plan initially goes well, but the ship is wrecked and Edward drowns. It is, ultimately, impossible to escape Mr Henry.

In her creation of Mr Henry, and her introduction of him into the quiet provincial world of *The Moorland Cottage*, Gaskell makes powerful use of contemporary legal developments. Attorneys were becoming more self-consciously and self-assertively professional, respectable, and were laying claim to higher social status. There is a palpable shock when an attorney of this new kind arrives and pitilessly exposes the long-standing hypocrisies and deceptions on which a provincial society is based. The truth is almost unbearable, and its revelation sets off the chain of events that drives the novella's narrative. How far Mr Henry himself can, or should, be blamed for this is only very lightly touched on, but he never evinces ulterior motives.[47] It is, rather, the surrounding characters' reactions, particularly Mr Buxton's reactions, to Mr Henry's findings that provide the main motivating force. Mr Buxton is seeing his whole way of life and understanding of the world crumble in front of him, which makes his rage understandable. What is more striking is the response of his son, who finds himself in line to inherit a position from which the hereditary respect and social influence has been worn away. Frank invokes legal ideas of a very different kind when he jokes about Maggie 'transport[ing]' him to Scotland and fantasises about escaping the 'mysterious corruptions and evils of an old state of society' by going to Australia (or Canada).[48] Unlike in *Mary Barton*, with its happy, escapist, Canadian ending, in the *Moorland Cottage* everyone ends up back where they started. We may hope that Frank will learn from his father's mistakes in his encounters with law, and also avoid the opposite extreme, but, in a novella often criticised for its conventionality, on this point Gaskell offers us not the slightest reassurance of a happy ending.[49]

[45] Contrast the effects of a threat to sue for breach of promise in H James, 'The Bench of Desolation' in H James, *Complete Stories 1898–1910* (D Donoghue (ed), Library of America, 1996) 847.

[46] Gaskell, *The Moorland Cottage* (n 9) 79.

[47] Contrast G Eliot, *The Mill on the Floss*, which may have been a response to *The Moorland Cottage*. In Eliot's novel the attorney, Mr Wakem, very explicitly has personal motives for his deployment of legal proceedings (see particularly, Book Third, Chapter VII, describing Wakem's 'parenthetic vindictiveness'). On the relationship between *The Moorland Cottage* and *The Mill on the Floss* see JG Sharps, *Mrs Gaskell's Observation and Invention* (Linden Press, 1970) 104–105; R Lumpkin, '(Re)Visions of Virtue: Elizabeth Gaskell's *Moorland Cottage* and George Eliot's *The Mill on the Floss*' (1991) 23(4) *Studies in the Novel* 432; J Billington, 'Reading and Writing Short Fiction: Elizabeth Gaskell and George Eliot' (2015) 29 *Gaskell Journal* 23.

[48] Gaskell, *The Moorland Cottage* (n 9) 57; 60–61.

[49] See eg E Wright, *Mrs Gaskell The Basis for Reassessment* (Oxford University Press, 1965) 116–17; Sharps (n 47) 104.

8

Attorneys II: *A Dark Night's Work*

I

A Dark Night's Work, first published in *Household Words* in 1863, sees Gaskell revisiting the fictional possibilities of attorneys' anxieties about their precarious status. The opening of the novel articulates the theme powerfully:

> In the county town of a certain shire there lived (about forty years ago) one Mr Wilkins, a conveyancing attorney of considerable standing.
>
> The certain shire was but a small county, and the principal town in it contained only about four thousand inhabitants; so in saying that Mr Wilkins was the principal lawyer in Hamley, I say very little, unless I add that he transacted all the legal business of the gentry for twenty miles round. His grandfather had established the connection; his father had consolidated and strengthened it, and, indeed, by his wise and upright conduct, as well as by his professional skill, had obtained for himself the position of confidential friend to many of the surrounding families of distinction. He visited among them in a way which no mere lawyer had ever done before; dined at their tables – he alone, not accompanied by his wife, be it observed; rode to the meet occasionally as if by accident, although he was as well mounted as any squire among them, and was often persuaded (after a little coquetting about 'professional engagements' and 'being wanted at the office') to have a run with his clients; nay, once or twice he forgot his usual caution, was first in at the death, and rode home with the brush. But in general he knew his place; as his place was held to be in that aristocratic county, and in those days.[1]

The tensions, difficulties and delicacies of the attorney's position are beautifully and economically delineated. As the opening sentence indicates, to be a conveyancing attorney is not automatically to be respectable. Strengthening and consolidating has only gained half-admission to society, the exclusion of the attorney's wife suggesting that his hosts regard the attorney as present essentially on business. He may consider himself a 'confidential friend', and his professionally acquired knowledge of the local gentry's affairs would seem to justify the adjective; but if he is a 'friend' to these families, it is patently not a friendship of equals, nor has confidence been reposed in him as a friend (as opposed to a professional advisor). There is, already, a troubling sense that the 'mere lawyer' is overreaching himself by imagining himself as a 'friend'.

[1] E Gaskell, *A Dark Night's Work* in E Gaskell, *A Dark Night's Work and Other Stories* (S Lewis (ed), Oxford University Press, 1992) 1.

The possibility that at some level he knows that he is deceiving himself is perfectly underlined by the hunting incidents: he knows that he has to stage his arrival as a happy coincidence, and to continue the fiction by pretending to have urgent commitments at the office. Possibly the clients recognise this 'coquetting' for what it is, but the sense remains that when the attorney forgets himself by being first to the kill, it is a breach of etiquette. After this elaborate description, 'But in general he knew his place' is nicely ambiguous. We know that he did not invariably act on this knowledge (when fox-hunting). And was the place he knew the place as a 'confidential friend' to the gentry? Or the place which the slightly supercilious narrator, seeming to echo the judgment of the gentry, would allocate to him? As the story develops, its most powerful narrative impetus will derive from the thwarted aspirations of the last of this line of attorneys, a man who had been destined for Oxford and a career at the Bar before his father's decision that 'his own business was too lucrative and brought too large an income to pass away into the hands of a stranger.'[2] The son is, therefore, left in the unhappy position of having to return to Hamley 'to assume the hereditary subservient position' to his former school-fellows.[3] If anything, his father's well-meaning attempt to compensate his son for the loss of career by sending him on a Grand Tour of Europe makes matters worse: there is now an even wider gap between the son's tastes and sensibilities and his professional position.

It can thus be seen immediately that, even though Gaskell is revisiting the theme of attorneys' social status that she explored so effectively in *The Moorland Cottage*, her treatment of it here is very different. What made Mr Henry so devastatingly effective was that he was an outsider (quite possibly from London); he had no desire to ingratiate himself with the gentry, as Mr Buxton is somewhat shocked to realise. Crucially, it is Mr Henry's professional persona that gives him power and authority – being an attorney is nothing to be ashamed of. For Mr Wilkins things are completely different. He desperately wants to be accepted by the gentry; his father wanted to be, and be seen to be, their 'friend'. There is also a nice contrast in Gaskell's use of artistic sensibility. Mr Henry has a refined taste in music, but does not allow artistic appreciation to interfere with his legal work. Mr Wilkins, by contrast, will indulge his artistic repulsion at the bright green of his clerk's coat, at the same man's provincial accent, and will resentfully envy the leisure of wealthier, less cultured, men, which he imagines he would spend more profitably. Henry can separate sense and sensibility; Wilkins cannot.

II

A Dark Night's Work also goes beyond *The Moorland Cottage* by deploying the fragile social status of attorneys as a narrative driver. We have already seen how

[2] ibid 2.
[3] ibid.

Gaskell creates the social parameters and terms on which the attorney operates. Into this society she then introduces Ralph Corbet, a young man who becomes engaged to marry Wilkins' daughter, Ellinor. Ralph provides a painful contrast with, and for, Wilkins: both men start out destined for university and a career at the Bar; as we saw above, Wilkins' course is altered, but Ralph will go on to succeed. Making Ellinor's lover the kind of man her father aspired to be sets the scene for mutual antipathy between the two men.

On Ralph Corbet's part that antipathy is fuelled by a keen awareness of the gentry's disdain for attorneys. In the novel's most quietly devastating moment, Ralph attends his brother's wedding, where he 'associated on equal terms with the magnates of the county, who were the employers of Ellinor's father, and spoke of him always as 'Wilkins', just as they spoke of the butler as 'Simmons''.[4] So much for friendship. After Ellinor hints to Ralph that her father has 'a possible shame' hanging over him, it is not long before Ralph starts to think about backing out.[5]

Ellinor has, here, been guilty of something of an understatement: her father has struck his partner, Dunster, in a rage, and Dunster has died from the blow. Ralph is prepared to think badly of Wilkins, but he stops short of suspecting homicide:

> [Corbet] thought he had pretty well ascertained the nature of this possible shame, and had little doubt that it would turn out to be that Dunster's disappearance to America, or elsewhere, had been an arranged plan with Mr Wilkins. Although Ralph Corbet was capable of suspecting him of this mean crime (so far removed from the impulsive commission of the past sin, which was dragging him daily lower and lower down), it was of a kind that was peculiarly distasteful to the acute lawyer, who foresaw how much base conduct would taint all whose names were ever mentioned, even by chance, in connection with it.[6]

It is not precisely spelled out here, but Corbet perhaps suspects Wilkins of trying to defraud his creditors in future bankruptcy proceedings by having Dunster 'abscond' with the partnership's assets. It is, otherwise, difficult to see how Dunster's disappearance with Wilkins' blessing could be any kind of 'crime', and Ralph Corbet is exactly the person not to make a mistake about that. But what Corbet is alert to, and troubled by, is the way that, as a matter of social practice rather than legal analysis, one can be guilty by association. A further complexity is added by Gaskell's reference to 'the impulsive commission of the past sin'. Is this to suggest that the impulsive homicide is more easily forgiven than a mean, planned fraud? And what should we make of the shift from 'crime' to 'sin'? The killing is clearly manslaughter, and almost certainly murder on the law as it stood – it is *both* a crime *and* a sin.[7] The passage is perhaps best read as a subtle deflation of the

[4] ibid 82.
[5] ibid at 79 and 86.
[6] ibid 86.
[7] K Smith, 'Offences Against the Person' in W Cornish et al, *Oxford History of the Laws of England: Volume XIII: 1820–1914 Fields of Development* (Oxford University Press, 2010) 392 at 422–26 emphasises that the defence of provocation (which would reduce a killing from murder to manslaughter) in this period would not be satisfied by proving only that the defendant experienced a loss of self-control.

'acute lawyer' point of view. Gaskell has already had Ralph almost stumble upon the true explanation when, after being told that Dunster had been reading travel books about America a decade earlier, he says, sardonically, 'Ten years is a long time beforehand … shows malice prepense with a vengeance.'[8] Malice prepense is the legal test for intention in murder; but Corbet lacks the imaginative capacity to revise his earlier conclusions – his is a merely rationalistic, lawyerly kind of cleverness. In the same way, in the passage quoted above, he flatters himself that his acute legal analysis has penetrated unerringly to the truth, and combines this conclusion with a knowingly cynical, worldly understanding of how his own reputation might be tarnished by broadbrush social attributions of guilt; but the compelling legal analysis is wrong, and its basic premise (thinking of 'crimes' rather than 'sins') sets him on the wrong track from the start. The only point on which he is capable of thinking really creatively is about what Wilkins' fraud might mean for his own social position as Wilkins' son-in-law.

As it turns out, Ralph Corbet will be guilty of the kind of mean-spirited calculation that he wrongly imputes to Wilkins. At first he holds firm against his family's opposition to the engagement, dismissing a threat by his mother to cut down timber on the estate he is due to inherit from her – he now knows (from his legal studies) that this threatened conduct is illegal. He also knows that breaking off the engagement would mean that 'he should lose all title to being a man of honour, and might have an action brought against him.'[9] 'Yet not the less for all this', the narrator continues, 'was the idea in his mind as a future possibility.' Corbet's commitment to Ellinor is provisional, subject, it becomes clear, to a calculation of likely costs and benefits at the moment performance is due. He seems to view his engagement in the same way that we might easily imagine him in his legal practice advising a commercial party about an awkward long-term contractual obligation; and it is, thus, the perfect expression when, on hearing of Wilkins' 'possible shame' from Ellinor, we are told that 'his heart contracted'.[10] The obvious meaning here is the physical sensation of the heart shrinking back; but 'contracted' ironically reminds us that, despite his unconditional proposal, Ralph the lawyer does not regard himself as having promised his heart for better, for worse. Rather like the addressee of *Shakespeare's Sonnets*, he is self-regardingly 'contracted' only to himself.[11]

It was necessary, in addition, to show that the provocative conduct fell within a recognised category and that there was some form of proportionality between the provocation and the mode of response. 'Affront by bare words or gestures' was insufficient. See further W Oldnall Russell, *A Treatise on Crimes and Indictable Misdemeanours* (London, 1826, vol 1) 486–89 (which is Smith's main source); and Hale, *Pleas of the Crown* (1800) vol 1, ch XXXVII.

[8] Gaskell, *A Dark Night's Work* (n 1) 75.

[9] ibid 81. His mother's assertion that 'Your father's disapproval is always a sufficient reason to allege' is incorrect as a matter of law. A father's disapproval might mitigate damages, but it did not justify a breach of promise. See references in ch 7, s IV, n 43 above – where a similar issue arises in *The Moorland Cottage*.

[10] Gaskell, *A Dark Night's Work* (n 1) 79.

[11] In Sonnet 1 the young man is described as 'contracted to thine own bright eyes.' For the Shakespearean allusions in *A Dark Night's Work* see below, s V.

Corbet quickly moves to asking himself 'What was to be gained by keeping his engagement with Ellinor?', the language of 'gain' speaking volumes; from thence it is a short step to finding an opportunity – or pretext – to free himself of his obligation. Wilkins, unhappily, provides it: he has been drinking heavily, and is subjected to some uncomfortably close questioning from Corbet about Dunster's disappearance. Wilkins tells Corbet to hold his tongue. It is the perfect excuse: '"Sir!" said Ralph, starting to his feet at being so addressed by "Wilkins the attorney".' Ralph's immediate response is to pull social rank: 'I, a Corbet of Westley ….'[12] He leaves Wilkins' house, never to return. For all the calculations, what spurs Ralph on finally to dispense with Ellinor is her father's failure to know his place, to remember that he is, merely, 'Wilkins the attorney.'

III

A Dark Night's Work not only revisits the place of attorneys – in doing so it also revisits and reworks elements of Gaskell's earlier novels (particularly *Mary Barton*); interweaves references to a wide range of poets; and it also seems to retell elements of *Hamlet* and *The Winter's Tale*. It is, in other words, strikingly intertextual.

Turning first to the allusions back to Gaskell's own work we can begin with the Wilkins family's basic configuration. Wilkins marries, he has two daughters; but his wife dies suddenly and his younger daughter shortly afterwards. His surviving daughter, Ellinor, grows up devoted to him. In a general sense Ellinor's position echoes that of many of Gaskell's heroines who lack a mother's care and guidance: Ruth Hilton (*Ruth*), Margaret Hale (from midway through *North and South*) and, especially, Mary Barton. But Ellinor's relationship with her father is something different – it has a morbidity absent in earlier novels. In a passage of disturbing intensity, Gaskell describes how the relationship develops after Ellinor's mother's death:

> From that time the tie between father and daughter grew very strong and tender indeed. Ellinor, it is true, divided her affection between her baby sister and her papa; but he, caring little for babies, had only a theoric regard for his younger child, while the elder absorbed all his love. Every day that he dined at home Ellinor was placed opposite him while he ate his late dinner; she sat where her mother had sat during the meal, although she had dined and even supped some time before on more primitive nursery fare. It was half pitiful, half amusing to see the little girl's grave, thoughtful ways and modes of speech, as if trying to act up to the dignity of her place as her father's companion …[13]

Readers of *The Moorland Cottage* will hardly need reminding that parental favouritism (paradoxically) tends to damage the more-favoured child more than the less-favoured. 'Half pitiful, half amusing' seems scarcely to do justice to the grotesque situation in which Wilkins insists on placing his grieving child.

[12] Gaskell, *A Dark Night's Work* (n 1) 92.
[13] ibid 9.

Then, when the baby dies, 'Her father put aside all business, all pleasure of every kind to win his darling from her grief. No mother could have done more, no tenderest nurse done half so much as Mr Wilkins then did for Ellinor.'[14] We might notice here that Wilkins' own grief over the loss of his baby daughter is not worth recording; and that he is made to sound uncomfortably like a lover until – in a characteristic move – the narrator steps back, in the second sentence, to compare him with a mother or a nurse. The impression remains, however, that the roles of daughter and wife are being troublingly confused.

The effect of all this on Ellinor is then set out:

> If it had not been for him she would have just died of grief. As it was, she overcame it – but slowly, wearily – hardly letting herself love anyone for some time, as if she instinctively feared lest all her strong attachments should find a sudden end in death. Her love – thus dammed up into a small space – at last burst its banks, and overflowed on her father. It was a rich reward to him for all his care of her, and he took delight – perhaps a selfish delight – in all the many pretty ways she perpetually found of convincing him, if he had needed conviction, that he was ever the first object with her.[15]

These formative events define the relationship: we are told that Wilkins is 'jealous' of anyone who gives Ellinor a present;[16] and that when choosing a governess for Ellinor, his 'first requirement' was 'someone who will not marry me, and who will let Ellinor go on making my tea.'[17] He doesn't need a wife: he has Ellinor. Predictably enough, when Ellinor wants to marry the young barrister, Ralph Corbet, Wilkins hesitates and delays making arrangements for the dowry: 'It was the usual struggle', the narrator assures us, 'between father and lover for the possession of love, instead of the natural and graceful resignation of the parent to the prescribed course of things.'[18] The nonchalance of 'the usual struggle' jumps out here. We might have been forgiven for thinking that the Wilkins family's misfortunes had been *unusual*, so it is rather wrong-footing to be told that this struggle is commonplace. The contrast between 'usual' and 'natural' also rather catches the eye: social conditions have deformed the proper attitudes of fathers toward their daughters – fathers are now routinely jealous and possessive, viewing suitors as love rivals. In a characteristically understated way, Gaskell hints here at the harms and distortions that a patriarchal society creates. The continuation of the sentence spells out exactly where this harm falls: 'and, as usual, it was the poor girl who bore the suffering for no fault of her own; although she blamed herself for being the cause of the disturbance in the previous course of affairs.'[19]

[14] ibid.
[15] ibid 9–10.
[16] ibid 10 – although the narrator again backs away from the most extreme implications by adding 'the first news of which did not come from or through him.'
[17] ibid.
[18] ibid 41.
[19] ibid.

After this crucial moment of narratorial intervention it is, perhaps, not easy to decide whether later events involving Ellinor and her father should be seen as abnormal or not. Two instances are particularly striking. The first comes after Wilkins has been involved in an altercation with his now business partner, Dunster, and has struck him. Dunster falls, and dies. Ellinor and the loyal family servant, Dixon, bury Dunster's body in the garden of Wilkins' house. Ellinor tries to kiss her father; 'No, Nelly', he says, 'you must never kiss me again; I am a murderer.'

> 'But I will, my own darling papa,' said she, throwing her arms passionately round his neck, and covering his face with kisses. 'I love you and I don't care what you are, if you were twenty times a murderer, which you are not; I am sure it was only an accident.'[20]

The second incident, at the conclusion of the novel, takes place in Ralph Corbet's study. Many years have passed since the engagement between Ralph and Ellinor was broken off; Ellinor shows Ralph a letter of apology from her father to Ralph, which was never completed. After Corbet has read the letter, Ellinor says: '"I may take this letter, I suppose …", casting envious loving eyes at her father's note.'[21]

In a novel where Ellinor is engaged to marry one man, and ends up marrying another, all the most powerfully passionate and emotional moments and language are with her father: neither her fiancé nor her husband are ever 'her first object', or seen having their faces smothered with kisses. And, as if the point needed amplifying, Ellinor's 'envious loving eyes' are directed at the symbol of her deceased father, not the living man to whom she was once engaged.

What has happened to make this relationship transgress 'the prescribed course'? Gaskell's language ('the usual struggle') suggests that the underlying factors are societal. The society she depicts is one in which social hierarchies are enforced with repressive zeal. Thus, the attorney's position remains precarious for decades: necessary but barely tolerated; admitted to society but only on pointedly restrictive terms. It is a society in which social status is immutable, its values backward-looking. It is perfectly expressive of these values when we are told that veneration is given to the Baronetage's record of patrilineal descent and that, when Wilkins makes attempts at social advancement he does so by seeking to prove a connection to the old De Winton family.[22] He can only hope to change his future by changing his forefathers' past.

In such a society, straightforward, fulfilling, spontaneous social interaction is impossible, and people like the attorney find themselves utterly isolated. It is, perhaps, then, not a surprise that they turn inwards – becoming morbidly obsessed with their own small family circle, prey to jealousy and discontent. In one of the most poignant moments in the novel, Gaskell gives us a glimpse of a different possibility. An assembly ball is being held; these are normally the preserve of

[20] ibid 55.
[21] ibid 161–62.
[22] ibid 5 (Baronetage); 16–17 (De Wintons).

the gentry, but Mr Wilkins senior has procured an invitation for his son. 'Many a squire glowered and looked black', but

> the duchess, to whom the _shire squires and their little county politics and contempts were alike unknown, saw no reason why her lovely Lady Sophy should not have a good partner, whatever his pedigree might be, and begged the stewards to introduce Mr Wilkins to her.[23]

The enticing vision of something close to natural selection is, however, no fairytale. The duchess' snobbery has merely temporarily trumped the gentry's: 'Edward was fully aware, if his fond father was not, that of all the young ladies who were glad enough of him as a partner at the Hamley assemblies, there was not one of them but would have considered herself affronted by an offer of marriage from an attorney, the son and grandson of attorneys.' This is a world in which your father and grandfather define who you are, and, with it, your life's opportunities and potential. Some of the features of Ellinor's relationship with her father are extreme, but, Gaskell seems to suggest, the attitudes of both father and daughter stem from the underlying values of the society of which they are part.

IV

Further reworkings of Gaskell's legal preoccupations can be seen as the plot develops. As in *Mary Barton*, an innocent man is tried for murder; also as in *Mary Barton*, the evidence against the accused is damning, particularly as the accused is unwilling to offer any defence. In both novels the law is shown being unable to imagine that those subject to it might have commitments that take priority over their treatment by the criminal law, and that love might lead them to sacrifice themselves.

Where, however, *Mary Barton* and *A Dark Night's Work* diverge, is that in *Mary Barton* the alibi evidence is obtained in the nick of time, and Jem Wilson is acquitted. Dixon is convicted – Ellinor being unable to return to England in time for his trial. This provides Gaskell with the opportunity to trace Ellinor's attempts to have the conviction overturned, which begin with Ellinor's going to Mr Johnson, the 'solicitor' (note, not 'the attorney') who had been charged with Dixon's defence. Immediately there is an obstacle – Johnson is holding an all-male dinner party for local lawyers. Ellinor cannot speak to him, but he sends her a note the gist of which is that she must wait until the following day to visit Dixon. Ellinor presents herself at the prison the next day, but she is turned away, first by the prison porter, then by the prison governor, as she lacks a sheriff's order. 'Her hope … that in her case there might be some exception to the rule' is 'of course', says the narrator, disappointed.[24] Ellinor returns, defeated, to Mr Johnson; it transpires, however,

[23] ibid 3.
[24] ibid 148.

that one of Johnson's dinner-party guests the previous evening was clerk to the magistrates, and that Johnson had asked this man to arrange a sheriff's order for Ellinor. The order is soon delivered, but 'Mr Johnson would come with her to see that she met with no difficulty or obstacle.'[25] Johnson's presence turns out to be invaluable – there is a rule that a turnkey must be present at any interview, but, Johnson explains to Ellinor, an 'obliging' turnkey will keep out of earshot. 'Mr Johnson quietly took care that the turnkey who accompanied Ellinor was "obliging".'[26] Perhaps Gaskell means here to hint at bribery. Whether she does so or not, the whole sequence eloquently illustrates what Ellinor is up against. The system is not necessarily corrupt, but it is bewildering: some rules are inflexibly enforced, others only in the letter but not the spirit. Above all, it is a system from which a single woman is essentially shut out – from Johnson's dinner party arrangements for the sheriff's order (which seem to bypass any formal application process), to the insider knowledge of how to secure an 'obliging' turnkey.

The process of having Dixon's conviction reviewed continues the theme. Ellinor is told that the decision is the Home Secretary's, but, at the same time, she 'cannot get access to him.'[27] She has to go to the trial judge – Judge Corbet (Ralph has been having a stellar legal career). Even then, Mr Johnson suggests that Ellinor will need more help, and offers to 'arrange and draw up what will have to be said.'[28] Ellinor, however, resolves to deal with matters herself, and hurries to London. She finds Corbet's address and goes to his home. Even before he has heard what she has to say, Corbet can offer some reassurance about Dixon's fate: 'the sentence is sure to be commuted to transportation, or something equivalent. I was talking to the Home Secretary about it only last night.'[29] We have previously been told that Corbet was out the previous evening at dinner – and it is rather striking quite how much crucial legal business seems to have been done by men at dinner-parties in the closing stages of this novel.

Ellinor then tells Corbet what really happened on the night of Dunster's death.

> The judge had been noting all down. He sat still now without replying to her. Then he wrote rapidly, referring to his own previous paper, from time to time. In five minutes or so he read the facts which Ellinor had stated, as he now arranged them, in a legal and connected form. He just asked her one or two trivial questions as he did so. Then he read it over to her, and asked her to sign it. She took up the pen, and held it, hesitating.
>
> 'This will never be made public?' said she.
>
> 'No! I shall take care that no one but the Home Secretary sees it.'
>
> 'Thank you. I could not help it, now it has come to this.'[30]

[25] ibid 151.
[26] ibid.
[27] ibid 150.
[28] ibid.
[29] ibid 155.
[30] ibid 160.

As Mr Johnson had anticipated, Ellinor cannot speak for herself, her truth needs to be 'arranged … in a legal and connected form', and is incomplete without the addition of trivial details. Dixon is reprieved, and all ends happily. Nevertheless, the means by which this conclusion is reached is somewhat disquieting. Gaskell hints at a labyrinthine, exclusively male, legal system where there are unpredictable gaps between form and substance that are traps for the uninitiated, but are capable of expert exploitation by the men in the know. Critical steps seem to take place in surprisingly informal, social contexts. Ellinor, we might feel, has been extremely fortunate to have Mr Johnson as her guide and advisor. It has also been a happy coincidence that the trial judge happened to be Ellinor's former fiancé: Ellinor has been warned by Johnson (who does not know about her previous relationship with Corbet) that 'you must be prepared with some kind of proof; for Judge Corbet will have to test your evidence.'[31] In the event, no such testing takes place, as Ellinor's honesty is already established. It seems all too easy to imagine things turning out differently.

Stephen Severn has gone further, describing the conclusion of the novel as a 'sudden and illogical closure … so patently absurd that it violates a central aesthetic tenet of nineteenth-century realist fiction.'[32] For Severn, Ralph's assurance of secrecy begins a series of implausibilities; it is impossible to believe that Dixon would be set free without public debate; and Ellinor and Dixon are accessories after the fact – they would not get away scot-free. The result is an ending that 'does not develop closure; it merely asserts it', with an ostentatiousness that makes it absurd.[33]

Gaskell's original readers could not have viewed the conclusion in this way. Indeed, in its depiction of the Home Secretary's review as a highly informal and secret process, in which the original trial judge's recommendation was often determinative, Gaskell's novel is rigorously realistic. Writing in the same year that *A Dark Night's Work* received its serial publication, James Fitzjames Stephen complained of precisely those features of the current law which Severn has claimed stretched credulity: 'The procedure is altogether informal. There is no open court, no examination of witnesses, no pleading of counsel on either side, and there is not even any parliamentary supervision.'[34] Stephen was convinced that 'the mode of administration is wrong, because under it a function which is really judicial is discharged by an irregular and irresponsible tribunal, consisting of a single statesman who has no

[31] ibid 150.

[32] S Severn, 'Narrative Cessation and Professional Culture in Elizabeth Gaskell's *A Dark Night's Work*' (2014) 40(1) *Victorian Review* 155, 156.

[33] ibid 170–71.

[34] J Fitzjames Stephen, *A General View of the Criminal Law of England* (Macmillan & Co, 1863) 224. For an excellent account of the Home Secretary's functions, and the arguments for reform in this period see K Smith, 'Sentencing and Review' in W Cornish et al, *Oxford History of the Laws of England Volume XIII: 1820–1914 Fields of Development* (Oxford University Press, 2010) 122, 128–34. On attempts to develop a more systematic approach to the Home Secretary's powers see R Chadwick, *Bureaucratic Mercy: The Home Office and the Treatment of Capital Cases in Victorian England* (Garland Publishing, 1992).

special acquaintance with law and no judicial experience.'[35] His proposed solution was to create a new court. Gaskell, however, has a rather different perspective: for her heroine the secret nature of the proceedings is crucial. Ellinor hesitates to sign until she is reassured about secrecy – she evidently still feels anxious about publicly betraying her father, and the fear of public shame that would be inevitable in an open court hearing would be a great discouragement to her coming forward. Gaskell's heroines are often intimidated by the prospect of public exposure in court;[36] by having the informal, secret Home Secretary procedure work so well for Ellinor, Gaskell subtly draws attention to an important, and gendered, benefit of the existing process, which legal writers on the subject had paid no attention to.

V

In addition to revisiting, elaborating and varying aspects of her own earlier work, Gaskell noticeably alludes to the work of others. Critics have noticed glancing references to Milton ('wisest, best'), Tennyson (Ralph Corbet's attraction to 'human stepping-stones') and, ironically, to Browning ('Oh, that she had been in England').[37] To these we may add an allusion to Chatterton when the narrator is describing Mr Livingstone, a clergyman who has grown a little stout, as having 'the type of holy innocence which some of the Romanists call the "sacerdotal face"'.[38] In *Kew Gardens* Chatterton describes a clergyman in the following terms:

> Within whose sacerdotal face,
> Add all the honorary signs of grace;
> Great in his accent, great in his size,
> But mightier still in turtle and mince pies.[39]

In his *Articles of Belief of Me Thomas Chatterton* the poet had identified himself as a Romanist when he declared that 'The Church of Rome (some Tricks of Priestcraft excepted) is certainly the true Church.'[40]

These allusions are characteristic of Gaskell's witty lightness of touch, but she also, in several allusions to Shakespeare, seems to be making a more ambitious,

[35] ibid 230.

[36] See eg Mary Barton, who suffers a nervous collapse after giving evidence; Margaret Hale, who fears exposure at an inquest into Leonards' death in *North and South*.

[37] Milton: S Lewis, notes to *A Dark Night's Work and Other Stories* (Oxford University Press, 1993) at 313, referring to 163 in the preceding text. The Milton text is *Paradise Lost*, Book VIII, 1.550 – 'wisest, virtuousest, discreetest, best'. The allusions to Tennyson and Browning are proposed in G Handley, '*A Dark Night's Work* Reconsidered' (2007) 21 *The Gaskell Society Journal* 65 at 69 and 70. The Tennyson allusion is to *In Memoriam*, 'That men may rise on stepping-stones/ Of their dead selves to higher things.' Browning's poem 'Home Thoughts from Abroad' begins 'Oh to be in England.'

[38] Gaskell, *A Dark Night's Work* (n 1) 116.

[39] Thomas Chatterton, 'Kew Gardens' in *The Complete Works of Thomas Chatterton: A Bicentenary Edition* (Donald S Taylor (ed), Oxford University Press, 1971) vol 1, 525 lines 457–60.

[40] 'Grevel Lindop, 'Introduction' to T Chatterton, *Selected Poems* (Carcanet, 1972) 7, 13.

and intriguing set of suggestions. After Dunster has been killed, Ellinor's father's health declines and he dies. Ellinor has to give up the house as her father has lost all his money, and her guardians (one of whom is Mr Johnson) make the decision in her best financial interests.[41] Ellinor moves to East Chester, where, on her arrival, rooks are seen flying to their nests in the elm trees.[42] Is Ellinor the crow flying to the rooky wood, as in *Macbeth*?[43] While she might look indistinguishable from other residents of East Chester, her traumatic past, and the terrible secret she still hides, make her very much a crow among the rooks.

To this subtle allusion can be added two direct references: to Autolycus's song from *The Winter's Tale*, and to Ellinor looking 'as woe-begone as Ophelia'.[44] In both cases there is an immediate explanation for the allusion. Autolycus's song, particularly the lines 'A merry heart goes all the day/ Your sad heart tires a mile-a', would explain why, as their engagement starts to unravel, Ellinor and Ralph look weary after a short stroll.[45] Wilkins describes Ellinor as looking like Ophelia when she has been caught in the middle of mutually unsatisfactory negotiations between Wilkins and Ralph over Ellinor's dowry. It is possible to read both allusions as merely illustrating self-contained, specific plot points.

However, both plays resonate more deeply with the novel. To take *Hamlet* first: there are many striking similarities between the world of *Hamlet* and the world of Hamley. One of the most immediate is characters' names. Hamlet and Fortinbras have the same names as their fathers, and there is the oppressive sense that this identicality brings with it inescapable duties and obligations to, and on behalf of, fathers from whose shadows both sons struggle to emerge.[46] The same goes for 'Wilkins the attorney', who, to the gentry, is indistinguishable from his predecessors. Gaskell beautifully makes the point at the very start of the novel (in the passage quoted at the start of this chapter). Who is being referred to when Gaskell says 'He visited among them' – father or son? Both in Shakespeare and in Gaskell the protagonist has attempted to escape from the stifling milieu by attending university – in both that escape is closed off. The pattern of naming children after parents applies also – in Gaskell – to girls. Ellinor's mother was called Lettice, like her grandmother. It amounts to a small act of resistance for Ellinor not to be named 'Lettice', and, even here, there is an echo of *Hamlet*: Elsinore becoming Ellinor, as Hamlet has become Hamley.

If, then, Gaskell has transposed *Hamlet* for the psychological setting of *A Dark Night's Work*, the structure of her novel seems also to be a response to *Hamlet*. Hamlet's closing words in Act I, scene 2, that 'foul deeds will rise/ Though all the earth o'erwhelm them to men's eyes' is a very accurate, indeed, a literal, plot summary of *A Dark Night's Work*. And, like *Hamlet*, the plot of the novel proceeds

[41] Gaskell, *A Dark Night's Work* (n 1) 101–102.
[42] ibid 108.
[43] W Shakespeare, *The Tragedy of Macbeth* 3.2.55–56.
[44] Gaskell, *A Dark Night's Work* (n 1) at 74 and 42.
[45] W Shakespeare, *The Winter's Tale* 4.3.123–124.
[46] This idea is very persuasively developed by E Smith, *This Is Shakespeare* (Penguin, 2019) ch 11.

by violent flurries of events interspersed with periods of uneasy stasis. The sense of everything suddenly happening too quickly in *Hamlet* (one of the ways in which 'the time is out of joint') is echoed in Gaskell, for instance when Ellinor's friend Miss Monro observes to her 'You have been travelling too much and too fast, my child.'[47] A further parallel can be seen in the discussion about how best to bury Dunster's body, when Dixon regrets that it cannot be in the churchyard; there has, of course, been a similar debate about Ophelia's burial.[48]

Where Gaskell departs from Shakespeare in her retelling of *Hamlet* is that in *A Dark Night's Work* 'Ophelia' suffers, but she does not die; her courage and heroism achieve a happy conclusion. In her transformation from passive victim to determined heroine, the railway, and the legal rules applying to it, play a crucial part. It is the new railway line that unearths Dunster's body in the garden of the Wilkins family's former home; the railway that transports Ellinor at speed to Ralph Corbet's house; and the absence of railway that retards and disrupts transmission of letters which would have warned Ellinor about the impending crisis.[49] The railway thus precipitates the final crisis, but also enables its resolution. At first glance, the sale of the land to the railway company seems to occur with improbably rapidity – Ellinor is, after all, only away from England for a couple of weeks. Here, however, as with her depiction of the informal process for reviewing convictions, Gaskell has drawn directly from life. Railway companies were empowered to acquire all land along their routes by compulsory purchase.[50] In practice they seem very rarely to have needed to exercise these powers, since they typically made landowners attractive offers: Mr Johnson's letter about the sale refers, very realistically, to 'the handsome sum the railway company had offered.'[51] Gaskell is also quite correct to envisage sale of the land going through without the beneficiary of the trust (ie Ellinor) needing to consent: under the Lands Clauses Consolidation Act 1845, section 7 trustees were empowered to sell land as if their ownership were absolute.[52] Hamlet's complaint about 'the law's delay' could not have been levelled at railway companies' land acquisitions.[53]

Questions of time run insistently throughout the novel. The Hamley in which the novel opens seems to be somewhere that time stands still – its values backward-looking and its inhabitants forever fixed in their social positions (and names). Dunster's death, then the railway, violently punctuates the stasis and makes time

[47] Gaskell, *A Dark Night's Work* (n 1) 162–63.

[48] ibid 54; *Hamlet* 5.1.

[49] ibid at 133, where the absence of a railway between Lyon and Marseilles is emphasised.

[50] W Cornish et al, *Law and Society in England 1750–1950*, 2nd edn (Hart Publishing, 2019) 155–57; RW Kostal, *Law and English Railway Capitalism 1825–1875* (Clarendon Press, 1994) ch 4.

[51] Gaskell, *A Dark Night's Work* (n 1) 133. Kostal (n 49) 147–61. Kostal's sympathy for railway companies' complaints that they were forced to pay more than the market value of land is challenged in S Jack and A Jack, 'Nineteenth-Century Lawyers and Railway Capitalism: Historians and the Use of Legal Cases' (2003) 24 *Journal of Legal History* 59 at 72–73.

[52] On the significance of the 1845 Act see FA Sharman, 'The History of the Lands Clauses Consolidation Act 1845' [1986] *Statute Law Review* 13 (Part I) and 78 (Part II).

[53] *Hamlet*, 3.1.71.

lurch forwards, while, rather oddly, time seems to pass differently for different characters. Miss Monro, the governess, is forty when she arrives in Hamley, but still only forty a dozen years later. Dixon, too, seems to be ageless.[54] Ralph Corbet, by contrast, ages prematurely[55] – although it is also true to say, as Graham Handley observes, that he was never really young at all.[56] The timing of other events also seems problematic: for instance, Ellinor discusses Ruskin's writings on the architecture of Salisbury Cathedral before they had been published.[57] Perhaps most strikingly, after the murder Ellinor spends 16 years in a kind of suspended animation, and then, as she finally reveals all to Corbet, time runs backwards.[58]

The sheer number, and systematic nature of these creative uses of time surely suggest that Gaskell's allusion to Autolycus' song is no casual coincidence, for *The Winter's Tale* is a work preoccupied with the same questions that interest Gaskell. Even the period of suspension (sixteen years) is the same for Shakespeare's Hermione as it is for Ellinor.[59] The feeling of time being suspended and stretched also casts light on Gaskell's tribulations with the work's title.[60] We are discussing it where Gaskell wanted to place it – at the end. If she had had her way, this radical formal innovation would have made the work unique.[61] Dickens, however, overruled her, and changed the title from *A Night's Work*. Gaskell was unable to persuade the book publisher to restore her choice. As critics have noticed, 'Dark' strikes a note of sensationalism which is ill-suited to the events of the novel, as the most sensational incident, Dunster's death, occurs about a third of the way through. What seems to have received less attention is the significance of Gaskell's original title. At first sight it seems an odd misdescription of a novel that covers several decades. The point, surely, is that, psychologically speaking, that dreadful night has lasted for years: the 'work' it generated was not the mere manual labour of digging a grave, but the psychological and spiritual struggles it imposed on Wilkins, Ellinor and Dixon. Not until the truth has been made known, Dixon exonerated, and Ellinor able to move on with her life is the 'work' created by that night truly over. Gaskell's original title captured a paradox about time – and was thus perfectly suited to a novel in which unsettlingly fluctuating experiences of time are so prominent.

[54] J Sutherland, 'Two-timing novelists' in *Is Heathcliff a Murderer? Puzzles in 19th-Century Fiction* (Oxford University Press, 1996) 123 at 130–31.

[55] Gaskell, *A Dark Night's Work* (n 1) 113 and, especially 153, where Dixon describes Judge Corbet as 'but a wizened old fellow in his grey wig. I should hardly ha' known him.'

[56] Handley (n 37) 65.

[57] Sutherland (n 53) 129.

[58] Gaskell, *A Dark Night's Work* (n 1) 161.

[59] Handley (n 37) 69.

[60] S Lewis, 'Introduction' to E Gaskell, *A Dark Night's Work and Other Stories* (Oxford University Press, 1993) ix–x.

[61] G Genette, *Paratexts* (JE Lewin tr, Cambridge University Press, 1997) 65 is not able to identify any literary work where the title appears at the end; the only example he can provide is the musical one of Debussy's *Préludes*, where the titles of individual preludes are placed at the end of each piece; even there, as he points out, the general title appears at the head of the work.

9

The Manchester Marriage

I

Gaskell's 1858 short story 'The Manchester Marriage' revisits, and elaborates on, aspects of her engagement with law that had preoccupied her since *Mary Barton*. The story concerns the unwittingly bigamous marriage of Alice Wilson (not to be confused with the Alice Wilson of *Mary Barton*) and Thomas Openshaw. It is bigamous because Alice's husband, Frank, was thought to have been lost at sea, but is in fact still alive, and eventually makes his way back to England. Frank tracks down Alice, comes to the Openshaws' house, but Alice and Thomas happen to be out, entertaining visitors. Frank, however, insists on speaking to Alice's longstanding and devoted servant Norah. Norah's attempt to conceal Frank's visit has the unhappy effect of placing her under suspicion for theft of a brooch belonging to a guest of the Openshaws, and the Detective Police are called. It turns out that the brooch has merely been mislaid, and Norah is soon exonerated. In the meantime, Frank has committed suicide in the Thames. Norah tells Thomas the whole story, but Alice never finds out. The story ends, shortly after Alice's death, with Thomas at Frank Wilson's grave, explaining to his step-daughter (Frank and Alice's daughter) that Frank had tried to return to see her. 'Sitting by the grave, Mr Openshaw told her the story, and for the sad fate of that father whom she had never seen, he shed the only tears she ever saw fall from his eyes.'[1]

Two aspects of this complex and disturbing story are particularly significant for understanding Gaskell's relation to law: her depiction of the Detective Police and her treatment of bigamy. The Detective Police enter the story when, the day after Frank's call at the Openshaws', one of the Openshaws' visitors believes that her valuable brooch is missing. The servants are questioned, and reveal that a mysterious man had called at the house and had been determined to speak to Norah. Norah refuses to reveal the man's identity, a refusal which prompts Thomas and his visitors to speculate that Norah must have a lover who is taking advantage of her. One of the visitors, Mr Chadwick, takes it upon himself to report the matter to the Detective Police. This is how Gaskell describes it:

> He went to the police-station, and made a statement of the case. He was gratified by the impression which the evidence against Norah seemed to make. The men all agreed in

[1] 'The Manchester Marriage' in E Gaskell, *Cousin Phillis and Other Stories* (H Glen (ed), Oxford World's Classics, 2010) 130 at 155.

> his opinion, and steps were to be immediately taken to find out where she was. Most probably, as they suggested, she had gone at once to the man, who, to all appearance, was her lover. When Mr Chadwick asked how they would find her out, they smiled, shook their heads, and spoke of mysterious but infallible ways and means.[2]

Norah has, indeed, gone to the hotel where Frank Wilson is staying. She is, somehow, followed there by a detective. When Norah learns that Frank has gone out, the landlady offers her a room to wait in. Norah accepts, and the landlady 'quietly' locks her in.[3] The narrative perspective then shifts to the view of the (unnamed) detective:

> Asking the landlady to detain [Norah] for an hour or so without giving any reason beyond showing his authority (which made the landlady applaud herself a good deal for having locked her in), he went back to the police-station to report his proceedings. He could have taken her directly; but his object was, if possible, to trace out the man who was supposed to have committed the robbery. He then heard of the discovery of the brooch; and consequently did not care to return.[4]

The Detective Police's involvement is confined to only three pages – but these pages are densely packed with incident and significance. We have already seen, in *Mary Barton*, and in 'Disappearances', that Gaskell has a somewhat ambivalent attitude towards the police.[5] Here, as in *Mary Barton*, the police busy themselves constructing a case against an innocent person. Unlike in *Mary Barton*, however, there is more professionalism and skill on show. The 'infallible ways and means' which allow them to track Norah recall Gaskell's awestruck description of police methods in 'Disappearances'. But, where 'Disappearances' was slightly regretful that all mysteries would now be solved with chilling efficiency, 'The Manchester Marriage' suggests that such regrets are unnecessary – the limits of police 'infallibility' are starkly displayed.

Those limits are immediately apparent from Mr Chadwick's visit to the police-station. Chadwick has very evidently made up his mind what has happened: his 'statement of the case' is coloured by the conviction that Norah has a lover of bad character, who has exploited Norah's position in the household to gain access to the property. 'The men all agreed' in this explanation, despite its being founded on nothing more than a clichéd stereotype of an older, single woman being blinded by insincere protestations of love. When events move to the hotel, the same unevidenced and patronising assumption entitles the detective to request Norah's temporary imprisonment. Here it seems that the police's suspicions overlap with, and are perhaps reinforced by, a more general prejudice that Norah has been subjected to. We never know why the landlady, who knows nothing of earlier events, takes it upon herself to lock Norah in the room, but Norah's surname is

[2] ibid 150–51.
[3] ibid 152.
[4] ibid.
[5] See ch 2, s VI.

Kennedy – she may well be, and sound, Irish. With investigative foundations like these, self-congratulatory claims of police infallibility become nothing less than ridiculous.

In 'Disappearances' Gaskell had worried that there might be no space for writers of fiction in a world where the Detective Police were on hand to solve all mysteries. As Stephen Severn has suggested, 'The Manchester Marriage' seems to be experimenting with the kinds of fiction that might co-exist with a detective police force.[6] Gaskell's answer is, effectively, that efficient methods of surveillance and evidence-gathering are all very well, but understanding the significance of that evidence requires nuanced, imaginative storytelling abilities which the police consistently lack. They do not even realise that they are falling back on the most banal stereotypes and clichés; they can imagine only the most crude, self-interested, sexual motives, and are entirely unable to conceive that things might not be quite as they seem. The novelist, Gaskell shows us, is very different: the complexities and unpredictabilities of human psychology are her raw materials, the multiplicity of motives for action (particularly, the varieties of love and altruism) key to narrative development. The novelist also offers a more rounded, humanising vision – people and events are not reduced to mere terms of a puzzle, to be cast aside if the puzzle no longer needs solving, as occurs when the detective 'did not care' to return to the hotel where Norah was being wrongly detained on his authority. Instead, the novelist shows her characters the courtesy of treating them with respect, and with an empathy that allows us to identify with their moral dilemmas and divided loyalties. Gaskell is, in short, asserting the centrality of narrative imagination in the successful analysis of human conduct, and (re-)asserting the novelist's supreme claim to that gift.

II

Bigamy is hardly an unusual subject-matter for mid-Victorian fiction, although it is worth noticing that 'The Manchester Marriage' significantly predates Mary Elizabeth Braddon's *Lady Audley's Secret* and the deluge of bigamy fiction that novel inspired.[7] Gaskell's treatment of the subject is characteristically (for her) unsensational, psychological and particularly interesting in its focus on how others are affected by the unintentional bigamy.

[6] S Severn, 'The Afterlife of Elizabeth Gaskell's "Disappearances": "Right at Last" and "The Manchester Marriage" as Experiments in Detective Fiction' (2015) 29 *Gaskell Journal* 37.

[7] *Lady Audley's Secret* was published in 1862, four years after 'The Manchester Marriage'. For a valuable discussion of the implications of bigamy plots see M McAleavey, 'Inconvenient Husbands and Superfluous Wives' (2013) 39 *Victorian Review* 35. The same author's 'The Plot of Bigamous Return' (2013) 123 *Representations* 87 brings out a longer view of bigamy as a crucial plot element, particularly in the ballad tradition, which she sees Gaskell drawing on in *Sylvia's Lovers*.

Gaskell sets the scene by explaining that Mr Openshaw and his wife, 'a pretty, gentle woman, of suitable age and character' have taken a house in London.[8] Alice Openshaw has been married before, the narrator explains, to a sailor named Frank Wilson with whom she had a daughter, Ailsie. After Frank's ship is reported lost at sea, Alice and her mother-in-law relocate from Liverpool to Manchester and open a boarding-house. One of the boarders is Thomas Openshaw, a rather brusque bachelor, whose kindnesses to Ailsie start to create a bond with Alice. Openshaw's proposal is, nevertheless, hardly designed to sweep Alice off her feet: 'Mrs Frank, is there any reason why we should not put up our horses together?'[9] Alice barely understands him. But, once she knows what is being asked, she accepts.

Several years go by – it is not quite clear how many – they have a son, they move to London. As we have seen, one night Frank reappears having been 'kept for years among savages' (again, how many years is never specified).[10] Frank immediately grasps the situation, briefly looks in at his sleeping daughter, then leaves. We learn later that he has gone to drown himself. Norah protects Alice from the knowledge that Frank was still alive, but she cannot avoid having to explain everything to Thomas Openshaw. Openshaw's response is admirable. He is, initially, guilt-stricken when he hears about Frank Wilson's suicide, and insists on accompanying Norah when she goes to identify Wilson's body: 'I must go with you and look on the face of the man I have so injured – unwittingly, it is true; but it seems to me as if I had killed him.'[11] Openshaw arranges a burial and tombstone for Wilson. On the last page of the story we are told that:

> Towards Alice he could hardly be more kind than he had always been; but he now seemed to look on her as someone sacred, and to be treated with reverence, as well as tenderness. He throve in business, and made a large fortune, one half of which was settled upon her.[12]

The love and concern that Alice's situation elicit from both Norah and Thomas can make it easy to forget that Alice could well have committed a felony. Assuming that the story is set at a date contemporaneous with its publication, the applicable legislation would have been the Offences Against the Person Act 1828, which, by section 22 made it a felony 'If any person being married, shall marry any other Person during the Life of the former Husband or Wife.' There was an exception for a 'Person marrying a Second Time, whose Husband or Wife shall have been continuously absent from such Person for the space of Seven Years then last past, and shall not have been known by such Person to be living within that time.' Alice of course satisfies the knowledge requirement for the exception; but what about the seven years? Gaskell does not tell us. For her purposes it hardly matters, and

[8] Gaskell, 'The Manchester Marriage' (n 1) 130.
[9] ibid 137.
[10] ibid 142–43.
[11] ibid 154.
[12] ibid 155.

that rather underlines and problematises the fact that it makes all the difference for the law. If seven years had not passed, it was not at all clear that Alice's innocent state of mind would have absolved her of criminal liability. Russell's 1828 treatise on crimes, which analyses the earlier offence laid down by the Bigamy Act 1604, gives no indication that an innocent mental state could prevent an accused from being guilty where the second marriage had taken place less than seven years after the first.[13] Later in the nineteenth century, cases on the materially identical offence of bigamy under the Offences Against the Person Act 1861 section 57 were divided on the issue. There was support for the view that an honest, or honest and reasonable, belief that the former spouse was dead prevented a finding of criminal liability;[14] but there was also authority to the opposite effect.[15] The issue was eventually determined in 1889 in favour of the requirement that a guilty mind was necessary.[16] Even on the assumption that a fair and reasonable belief did prevent a finding of criminal guilt, Alice's position would have remained precarious. In a case heard in 1871, a man whose wife had left him, and gone to France, made efforts to ascertain whether the wife was still alive by calling on her mother for information, making inquiries in local towns and consulting a detective (not, evidently, of the 'infallible ways and means' kind). A jury, nevertheless, found that, in the absence of any categorical information from these sources, his belief that his wife was not alive was 'not reasonable.'[17] Alice's belief that her husband has died rests only on the report of the Shipping Office and the fact that the ship's owners had claimed against their insurers for the loss of the ship.[18]

The fact that Alice may well have committed a serious criminal offence, yet no one in the story for a moment invokes criminality, indicates that we are in a fictional territory which Gaskell found particularly rich – namely, a world in which legal rules and requirements are radically at odds with her characters' values. The law's criminalisation of Alice and, at the very least, its position that the Openshaws' marriage is void could hardly be further from the characters' lived experience and values.[19] It has been suggested that Mr Openshaw's decision to settle half of his fortune on Alice (in the paragraph quoted above) was undertaken so as to provide for her 'in a manner that does not depend on her being his wife'.[20]

[13] WO Russell, *A Treatise on Crimes and Indictable Misdemeanours* (Joseph Butterworth and son, 1828) vol 1, ch 23 'Of Bigamy'.

[14] *R v Turner* (1862) 9 Cox CC 145 (honest belief); *R v Turner* (1871) 11 Cox CC 670 (honest belief on fair and reasonable grounds).

[15] *R v Gibbons* (1872) 12 Cox CC 237.

[16] *R v Tolson* (1889) 23 QBD 168. The relation between these cases and broader developments in criminal law is explored in W Cornish et al, *Law and Society in England 1750–1950*, 2nd edn (Hart Publishing, 2019) 585–87.

[17] *R v Horton* (1871) 11 Cox CC 670.

[18] Gaskell, 'The Manchester Marriage' (n 1) 133.

[19] W Cornish, 'Marriage' in W Cornish et al, *The Oxford History of the Laws of England Volume XII, 1820–1914, Fields of Development* (Oxford University Press, 2010) 748; WO Russell, *A Treatise on Crimes and Indictable Misdemeanours* (Joseph Butterworth and son, 1828) vol 1, 191.

[20] H Glen, notes to 'The Manchester Marriage' in E Gaskell, *Cousin Phillis and Other Stories* (Oxford World's Classics, 2010) 260.

If so, this might be some acknowledgement on Openshaw's part that his marriage was not quite all it should have been. Interestingly, however, it was settled law that a testamentary provision 'to my wife Alice' in Openshaw's circumstances would have been perfectly effective.[21] The courts recognised, of course, that the person named was not a wife according to the legal definition, but their overriding objective was to give effect to the testator's intention. In ascertaining that intention, the judges accepted that 'wife' could be used in the secondary sense of a person reputed to be, or treated as, a wife. Openshaw's creation of a settlement, then, is not necessitated by law – it is, surely, prompted by his devotion to Alice, and it is expressive precisely because it is unnecessary, and, therefore, highly unusual. Settlements were typically used only by the wealthiest, aristocratic families, and were created at the time of the marriage, not after it.[22] Openshaw travels far beyond the conventional expectations of his class and wealth when he becomes a settlor.

By the end of the story, we can be in no doubt that Openshaw is a man whose choices and values are admirably independent-minded. His sense of guilt, and responsibility, in the aftermath of Frank Wilson's suicide, for instance, exceeds any legal rules of causation or liability. The revelation of Alice's bigamy has not the slightest effect on his devotion to her; if anything, he cares for her more than before. There is the very clear sense in Gaskell's story that Openshaw's values are not some mere eccentric aberration. On the contrary, it is the law that is made to look eccentric when it denies the validity of such a happy, committed union. And that makes Gaskell's title for the story particularly intriguing. Alice and Thomas have got married in Manchester, but clearly some more significant characteristic of their relationship is being emphasised. Elsewhere in Gaskell, Manchester is the source of direct, plain-speaking common-sense, of self-reliance, advancement through diligence and hard work; all of these qualities can be seen with the Openshaws. There might also, perhaps, be a glancing allusion to the 'Manchester School' of laissez-faire economists; at least, there is an element of economic dependency in the background.[23] The most illuminating sense of the expression, though, is surely as an echo of 'Manchester goods' – the domestic sheets, linen, pillowcases, etc which the Manchester textile industry was famous for. Rather like those goods, the Openshaws' marriage is durable, practical, dependable, comfortable and, above all, functional – it makes both parties happy, and visibly makes Thomas Openshaw a more caring, thoughtful and sympathetic person, not only in his love for Alice, but also in his devotion to Ailsie. Paradoxically, though, this 'Manchester marriage' is, in legal terms, no marriage at all. By the end of the story it is absurd to claim that there is anything counterfeit or shoddy about it, since

[21] *Doe d Gains v Rouse* (1848) 5 CB 422. The proposition was confirmed in *Re Smalley* [1929] 2 Ch 112, and remains good law today: see A Learmonth et al (ed), *Theobald on Wills*, 19th edn (Sweet & Maxwell, 2021) at 29-002.

[22] See eg Cornish et al, *Law and Society* (n 16) at 350, describing settlement as being 'For the upper stratum of society.'

[23] The expression seems to have been first coined in the late 1840s: WD Grampp, *The Manchester School of Economics* (Stanford University Press, 1960) 3.

in all respects that matter it is so much the real thing. Gaskell's story can, in that sense, be seen as ironically juxtaposing Alice's first, short-lived, and not especially happy 'legal' marriage with her 'Manchester' sequel. The story is, however, more than a critique of heavy-handed legal rules. What, applying the pervasive values of the story, makes Thomas and Alice husband and wife is not law, or status, it is that they are committed to each other and behave as spouses; it is the performance, not the source, of obligations that matters. The point is not limited to spouses: Thomas acts as father to Ailsie, finding toys for her, taking her for walks in a wheeled chair. Frank, Ailsie's biological father, sees her once, on his brief return, when he thinks that she is asleep; Ailsie is in fact awake, but, understandably terrified by the appearance of a strange man in her bedroom, she is feigning sleep. In the final sentence of the story (quoted in full in the opening paragraph of this chapter), Frank is described as 'the father [Ailsie] had never seen.' At first glance it looks like a careless mistake by the author: she has seen him before.[24] But surely Gaskell is suggesting an important point here. For her, being a father, like being a husband or wife, is not about rules, or law, or biology – it is about performing the role. Ailsie has never seen Frank being her father – his biological relationship merely gave him the opportunity to be her father in the only sense that (for Gaskell) really counts. The slippery syntax of that final sentence – in which it is all too easy, on first reading, to think that it is Ailsie who will be shedding the tears for the lost father – underlines the point. Her father is Openshaw – he has performed, and continues to do so: in his happy Manchester marriage he has also been an exemplary Manchester father.

[24] C Mitchell, n 19 in E Gaskell, *The Works of Elizabeth Gaskell Volume 3 Novellas and Shorter Fiction II* (C Mitchell (ed), Routledge 2016) 455.

10

My Lady Ludlow

She neither saw, nor heard, nor was in any way cognisant of the existence of those who had no legal right to exist at all.

I

In *My Lady Ludlow* an elderly narrator recounts her experiences in the household of Lady Ludlow several decades earlier. The setting is rural Warwickshire. The novel thus immediately distances itself from Gaskell's contemporary urban fictions. It also, at the very outset, announces that the world in which the story is set is now irretrievably lost: railways and regular postal services, the narrator tells us, have seen it off.[1] The result of these introductory remarks is, therefore, an invitation to the reader to notice, and reflect on, what has changed; perhaps, also, to take issue with the narrator's assertion that all the changes are irreversible.

Among the elements of social life that we observe in rural Hanbury over the course of the novel are the activities of lawyers, justices of the peace and, as *de facto* supreme magistrate, Lady Ludlow herself. We also witness the application and consequences of legal rules (which are almost invariably depicted with perfect doctrinal and historical accuracy). It is a novel in which law is prominent, and which is preoccupied with the question of how law, legal institutions and legal professionals might contribute to the formation of a happy, caring and inclusive society.

Gaskell's interest in this question can be seen even before the novel as such begins: although first published as a freestanding story in 1858, *My Lady Ludlow* was collected in *Round the Sofa and Other Tales* the following year, when Gaskell added a framing narrative.[2] *My Lady Ludlow* became only one, although by far the longest, of the tales told by a circle of acquaintances who had found themselves thrown together in Edinburgh. Other tales included 'An Accursed Race' (discussed further in chapter twelve, section IV). The Edinburgh frame narrative (relegated to an appendix in the World's Classics edition) describes how one of this circle of acquaintances has come to hear the story of Lady Ludlow: she is

[1] E Gaskell, *My Lady Ludlow and Other Stories* (E Wright (ed), Oxford University Press, 1989) 1.
[2] ibid 433.

staying in lodgings, where her landlord's miserliness makes her uncomfortable, so she gladly seizes the opportunity to be elsewhere in the evening. This is how Gaskell describes the landlord:

> the old man – sly, miserly, and intelligent – popping out upon us from his room … with some civility which we learnt to distrust as a mere pretext for extorting more money, yet which it was difficult to refuse: such as the offer of any books out of his library, a great temptation, for we could see into the shelf-lined room; but just as we were on the point of yielding, there was a hint of the 'consideration' to be expected for the loan of books of so much higher a class than any to be obtained at the circulating library, which made us suddenly draw back.[3]

We shall see that this vignette epitomises precisely the set of values and way of life that *My Lady Ludlow* defines itself against. The landlord is all too plainly pursuing his own self-interest, and evidently has no scruples about exploiting the lodger (whom we know is a young woman staying in Edinburgh for medical treatment) and her governess. His invocation of 'consideration', in its legal sense, is perfectly ironic: it is he who should be showing consideration to them, not them providing it to him. Yet, of course, as a matter of legal analysis, the landlord is strictly correct, and it is not as if consideration in the law of contract is some archaic doctrinal survival: it represents the basic feature of free-market economics. What we have here, in microcosm, is the conflict of values that will animate *My Lady Ludlow*: on the one hand the maximisation of self-interest as permitted, and encouraged, by law; on the other hand, an ethic of altruism and empathy. 'Consideration' is fundamental – but 'consideration' in which sense?

II

At the heart of *My Lady Ludlow* there is a commitment to an ethic of consideration in the second sense. It is personified by Lady Ludlow herself, into whose orbit the narrator drifts after the death of her father, to whom Lady Ludlow is distantly related. Lady Ludlow supports six resident companions, one of whom has recently passed away, and the narrator is offered the chance to take her place. She is, in effect, a substitute for a substitute, the companions filling the places of Lady Ludlow's children, who have died in infancy. Lady Ludlow's displaced maternal love extends far beyond any legal obligation, and there is never any risk of 'consideration' in its legal sense intruding. Instead, when, later in the novel, financial constraints are forced upon Lady Ludlow, and her lawyer urges rationalisation including the dismissal of the companions, Lady Ludlow is steadfast: 'she would not listen to the proposal for a moment.'[4] She would, of course, have been perfectly within her legal rights to accede to it.

[3] ibid 435.
[4] ibid 169.

Lady Ludlow's relationships with her servants are, similarly, coloured by care and consideration. At the same time that her lawyer is urging her to dismiss her companions, he also proposes streamlining the servants:

> Her establishment consisted of somewhere about forty servants, of whom nearly as many as twenty were unable to perform their work properly, and yet would have been hurt if they had been dismissed; so they had the credit of fulfilling duties, while my lady paid and kept their substitutes. Mr. Smithson made a calculation, and would have saved some hundreds a year by pensioning off these old servants. But my lady would not hear of it.[5]

What might perhaps look eccentric or irrational in Lady Ludlow's behaviour only appears so when assessed by the standards of selfish economic efficiency. Lady Ludlow is not such a fool as to think that all forty servants are economically necessary; she sees herself as owing them obligations which run far beyond her economic self-interest. Both the narrator and, implicitly, Lady Ludlow herself, register that the servants' engagement is similarly extensive – they would be 'hurt' to be retired, even though they would be financially compensated by a pension. Perhaps most strikingly, the description of Lady Ludlow's household reveals two radically different kinds of transaction on ostensibly identical terms. The first type is the orthodox, legal, contractual exchange of wages for service; the second, in which the form belies the content, is a paralegal, unorthodox conferment of benefit, inspired by earlier service. Contractual forms are being subverted, so that what is typically thought of as an instrument to further both parties' self-interest is in fact being used to pursue altruism, while, at the same time, preserving the dignified fiction that the payment is being made for valuable work. This truly is considerate consideration.

Lady Ludlow is not the only character to be seen deliberately distorting and subverting contracts of service. The entertainingly eccentric Laurentia Galindo has a settled practice, we are told, of recruiting as her one servant an individual incapable of performing the role. She then happily devotes herself to serving her 'servant'. The result is a joyously comical, informal relationship where social deference is replaced by feisty equality – there would be no way of knowing, from their dialogue, who was the mistress and who the servant.[6] Similarly, when Lady Ludlow's steward seems to need clerical assistance, Miss Galindo is happy to oblige, but unhappy to be offered payment by Lady Ludlow.[7] Money cheapens.

By making use of legal forms in such idiosyncratic and subversive ways, both Lady Ludlow and Miss Galindo practise the 'perverse economies' that we have seen elsewhere in Gaskell's work. They closely resemble, for instance, Thurston and Faith Benson and their servant, Sally, in *Ruth*.[8] But where the Bensons' ability

[5] ibid.
[6] See eg ibid, 137–39.
[7] ibid 178.
[8] See ch 3, ss VI–VII.

to give wider social effect to their values is constrained by their limited finances and the ever-intrusive, insistent contrast of Mr Bradshaw (the successful manufacturer), in *My Lady Ludlow* Lady Ludlow has both the means and opportunity to give institutional expression to her values. The result is a household that in many ways sounds like a secular convent (we are told in the opening pages that the buildings resemble a convent, the house was once a priory, the narrator's room is a 'cell').[9] Crucially, it is not a mere charity, but a community. Lady Ludlow and Miss Galindo's values also have the effect of refocusing social priorities; where the dominant ethic is one of care for others, those most in need of care move from the margins of society to its centre. The narrator herself is a perfect illustration: soon after her arrival at Lady Ludlow's she starts to suffer from mobility problems which soon make her unable to walk. The narrator becomes Lady Ludlow's 'especial charge' and, as an acute observer from her sofa in Lady Ludlow's room, gains the insights that inform her story.[10]

The narrator's incapacity also brings in further legal questions, when she is seen by a doctor. The doctor is evidently engaged by Lady Ludlow, and he reports back to her. If the narrator ever learns what the doctor's diagnosis was, she does not share that information with us; the most likely inference is that she is not told.[11] We might perhaps feel that Lady Ludlow, as a parent-substitute, may have good, compassionate reasons for holding back the doctor's assessment. But is it Lady Ludlow's decision to make? Does the assumption of quasi-parental duties bring with it an entitlement to parental rights? Here the legal analysis – Lady Ludlow contracts with the doctor and his report is her information, to deal with as she sees fit – aligns with her parental instincts perhaps a little too conveniently for comfort.

III

Two incidents in the novel revolve around specific points of legal doctrine. The first is Mr Horner's will. Mr Horner is Lady Ludlow's steward, and is devoted to her and her estate. He is also keen to educate Harry Gregson, an intelligent boy from a poor background who lives close by; but unfortunately this initiative brings Horner into conflict with Lady Ludlow. The boy suffers a serious injury while running an errand for Mr Horner. The accident, we later learn, prompts Mr Horner to make a will by which he leaves all his money in trust for the boy's education. Several years then pass, during which the financial position of the Ludlow estate becomes weakened as a result of Lady Ludlow having deliberately, and against Mr Horner's

[9] Gaskell, *My Lady Ludlow* (n 1) at 4, 7 and 9.
[10] ibid 33.
[11] ibid 34.

advice, refused to secure repayments due under a mortgage of her lands. After Mr Horner's death, it is discovered that he has amended his will:

> there was a codicil to the will … – feebly written by Mr. Horner himself, as if in preparation only for some more formal manner of bequest; or, perhaps, only as a mere temporary arrangement till he could see a lawyer, and have a fresh will made. In this he revoked his previous bequest to Harry Gregson. He only left two hundred pounds to Mr. Gray [the local clergyman] to be used, as that gentleman thought best, for Harry Gregson's benefit. With this one exception, he bequeathed all the rest of his savings to my lady, with a hope that they might form a nest-egg, as it were, towards the paying off of the mortgage which had been such a grief to him during his life.[12]

The revised will is, of course, a powerful expression of the loyalty Lady Ludlow inspires. It is also legally interesting. When Gaskell was writing *My Lady Ludlow*, in 1853, the situation would have been regulated by the Wills Act 1837, and the legal position would have been simple. The codicil had not been attested by two witnesses; it was not, therefore, legally effective.[13] *My Lady Ludlow*, however, is set prior to 1837, and the validity of the codicil under the earlier law is a nice question. Since it concerns the transmission of personal property, the basic (and deceptively simple) question is whether it represented the final will of the deceased.[14] The codicil being found in Mr Horner's papers is a point in its favour.[15] But the fact that the rest of the will is formally correct is problematic. The situation is not, perhaps, as suggestive as where a testator has indicated that only formally approved documents are to be taken to be expressive of his final will.[16] Yet nor does this seem to be a case of the formalities not being effected due to lack of time, or an emergency, where the courts had found the lack of formality immaterial.[17] We simply do not know how long there was between Mr Horner's drafting of the codicil and his death, and even if we did know it would not necessarily resolve the question, as a delay would be as consistent with not getting around to seeing an attorney as it would with deliberately not taking the final step of altering the will. We might also wonder whether Mr Horner, as a former attorney's clerk and a man of business, at some level appreciated that the informality of the codicil left him not entirely committed to its provisions.[18] Though the codicil expresses his loyalty, both the legal and fictional contexts

[12] ibid 166.

[13] Wills Act 1837, s 21 required any alteration to a will to comply with the formal requirements for making a will, which were set out in s 9 of the Act. See further A Learmonth et al, *Theobald on Wills*, 19th edn (Sweet & Maxwell, 2021) ch 6, 'Alterations'. On the effect of the 1837 Act see S Anderson, 'Succession, Inheritance and the Family' in W Cornish et al, *Oxford History of the Laws of England. Volume XII: 1820–1914 Private Law* (Oxford University Press, 2010) 3 at 3–4.

[14] T Jarman, *A Treatise on Wills* (Sweet & Maxwell, 1844) vol 1, ch VI, 'Execution and Attestation of Wills Made Before the Year 1838'.

[15] Jarman (n 14) 91.

[16] ibid 93–94.

[17] ibid 95.

[18] *My Lady Ludlow* (n 1) 44. Although we are also told, more generally, that Horner's 'own personal affairs were not in the order in which they had been a year or two before' (168).

work together to suggest the very complex, and conflicted state of indecision that has given rise to it.

There is never any debate in the novel about the validity of the codicil; there is, perhaps, such an ingrained deference to Lady Ludlow's entitlements that no one dreams of challenging them. But the ultimate fate of Mr Horner's 'nest-egg' is characteristic of the novel. Lady Ludlow accepts the money, but only conditionally. As she explains to Harry Gregson: 'Mr. Horner intended you to have this money first. I shall only call it borrowing it from you, Harry Gregson, if I take it and use it to pay off the debt. I shall pay Mr. Gray interest on this money, because he is to stand as your guardian, as it were, till you come of age ...'[19] There are, again, echoes here of *Ruth*, with gifts being reconceived by their recipients as loans. But whereas in *Ruth* the change in the transaction frustrated the donor's intention, here Lady Ludlow has perceived the intention and arrived at a happier way to give effect to it than Mr Horner himself had been able to. By the end of the novel Harry Gregson has been to school and grown up to be a clergyman; thanks to Lady Ludlow, law has not got in the way.

IV

Harry Gregson's rise to the clergy is particularly impressive given his background. He is the son of Job Gregson, a 'notorious poacher', whose committal for trial on a charge of theft is the second of the two law-related incidents mentioned at the start of the previous section. The committal is highly contentious. It has been instigated by a newly-appointed justice of the peace, Harry Lathom, who, it seems, has been overzealous. Mr Gray, the local clergyman, explains what has happened when he comes to see Lady Ludlow to ask her to intervene:

> he has committed Job Gregson for stealing – a fault of which he is as innocent as I – and all the evidence goes to prove it, now that the case is brought before the Bench; only the Squires hang so together that they can't be brought to see justice, and are all for sending Job to gaol, out of compliment to Mr. Lathom, saying it is his first committal, and it won't be civil to tell him there is no evidence against his man. For God's sake, my lady, speak to the gentlemen; they will attend to you, while they only tell me to mind my own business.[20]

The narrator has not been with Lady Ludlow long, but she can immediately see the problems with Mr Gray's request: it is not that intervention would be improper, but that 'my lady was always inclined to stand by her order' and that 'it was rather a point of honour in those days to encourage a young magistrate, by passing a pretty sharp sentence on his first committals.'[21] She stops short of putting it starkly,

[19] ibid 177.
[20] ibid 23.
[21] ibid.

but this is class solidarity overriding the most basic elements of judicial process. It even seems that the justices themselves, in dismissing Mr Gray's concerns, have expressly relied on 'this custom of paying a compliment to a newly-appointed magistrate as their only reason.'[22]

Lady Ludlow is inclined to let events take their course. Her servants seem to have other ideas – as she is out for a drive, the coachman just so happens to take her right past Gregson's home. Lady Ludlow speaks to Gregson's wife; what she hears makes her decide to go to see Lathom. Lathom acknowledges that he issued the warrant, adding 'You are doubtless aware of his character; a man who sets nets and springes in long cover, and fishes wherever he takes a fancy. It is but a short step from poaching to thieving.' Lathom obviously intends this as a persuasive supplementary justification, but Lady Ludlow's reply is surprising:

> 'That is quite true,' replied Lady Ludlow … 'but I imagine you do not send a man to gaol on account of his bad character.'
>
> 'Rogues and vagabonds,' said Mr. Lathom. 'A man may be sent to prison for being a vagabond; for no specific act, but for his general mode of life.'
>
> He had the better of her ladyship for one moment; but then she answered:
>
> 'But in this case, the charge on which you committed him was theft; now his wife tells me he can prove he was some miles distant from Holmwood, where the robbery took place, all that afternoon; she says you had the evidence before you.'[23]

This puts Lathom on the defensive. He tells Lady Ludlow that no such evidence was before him; it may have been before other magistrates at later hearings, but he is not responsible for their decisions. It is an ill-judged reply:

> 'And do you mean to say, Mr. Lathom, that you don't consider yourself responsible for all injustice or wrong-doing that you might have prevented, and have not? Nay, in this case the first germ of injustice was your own mistake …'
>
> … Lady Ludlow caught the look of stubbornness in his face, and it roused her as I had never seen her roused.
>
> 'I am sure you will not refuse, sir, to accept my bail. I offer to bail the fellow out, and to be responsible for his appearance at the sessions. What say you to that, Mr. Lathom?'
>
> 'The offence of theft is not bailable, my lady.'
>
> 'Not in ordinary cases, I dare say. But I imagine this is an extraordinary case. The man is sent to prison out of compliment to you, and against all evidence, as far as I can learn. He will have to rot in gaol for two months, and his wife and children to starve. I, Lady Ludlow, offer to bail him out, and pledge myself for his appearance at next quarter-sessions.'
>
> 'It is against the law, my lady.'
>
> 'Bah! Bah! Bah! Who makes laws? Such as I, in the House of Lords – such as you, in the House of Commons. We, who make the laws in St. Stephen's, may break the mere

[22] ibid 24.
[23] ibid 29.

> forms of them, when we have right on our sides, on our own land, and amongst our own people.'
>
> 'The lord-lieutenant may take away my commission, if he heard of it.'
>
> 'And a very good thing for the county, Harry Lathom; and for you too, if he did, – if you don't go on more wisely than you have begun. A pretty set you and your brother magistrates are to administer justice through the land! I always said a good despotism was the best form of government; and I am twice as much in favour of it now I see what a quorum is …[24]

In our final glimpse of Harry Lathom, he is getting into Lady Ludlow's coach 'with the air of a whipped hound'.[25] We hear no more of Job Gregson being prosecuted for theft.

This is an extraordinarily suggestive and rich passage of dialogue. Gaskell's depiction of rural justices of the peace using their position to settle scores with poachers had powerful historical precedent. Lord Brougham, in 1828, had famously said there was 'not a worse constituted tribunal on the face of the earth' than 'a brace of sporting justices' prosecuting a poacher, and there had been notorious abuses.[26] Gaskell seems to have invented the custom of complimenting a magistrate by imposing a swingeing sentence on his first committal – at least, there is no mention of it by historians;[27] but as an expression of class solidarity, and an example of the criminal law being administered in an inappropriately instrumental way, it seems to make explicit the underlying values in play.

In the discussion about bail, by contrast, there is no novelistic embellishment. As the standard manual for justices of the peace explained, in its 1810 edition, a statute dating back to the reign of Edward I instructed bail to be denied on a charge of felony (of which larceny was an example) where the accused was a thief 'openly defamed and known.'[28] In order to satisfy this requirement it seems not to have been necessary to show that the accused had previously been convicted of an offence; and it is, therefore, easy to see why Justice Lathom would have concluded that Job Gregson could not be bailed.[29] It is worth noticing, however, that although any decision to deny bail would have been justified on the facts, Lathom's broader assertion that theft was not bailable was incorrect. Under the statute, it was only charges of certain kinds of theft, and against

[24] ibid 30–31.

[25] ibid 32.

[26] H Brougham, *Speeches of Henry Lord Brougham* (Adam and Charles Black, 1838) vol 2 at 373; see discussion in JL Hammond and B Hammond, *The Village Labourer 1760–1832* (Longman, Green & Co, 1912) 186–88. The Hammonds' tendency to rely uncritically on fiction as historical evidence is highlighted in PB Munsche, *Gentlemen and Poachers The English Game Laws 1671–1831* (Cambridge University Press, 1981) at 2.

[27] It is not mentioned by the Hammonds (n 26), by Munsche (n 26) ch 4, or by P Polden, 'Justices of the Peace and their Courts' in W Cornish et al, *Oxford History of the Laws of England: Volume XI: 1820–1914 English Legal System* (Oxford University Press, 2010) ch XIII.

[28] R Burn, *The Justice of the Peace and Parish Officer*, 21st edn (Strahan, 1810) vol 1, 210.

[29] ibid 213.

certain kinds of people, that were excluded.[30] Lathom is also rather quick to downplay the extent to which he had a discretion: again, the justices' manual indicates that when dealing with a charge against a person openly defamed as a thief, 'this seems in a great measure to be left at the discretion of the person who has power to bail them.'[31]

A final point to note about Gaskell's treatment of bail is that, rather like her treatment of Mr Horner's will, a legally informed reader would have registered that the law was now radically different. Just as the requirements for a valid will had been transformed and rationalised by the Wills Act 1837, the rules for bail had been streamlined, and made far simpler, by the Indictable Offences Act 1848. At the time *My Lady Ludlow* was published, bail was generally available for any felony except treason.[32] This change in the law gives Lady Ludlow's position an additional dimension. There are not many moments when she is ahead of her time – but here, acting on her instinctive sense of justice – she adopts a position that was pure orthodoxy for Gaskell's readers.

Pure orthodoxy, however, is no way to describe Lady Ludlow's approach to statutes. Her radical atomisation of the basis of statutory authority into the decisions of people like herself and Harry Lathom, and the logical corollary that she and Lathom are free to depart from such decisions when circumstances allow, hardly withstands close analysis. It is, of course, the constitutional significance accorded to such decisions that gives them the force of law. Less strident, but more interesting, is what Lady Ludlow sees as the justification for setting statutes aside: right, her 'own land' and her 'own people'. The latter two factors hint at Lady Ludlow's position as a kind of sovereign. It is a theme to which the novel will return explicitly (when describing Lady Ludlow as 'queen regnant', 'little queen' and 'fairy queen'[33]) and implicitly (describing her approach to disputes with tenants). Such ideas of sovereignty over one's own land, we might notice, are enabled by lack of communication with the outside world: the opening of the novel has emphasised the absence of railways and regular postal deliveries. Nor does it seem that Lady Ludlow needs to assert her sovereignty – it is other characters who describe her as a queen, and the incident with Lathom is exceptional.

But while Lady Ludlow is a kind of sovereign, she is not, despite her expressed admiration for 'good despotism', an autocrat. She regards herself as constrained by what is 'right', which, as we have seen, commits her to conduct which is

[30] See discussion in ibid 212–13.

[31] ibid 213.

[32] Indictable Offences Act 1848, s 22. The section is helpfully explained in S Stone, *The Justices' Pocket Manual*, 8th edn (Shaw and Sons, 1860) 16. The Act was part of the statutory code of criminal procedure introduced by Sir John Jervis: Cornish, Banks et al, *Law and Society in England 1750–1950*, 2nd edn (Hart Publishing, 2019) 37. See also D Freestone and J Richardson, 'The Making of English Criminal Law: (7) Sir John Jervis and His Acts' [1980] *Crim LR* 5.

[33] Gaskell, *My Lady Ludlow* (n 1) 168, 155 and 208. Also, 'Lady Ludlow's invitations were like royal commands' (126).

altruistic and disadvantageous to her own interests. The idea is developed a little in the description of Lady Ludlow's disputes with tenants. Though she acts as judge in her own causes, she, to her steward's occasional dismay, adheres to 'her hereditary sense of right and wrong between landlord and tenant.'[34] It is a sense derived not only from her own experience, but from her father's guidance and instructions.

The world of *My Lady Ludlow* is, then, not merely historically remote and far from the city, it is a microcosm with, in effect, its own distinctive form of government – a kind of altruistic monarchy – and own laws. Those laws' basis in the 'hereditary sense of right and wrong' pitches them against statute; it also gives them the feel of an idealised common law. Like the common law, Lady Ludlow's precepts gain authority from tradition, acceptance, and previous application to materially identical circumstances. And it is perhaps only an accident, but as it happens Lady Ludlow's assertions about bail being available on charges of theft reflected the old common law position (which only categorically denied bail for homicide).[35] Gaskell thus has Lady Ludlow taking up a position that is Janus-faced: it harks back to the early common law, but also anticipates the Victorian reforms of 1848. The result is rather unsettling; the story can no longer be neatly, and condescendingly, placed in a quaint, unmodernised past.

V

Lady Ludlow's assertion of sovereignty is a direct challenge to legal orthodoxy, and it is not the only one. Elsewhere in the novel Gaskell explores, probes and satirises the way that the law's, and the lawyers', perspective misleads and distorts. To begin at the happier, comical end of the scale – after Mr Horner's death, the family lawyer, Mr Smithson arrives. It falls to Miss Galindo, as Mr Horner's former assistant, to present the accounts to him. We already know that Miss Galindo is warm-hearted, loquacious and a little eccentric; but she is also astute, and knows that the fact that the accounts are all correct will probably not be enough for the lawyer. She explains her strategy:

> That man is a good man – a sensible man – and, I have no doubt, he is a good lawyer; but he can't fathom women yet … I read the man … Here was a man who thought that a woman in a black silk gown was a respectable, orderly kind of person; and I was a woman in a black silk gown. He believed that a woman could not write straight lines, and required a man to tell her that two and two made four. I was not above ruling my

[34] ibid 169. See similarly the detail in Gaskell's 1865 novel *Wives & Daughters* about Lord Cumnor, a 'forbearing landlord' occasionally overturning his agent's decisions regarding tenants: Elizabeth Gaskell, *Wives & Daughters* (Pam Morris (ed), Penguin, 2003) 7.
[35] Burn (n 28) 210.

> books, and had Cocker a little more at my fingers' ends than he had. But my greatest triumph has been holding my tongue.[36]

There is a sense here that the good lawyer's failings are inextricably tied to his profession: there is an ingrained way of doing things, any departure from which, no matter how superficial, causes concern. The black silk gown and the silence are read as signs of probity, respectability, competence, reliability. It is fortunate for Mr Smithson that Miss Galindo's performance is an accurate portrayal of her character – one catches a momentary glimpse of how easily the good lawyer could be deceived.

The law's expectations of how the world works, however, can have more serious consequences, as has been the case for Miss Galindo's parents, and, indirectly, for herself. Miss Galindo's father, Hubert, was a second son. His elder brother, Lawrence, inherits the family estate, but Lawrence has gone on a grand tour to Italy, has loved it, and stayed there. Lawrence falls ill and dies in Italy: 'Mr Galindo received a formal letter from his brother's bankers, announcing Sir Lawrence's death, of malaria fever, at Albano, and congratulating Sir Hubert on his accession to the estates and the baronetcy.'[37] 'The London bankers had managed everything well. There was a large sum of ready money in their hands, at Sir Hubert's service ….'[38] Hubert and his wife begin spending the money. But then they:

> had a letter from the lawyer, whom they had employed, saying that Sir Lawrence had left an heir, his legitimate child by an Italian woman of low rank; at least, legal claims to the title and property had been sent into him on the boy's behalf. Sir Lawrence had always been a man of adventurous and artistic, rather than of luxurious tastes; and it was supposed, when all came to be proved at the trial, that he was captivated by the free beautiful life they lead in Italy, and had married this Neapolitan fisherman's daughter, who had people about her shrewd enough to see that the ceremony was legally performed. She and her husband had wandered about the shores of the Mediterranean for years, leading a happy, careless, irresponsible life, unencumbered by any duties except those connected with a rather numerous family.[39]

Lawrence's heirs are soon in touch,

> calling upon Sir Hubert to relinquish title and property, and to refund what money he had expended. He was vehement in his opposition to this claim. He could not bear to think of his brother having married a foreigner – a papist, a fisherman's daughter; nay, of his having become a papist himself. He was in despair at the thought of his ancestral property going to the issue of such a marriage. He fought tooth and nail, making enemies of his relations, and losing almost all his own private property; for he would go

[36] ibid 167. 'Cocker' is *Cocker's Arithmetick*, a hugely successful mathematics textbook, which went through over 130 editions after its first publication in 1678.

[37] ibid 180–81.

[38] ibid 181.

[39] ibid 183.

> on against the lawyer's advice, long after every one was convinced except himself and his wife.[40]

The thread linking together this tumultuous sequence of events is the concept of legitimacy, not merely (although not insignificantly) as a legal rule, but also as a social expectation and societal norm. When Sir Lawrence passes away in Italy it simply does not occur to the bankers, nor to his younger brother, that he might have a wife and children. In rather the same way that Mr Smithson *knows* what a respectable, trustworthy woman looks like, the bankers and Hubert know a Lady Galindo when they see one. They cannot imagine Lawrence departing so much from the type of the English baronetcy into which he is born – his stay in Italy is, for them, merely an aberration, not the result of self-discovery or love. Gaskell makes the point beautifully in her brief description of the trial: 'it was supposed … that he was captivated by the free beautiful life.' 'Captivated' has a note of enchantment, of involuntariness; and 'it was supposed' – by, we assume, observers of the trial – suggests an unsolved mystery, to which this proposed solution is advanced tentatively. The truth is that no one knows. Not that that prevents speculation – the little detail about the 'shrewd' people ensuring a proper marriage is perfect – again, this is pure supposition, and is inspired by the laziest of clichéd assumptions about the kind of relationship an English aristocrat would (or should) have preferred with an Italian fisherman's daughter. It makes the marriage sound like a kind of trick, as if its technical validity was undermined by its inconsistency with wider and deeper ideas of legitimacy. It is, precisely, Sir Lawrence Galindo's failure to defer to these norms of legitimacy that makes his life quite literally incomprehensible to his brother, his bankers and other observers.

Hubert's response to the revelation of his brother's wife and children shows us how deeply held his views of legitimacy are. It becomes more than a matter of law – he persists against legal advice, and we might here be reminded of *The Moorland Cottage* where Mr Buxton, rocked by revelations of his tenants' fraud, insists on suing despite legal advice against it.[41] In both instances it is a dispute, for these two men, about far more than money; their whole worldview is in jeopardy. Hubert's claim to the estate is indeed hopeless, but in making him liable to repay the money advanced by the bankers, Gaskell may have visited even greater humiliation on him than the law would have required. The basis of any claim for that money against Hubert would have been the eighteenth-century equivalent of a claim in unjust enrichment – an action for money had and received. Hubert has, of course, been enriched by the receipt of the money. The payment was made pursuant to a shared understanding that Hubert was entitled to inherit Lawrence's property (ie that Lawrence had no legitimate children). This shared understanding being shown to be false – there being, in eighteenth century legal terms a 'failure

[40] ibid 184.
[41] Discussed in ch 7, s IV.

of consideration' for the payment – a valid reason for restitution is established.[42] However, Hubert has not been enriched at the true heir's expense. The bankers paid without Lawrence's or his heir's authority; the payment does not, therefore, go to reduce the amount by which the bankers are indebted to the heirs – the bankers remain liable to the heirs in the full amount, and the heirs cannot claim any of the money advanced from Hubert.[43] It is, perhaps, little consolation for the loss of the baronetcy.[44]

Hubert's dashed hopes have further ramifications. Miss Galindo had been courted by Mark Gibson, a barrister. When Hubert and his wife thought that they were about to become Sir Hubert and Lady Galindo, they decided that their daughter could do better, and turned Gibson away. He seems to lead an unhappy life, and at his early death leaves behind an illegitimate daughter. The little girl is an orphan. Miss Galindo adopts her, and this precipitates something of a social crisis, as Lady Ludlow cannot countenance illegitimacy. As is said of her, in the passage quoted in the epigraph to this chapter, 'she neither saw nor heard, nor was in any way cognisant of the existence of those who had no legal right to exist at all.'[45] It is a jarringly hard line, which comes as something of a surprise, perhaps, given Lady Ludlow's previous refusal to be dictated to by legal rules. Fortunately her attitude soon softens; but the incident is a reminder of how all-pervasive legal rules, and the social expectations built upon them, can be, even for the most independent-minded of characters.

VI

We began this chapter by reflecting on the remoteness, in both time and place, of this novel, from the mid-nineteenth century urban situation of its creation. The narrator's own remarks seem to invite a reading of the novel as an escapist, rather whimsical, story: the world in which it takes place, we are told, emphatically, has disappeared. But as the novel unfolds we may begin to wonder whether the world Gaskell depicts could ever have existed – it is as much allegorical as historical. At its centre is an imagined community in which the dominant ethic is altruism,

[42] For the classic exposition of the grounds on which a claim for money had and received was available in the eighteenth century see *Moses v Macferlan* (1760) 2 Burr 1005.

[43] C Mitchell, 'Banks, Agency and Unjust Enrichment' in J Lowry and L Mistelis (ed), *Commercial Law and Commercial Practice* (Butterworth, 2006) 109; C Mitchell, P Mitchell and S Watterson (ed) *Goff and Jones on Unjust Enrichment*, 10th edn (Sweet & Maxwell, 2022) at 6–53: 'if the bank has no right to be reimbursed by the customer for the payment it has made, eg because it acted without mandate, and the bank must recredit its customer, the payment is at the expense of the bank alone Hubert would be liable to the bankers, but there is nothing to suggest that the bankers bring a claim against him.

[44] The fact that Hubert had spent some of the money would not have been relevant to liability, since the defence of change of position in unjust enrichment was not recognised until the 1990s (in *Lipkin Gorman (A Firm) v Karpnale Ltd* [1991] 2 AC 548).

[45] Gaskell, *My Lady Ludlow* (n 1) 189.

and which distinguishes itself by resistance to the pressures of selfishness and self-interest. In this radically different community there is a radically different place for law – legal rules have no presumptive authority, let alone value as guides to correct conduct. They can be made use of to accomplish ends entirely different to their ostensible purposes (as in Lady Ludlow's fictional contracts of service) and even set entirely aside (as in Job Gregson's bail). The dangers of internalising legal rules, and building social structures on them, are eloquently illustrated by the contentions in the latter stages of the novel over legitimacy. It is as if it was only by retreating to a setting distant in time and location that Gaskell could find the imaginative space to develop these critical ideas, which speak to so many aspects of Victorian society, with complete freedom.

11

Sylvia's Lovers

I

In *Sylvia's Lovers* Gaskell takes her fiction in a new direction.[1] The novel is set in the 1790s, and mostly takes place in Monkshaven, a fictional town on the north Yorkshire coast with a strong resemblance to Whitby.[2] Its events are driven by Britain being at war with France: several key plot points are triggered by the activities of the press-gangs, who were tasked with finding sailors to man naval vessels. As the narrator sardonically points out, in the opening chapter of the novel, there was a particular need for more sailors 'after every great naval victory of that war.'[3] The tone of the comment reflects the tone of the book, which, more noticeably and insistently than Gaskell's earlier work, dwells on irreconcilably opposed valuations of events. Gain is as inextricably linked with loss as happiness with disappointment, and fulfilment with frustration. It is sometimes a matter of bitter paradox for one character; but often, and more simply, that gain in one quarter inevitably brings loss in another, and that, as Terry Eagleton has pointed out, there is no systematically controlling ideology to adjudicate on events.[4] In a novel concerned with politically controversial subject-matter, the refusal to commit to a controlling ideology, or to propose a solution or, at least, some kind of first steps towards a *rapprochement* (by contrast with, say, *Mary Barton* and *North and South*) give the novel a pervasive air of bleakness.[5]

If the historical setting and the attitude of the novel mark it out as something new in Gaskell's career, there are still elements of continuity – and, among these, are Gaskell's interest in legal rules, legal processes and legal personnel. Indeed, as we shall see, some of the law-related material in *Sylvia's Lovers* directly mimics specific legal incidents in *Ruth*, and Daniel Robson, Sylvia's father, will fail to help himself in his criminal trial, in a way which is reminiscent of Jem Wilson's

[1] T Eagleton, '*Sylvia's Lovers* and Legality' (1976) 26 *Essays in Criticism* 17; C Pettitt, 'Time Lag and Elizabeth Gaskell's Transatlantic Imagination' (2012) 54 *Victorian Studies* 599.

[2] Early readers of the novel, assuming that Gaskell was aiming to create Whitby in all but name, were quick to point out discrepancies: FE Twinn, 'Unpublished Letters and Geographical Errors in *Sylvia's Lovers*' (2001) 48 *Notes and Queries* 149.

[3] E Gaskell, *Sylvia's Lovers* (Francis O'Gorman (ed), Oxford University Press, 2014) 9.

[4] Eagleton (n 1).

[5] E Wright, in *Mrs Gaskell The Basis for Reassessment* (Oxford University Press, 1965) at 172 notes a turn to bleakness in shorter fiction written immediately before *Sylvia's Lovers*.

behaviour in *Mary Barton*.[6] But Gaskell also takes her legal interests in new directions, making unexpectedly detailed references to relevant statutory provisions, and reflecting on the partial, inconsistent effects of law in the society she is depicting. Indeed, law can be seen as a central aspect of the book's overarching theme of the pathologies of repression.

II

From the very first chapter of the book, Gaskell makes it clear that law will have a central, structural and deeply problematic part to play. Having established the setting of the novel as Monkshaven, and having sketched in the threat from France, she continues:

> We had our ships; but where were our men? The Admiralty had, however, a ready remedy at hand, with ample precedent for its use, and with common (if not statute) law to sanction its application. They issued 'press warrants,' calling upon the civil power throughout the country to support their officers in the discharge of their duty. The sea-coast was divided into districts, under the charge of a captain in the navy, who again delegated sub-districts to lieutenants; and in this manner all homeward-bound vessels were watched and waited for, all ports were under supervision; and in a day, if need were, a large number of men could be added to the forces of his Majesty's navy. But if the Admiralty became urgent in their demands, they were also willing to be unscrupulous. Landsmen, if able-bodied, might soon be trained into good sailors; and once in the hold of the tender, which always awaited the success of the operations of the press-gang, it was difficult for such prisoners to bring evidence of the nature of their former occupations, especially when none had leisure to listen to such evidence, or were willing to believe it if they did listen, or would act upon it for the release of the captive if they had by possibility both listened and believed. Men were kidnapped, literally disappeared, and nothing was ever heard of them again. The street of a busy town was not safe from such press-gang captures, as Lord Thurlow could have told, after a certain walk he took about this time on Tower Hill, when he, the attorney-general of England, was impressed, when the Admiralty had its own peculiar ways of getting rid of tiresome besiegers and pensioners.[7]

This extraordinary, detailed, and cutting account of the legal basis for impressment, and its operation in practice, casts a shadow over the rest of the novel. In its legal detail it is impeccable. It was notorious that there was no statutory authority for impressment;[8] the point was made forcefully in what seems to have been the

[6] For discussion of Jem Wilson's trial, see above, ch 2, s V.

[7] Gaskell, *Sylvia's Lovers* (n 3) 9.

[8] See eg W Waterson, *A Cyclopedia of Commerce, Mercantile Law, Finance, Commercial Geography and Navigation*, 2nd edn (Henry G Bohn, 1863) at 374: 'Parliament has never yet, except incidentally, entered upon this subject, probably from a feeling that any legislation regarding it which did not involve abolition of the practice would be very unpopular.'

only attempt to challenge the practice in *R v Broadfoot*.[9] In that case, however, the Recorder of Bristol, Sir Michael Foster, had held that no such statutory authorisation was necessary, since the Crown's right to impress sailors was inherent in its prerogative powers, and was part of the common law.[10] Statute, it was held, was relevant only insofar as a long line of statutes could be identified in which it was assumed that impressment was lawful.[11] As regarded common law, authority for impressment could not be found in any earlier decided cases, but, rather, in the necessity of impressing sailors for 'publick safety':[12] 'it is a maxim in law, and good policy too, that all private mischiefs must be borne with patience for preventing a national calamity.'[13] 'A general immemorial usage', he continued, 'not inconsistent with any statute especially if it be the result of evident necessity and withal tendeth to the publick safety is, I apprehend, part of the common law of England.'[14] This common law position was supported by 'precedents' only in the sense that there were formal documents such as commissions and mandatory writs which asserted the right to impressment.[15] As one commentator caustically observed, 'this formidable exercise of the royal prerogative has no better foundation than vague usage.'[16]

The judgment in *Broadfoot* did, at least, lay down some limits on the power of impressment. On the facts of the case, a press-gang had been sent out from a naval ship while the ship's captain and lieutenant remained on board. The captain's authority to impress sailors was in the form of a document issued by the Admiralty Commissioners, which required either the captain or his lieutenant to be present when sailors were apprehended. It followed that there was no legal justification for the activities of the gang.[17] Similarly, Sir Michael Foster was very careful to make it clear that impressment could only be legally effective against seamen; landsmen could not be impressed into the navy.[18] In Gaskell's account, however, there is a terrifying gap between theory and practice: once seized, a man has no opportunity to contest the legal basis for his apprehension, which means, in effect, that anyone is vulnerable to being 'kidnapped' (with that word being used in its correct legal sense of a taking without legal justification). The anecdote about Lord Thurlow is colourful and entertaining, but it also invites a symbolic reading: when a personification of the legal system can be swept up, with impunity, on a busy street, where is the rule of law?

[9] (1743) Foster 154.
[10] ibid 159: 'a great mistake' to think that statutory authority for impressment was needed.
[11] ibid 169–71.
[12] ibid 157–58. See also Sir Michael Foster's introductory note to the report at 154: 'If it be asked, where are the adjudged cases on which the author groundeth his opinion? he freely confesseth, that he hath not met with one.'
[13] ibid 159.
[14] ibid 159.
[15] ibid 160.
[16] Waterson (n 8).
[17] *R v Broadfoot* (1743) Foster 154 at 155.
[18] ibid 157–58. See also *R v Tubbs* (1776) 2 Cowp 512.

In theory, an important limitation on the Crown's prerogative to impress seamen was provided by statutory exemptions.[19] In *Sylvia's Lovers* a relevant exemption covers Charley Kinraid, a harpooner (or specksioneer) aboard a whaling vessel. Statutory provisions singled out harpooners, line managers and boat steerers of Greenland whaling vessels for automatic exemptions. Ordinary seamen attached to such vessels were also protected, although, at times, their protection was conditional on registration.[20] However, on the two occasions that Kinraid and his shipmates seek to assert their exemptions, it is to no avail. On the first occasion the crew of the Greenland whaling ship refuse an impressing naval captain's order to come on deck; the result is a stand-off, followed by a fight in which Kinraid apparently kills members of the press-gang, and one of Kinraid's shipmates is fatally wounded.[21] On the second occasion, when Kinraid is making his way to his vessel shortly after his engagement to Sylvia, he states his exemption and produces his documents immediately.[22] The gang, however, has not the slightest interest in such technicalities, and Kinraid is kidnapped – although not before entrusting Philip Hepburn, Sylvia's other lover, with a message for Sylvia about what has happened to him. Hepburn's deliberate failure to deliver the message will shape his life, both for better and for worse.

Gaskell's depiction of the press gang in action gives the legal sources, with their earnest analyses of public utility and history, their meticulous examination of questions of statutory construction, an air of fantasy. She is, of course, forcefully making the point that legal rights are essentially meaningless – literally, just pieces of paper – unless there are readily available legal mechanisms to assert them. But she is also going further, by creating for her novel a world in which regard paid to law is bafflingly inconsistent. The press-gang systematically disregard the limits of the prerogative power of impressment and nothing ever comes of it – in Gaskell's novel we never, for instance, hear of naval officers being disciplined or even reprimanded, let alone facing trial for assault, kidnap, or manslaughter, even though, historically, such prosecutions were brought.[23] Neither, strikingly, do there ever seem to be legal consequences in the novel for resisting impressment. Kinraid has, apparently, shot at least two men, and though Philip Hepburn says 'he'll have to stand his trial', no one else even pauses to consider whether he might be charged with murder or manslaughter.[24] He comes and goes freely, until the press gang happen, by chance, to catch him. Hence, when the narrator says,

[19] Exemptions at common law were also theoretically possible, although none seemed to exist: *R v Tubbs* (1776) 2 Cowp 512.

[20] Stat 13 Geo 2 c 28, Continuance of Acts, etc 1739 s 5; Stat 26 Geo 3, c 41, Fisheries Act 1786, s 17; Stat 26 Geo 3 c 50, Southern Whale Fishery Act 1786 s 25; Stat 35 Geo 3 c 92, Southern Whale Fisheries Act 1795. These provisions' application to a ship's carpenter is discussed in *Ex parte John Caruthers* (1807) 9 East 44.

[21] Gaskell, *Sylvia's Lovers* (n 3) 66–67. Philip Hepburn's observation at 67 that 't' press gang had law on their side, and were doing nought but what they'd warrant for' is incorrect.

[22] ibid 189.

[23] C Lloyd, 'The Press Gang and the Law' (1967) 10 *History Today* 683, 688–89.

[24] Gaskell, *Sylvia's Lovers* (n 3) 66.

of the press gang, that 'They had the law to back them, therefore their business was lawful', it is only partially true. They have 'the law' in the sense of the Crown's common law prerogative, to justify some of their activities; in a more intimidating way they have 'the law' in the sense of the support of the authorities (including the armed forces), which allows them to act with impunity. But it does not 'therefore' follow that everything they do is 'lawful', certainly not if 'lawful' carries any note of rightfulness or justification. And the fact remains that, in the skirmishes between the press-gang and the sailors, the law seems to be suspended – neither side thinks of having recourse to it, it would seem.

III

A very different kind of significance for law can be seen in the early chapters' treatment of taxation and smuggling. Monkshaven's main shop is run by two Quaker brothers, who have very exacting standards of honesty. 'Yet', says the narrator,

> though scrupulous in most things, it did not go against the consciences of these good brothers to purchase smuggled articles. There was a back way from the river side, up a covered entry, to the yard-door of the Fosters, and a peculiar kind of knock at this door always brought out either John or Jeremiah, or if not them, their shopman Philip Hepburn; and the same cake and wine that the excise officer's wife might just have been tasting, was brought out in the back parlour to treat the smuggler. There was a little locking of doors, and drawing of the green silk curtain that was supposed to shut out the shop, but really all this was done very much for form's sake. Everybody in Monkshaven smuggled who could, and every one wore smuggled goods who could, and great reliance was placed on the excise officer's neighbourly feelings.[25]

Although the press-gang and the Foster brothers are both flouting the law, their modes of operation could not be more different. The Fosters' is a friendly, sociable, polite criminality, with refreshments. Its etiquette of concealment (drawing the curtain) is, in effect, a semaphore, announcing 'Smuggling in Progress', and the cake and wine being shared between the excise officer's wife and the smugglers make it almost the same social occasion. Philip Hepburn's complicity, juxtaposed soon afterwards with some moralistic preaching which he mistakenly thinks will impress Sylvia, highlights his rather patchy, self-serving values, but, at least as far as smuggling is concerned, Hepburn seems to be sharing in the general hypocrisy – 'every one did that, only it was considered polite to ignore it.'[26]

Gaskell's portrait of the Foster brothers' smuggling activities seems initially focused on luxury items for sale in their shop, like silks and laces.[27] But a little

[25] ibid 23–24.
[26] ibid 41.
[27] ibid.

further on in the book, when Kinraid and Sylvia's father are discussing smuggling, a very different aspect of the issue is highlighted:

> There was no question of the morality of the affair; one of the greatest signs of the real progress we have made since those times seems to be that our daily concerns of buying and selling, eating and drinking, whatsoever we do, are more tested by the real practical standard of our religion than they were in the days of our grandfathers. Neither Sylvia nor her mother was in advance of their age. Both listened with admiration to the ingenious devices, and acted as well as spoken lies, that were talked about as fine and spirited things. Yet if Sylvia had attempted one tithe of this deceit in her every-day life, it would have half broken her mother's heart. But when the duty on salt was strictly and cruelly enforced, making it penal to pick up rough dirty lumps containing small quantities that might be thrown out with the ashes of the brine-houses on the high-roads; when the price of this necessary was so increased by the tax upon it as to make it an expensive, sometimes an unattainable, luxury to the working man, Government did more to demoralise the popular sense of rectitude and uprightness than heaps of sermons could undo. And the same, though in smaller measure, was the consequence of many other taxes. It may seem curious to trace up the popular standard of truth to taxation; but I do not think the idea would be so very far-fetched.[28]

This passage brilliantly exploits some of the possibilities of historical realism,[29] as the smugly satisfied self-congratulation about 'real progress' and the 'practical standard of our religion' today gives way to an acknowledgement that moral purity is much more easily achieved in conditions of material comfort.[30] It is, in particular, the point about taxation on salt as 'demoralising' that is so perfectly judged, for here we can see Gaskell's alertness to the social repercussions of statutory provisions, the potential for law to shape, indeed, to deform, behaviour and to distort values.

IV

Amidst this array of laws pushing those subjected to them to extremes of violence and dishonesty, Gaskell introduces yet another kind of engagement with law when Alice Rose writes her will. Alice is a relatively minor character, the mother of Hester who works in the Fosters' shop; Hester loves Philip Hepburn from afar. Alice presses her lodger, William Coulson, to write the will for her. Coulson agrees,

[28] ibid 89.

[29] On the importance of seeing *Sylvia's Lovers* as a work of historical realism see two essays by M Shaw, '*Sylvia's Lovers*, then and now' (2004) 8 *Gaskell Society Journal* 37, and '*Sylvia's Lovers* and other historical fiction' in J Matus (ed), *The Cambridge Companion to Elizabeth Gaskell* (Cambridge University Press, 2007) 75.

[30] In this respect Gaskell anticipates Brecht's 'Erst kommt das Fressen, dann kommt die Moral' in his own venture into the eighteenth century, *Der Dreigroschenoper (The Threepenny Opera)*, Act two scene 6, translated as 'Food is the first thing. Morals follow on' in B Brecht, *Collected Plays: Two* (J Willett and R Manheim (ed and tr), Methuen, 1979) 145.

despite his misgiving 'that he was infringing on a lawyer's prerogative, and that, for aught he knew, he might be prosecuted for making a will without a licence, just as a man might be punished for selling wine and spirits without going through the preliminary legal forms that give permission for such a sale.'[31] Alice proceeds to instruct him to 'make the sign of the Trinity, and write, 'In the name of the Father, the Son and the Holy Ghost.''

> 'Is that the right way o' beginning a will?' said Coulson, a little startled.
>
> 'My father, and my father's father, and my husband had it a-top of theirs, and I'm noane going for to cease fra' following after them, for they were godly men … I give and bequeath – did thee put 'give and bequeath' at th' beginning?'
>
> 'Nay,' said William, looking back. 'Thee didst not tell me 'give and bequeath'!'
>
> 'Then it won't be legal, and my bit o'furniture 'll be taken to London, and put into chancery, and Hester will have noane on it.'[32]

The scene is very reminiscent of *Ruth*, where Sally, the Bensons' long-standing servant, puts her affairs in order.[33] As in *Ruth*, the testatrix mistakenly, and comically, insists on certain formal language in the belief that only with such language can the will be effective. Also as in *Ruth* the comedy light-heartedly makes serious points. Alice is the first character we have met in *Sylvia's Lovers* who is deeply committed to the idea that legal words matter, but it is a commitment that makes her ridiculous. Coulson's anxiety seems to represent a complementary concern – that legal matters are so highly esoteric and specialised, that even as simple a transaction as leaving everything you own to your child is fraught with complexity. Neither Alice nor William can imagine that the law would interpret her words and wishes in their ordinary plain meaning; and this, we might feel, is yet a further sign that the law is going wrong.

V

As the novel progresses, Philip Hepburn rises from shopman to be the Foster brothers' joint successor. The brothers arrange a dinner, at which they plan to make their offer to him; but before they get down to business there is some small-talk:

> Politics in those days were tickle subjects to meddle with, even in the most private company. The nation was in a state of terror against France, and against any at home who might be supposed to sympathise with the enormities she had just been committing. The oppressive act against seditious meetings had been passed the year before, and people were doubtful to what extremity of severity it might be construed. Even the law authorities forgot to be impartial, but either their alarms or their interests made

[31] Gaskell, *Sylvia's Lovers* (n 3) 72.
[32] ibid 73–74.
[33] See ch 3 above, s VII.

> too many of them vehement partisans instead of calm arbiters, and thus destroyed the popular confidence in what should have been considered the supreme tribunal of justice. Yet for all this, there were some who dared to speak of reform of Parliament, as a preliminary step to fair representation of the people, and to a reduction of the heavy war-taxation that was imminent, if not already imposed. But these pioneers of 1830 were generally obnoxious.[34]

Gaskell then moves from the general to the particular:

> At such a place as Monkshaven all these opinions were held in excess. It had been not unfrequently found that the public duty of prosecuting opinions not your own overrode the private duty of respecting confidence. Most of the Monkshaven politicians confined themselves, therefore, to such general questions as these: 'Could an Englishman lick more than four Frenchmen at a time?' 'What was the proper punishment for members of the Corresponding Society (correspondence with the French Directory), hanging and quartering, or burning?' 'Would the forthcoming child of the Princess of Wales be a boy or a girl? If a girl, would it be more loyal to call it Charlotte or Elizabeth?'
>
> The Fosters were quite secure enough of their guests this evening to have spoken freely on politics had they been so inclined. And they did begin on the outrages which had lately been offered to the king in crossing St James's Park to go and open the House of Lords; but soon, so accustomed were their minds to caution and restraint, the talk dropped down to the high price of provisions.[35]

In these passages Gaskell beautifully illustrates how certain kinds of law, in the right environment, can become all-pervasive. She begins with a reference to the Seditious Meetings Act 1795, which imposed extensive restrictions on meetings of 50 or more people; it is not immediately clear how that legislation could have been construed to an 'extremity of severity.' The Treasonable and Seditious Practices Act 1795, however, which was closely associated with the Seditious Meetings Act, was susceptible to expansive interpretation. For instance, under section 2 of the Treasonable and Seditious Practices Act, it was an offence 'maliciously and advisedly, by Writing, Printing, Preaching, or other Speaking [to] express, publish, utter, or declare any Words or Sentences to stir up the People to Hatred or Contempt of the person of his Majesty, his Heirs or Successors, or the Government and Constitution of this Realm, as by Law established.'[36] With statutory wording this broad, no political critique is safe. The Act was passed on 18 December 1795, so that at the time of the Foster brothers' dinner-party, in early 1796, there would have been understandable anxiety about its scope.[37] The uncertainty would continue – there were no prosecutions under the Treasonable

[34] Gaskell, *Sylvia's Lovers* (n 3) 148.
[35] ibid 148–49.
[36] The texts of both Acts can conveniently be accessed in HT Dickinson (ed), *Constitutional Documents of the United Kingdom 1782–1835* (KG Saur, 2005) 27 (Treasonable and Seditious Practices Act 1795) and 31 (Seditious Meetings Act 1795).
[37] For the chronology relating to the dinner-party see G Handley, 'The Chronology of Sylvia's Lovers' (1965) 12 *Notes and Queries* 302.

Practices Act in the 1790s[38] – and an environment in which the prosecuting authorities make untested assertions about such a statute's reach very effectively closes down political discussion. Indeed, we might feel that such a law, almost paradoxically, is at its most potent when it is all potential, that is, in the period between enactment and judicial interpretation when there have been no convictions or acquittals. It is the looming, threatening possibilities of the broad statutory language that intimidate and deter the widest circle of speakers.

The result, in Monkshaven at least, is that any political conversation is reduced to the most stilted, jingoistic clichés. Gaskell also points out, however, that such changes do not happen overnight: 'It had not been unfrequently found …' indicates a readiness to prosecute for sedition prior to 1795, and here it is worth reminding ourselves that most prosecutions were initiated and funded by individuals.[39] There is, in other words, already a culture of suppressing political speech which the 1795 Act complemented. Here, again, Gaskell nicely illustrates the effects of such culture: the Fosters have no fear that Philip and their other guest William Coulson might bring a prosecution for sedition against them, but their habit of avoiding political controversies is ingrained – self-censorship has become internalised, it is second nature. It is also, finally, worth noting the ironical twist with which Gaskell ends this passage. It was high bread prices in autumn 1795 that prompted protests, mass-meetings and the insults directed at the King when he was on his way to open Parliament. These, in turn, led to the Seditious Meetings Act and the Treasonable and Seditious Practices Act.[40] The high price of provisions was, therefore, explosively provocative material, but only when addressed to the right (or wrong?) audience; it was entirely inert, indeed, it was positively benign, in the hands of a quartet of shopkeepers.

VI

One of the novel's great dramatic crises brings Daniel Robson into direct conflict with the criminal law. The press-gang have been intensifying their operations in Monkshaven, making local sailors furtive and suspicious, despite their legal privilege against impressment. One night the town's fire-bell is sounded. Men instinctively rush to the rescue, only to discover that it is a false alarm, and a trick to bring sailors out into the open. Several men are seized, and taken to the gang's base at the Mariner's Arms, known as the 'Randyvowse'. Daniel, whose past experiences give him good reason to detest press-gangs, is incensed by the trickery;

[38] C Emsley, 'An Aspect of Pitt's "Terror": Prosecutions for Sedition during the 1790s' (1981) 6 *Social History* 155, 156–57.

[39] Emsley (n 38) 166.

[40] For an outline of the historical background see the entry on 'Seditious Meetings Act' in R Crowcroft and J Cannon, *The Oxford Companion to British History*, 2nd edn (online ed, Oxford University Press, 2015).

and leads an attack on the Randyvowse.[41] The impressed men are freed, the gang is chased off, and the mob Daniel has led set about destroying the Randyvowse's furniture. They have just set fire to it as Daniel starts to make his way home, highly satisfied with his night's work.

Sylvia and her mother, Bell, admire Daniel's daring and heroism; but a rather different note is struck by the arrival of Philip Hepburn, who reports that the authorities have mobilised the militia, and that the perpetrators are sure 'o' being clapt int' prison and tried for it.'[42] 'The women looked at each other with blank eyes, as if they were as yet unable to take in the new idea that the conduct which had seemed to them a subject for such just pride could be regarded by anyone as deserving of punishment or retribution.'[43] What exactly Daniel is being charged with will only be revealed after he has been arrested, and Philip has sought legal assistance for him.

Philip's first recourse is to a Mr Donkin, 'the oldest established and most respected attorney in Monkshaven – he who had been employed to draw up the law papers and deeds of partnership consequent on Hepburn and Coulson succeeding to the shop of John and Jeremiah Foster, Brothers.'[44] Gaskell may be hinting at the smallness of the Monkshaven world when she gives this attorney the same surname as the captain of Kinraid's whaling-ship, and the tailor who visits the Robsons earlier in the novel.[45] The interview gets off to a bad start:

> 'You are aware that I am the clerk to the magistrates?'
>
> 'No, sir', in a tone that indicated the unexpressed 'What then?'
>
> 'Well, but I am. And so of course, if you want my services or advice in favour of a prisoner whom they have committed, or are going to commit, you can't have them, that's all.'[46]

Donkin's position does, at least, enable him to tell Philip exactly what the charge is:

> 'The evidence is clear as to his being present, aiding and abetting, – indicted on the 4th section of 1 George I, statute 1, chapter 5. I'm afraid it's a bad look-out …'
>
> 'What can they do to him, sir?'
>
> 'Do?' Mr Donkin half smiled at the ignorance displayed. 'Why, hang him, to be sure; if the judge is in a hanging mood. He's been either a principal in the offence, or a principal in the second degree, and, as such, liable to the full punishment. I drew up the warrant myself this morning, though I left the exact name to be filled up by my clerk.'[47]

[41] Gaskell, *Sylvia's Lovers* (n 3) 48–49 – where it is made clear that Daniel maimed his own hand to avoid impressment; this put an end to his life as a sailor.

[42] ibid 238.

[43] ibid.

[44] ibid 248.

[45] ibid 189 and 44. Donkin is also the surname of the Hales' Milton landlord in *North and South*: E Gaskell, *North and South* (A Shelston (ed), Norton, 2005) 58.

[46] ibid 248–49.

[47] ibid 249.

Philip begs Donkin for help, saying that Daniel 'thought he was doing such a fine deed.' The response is terse:

> 'Demolishing and pulling down, destroying and burning dwelling-houses and outhouses,' said Mr Donkin. 'He must have some peculiar notions … Well; you must try and get a good lawyer to bring out all that side of the question. There's a good deal to be said on it; but it's my duty to get up all the evidence to prove that he and others were present on the night in question; so, as you'll perceive, I can give you no help in defending him.'[48]

However, as Philip persists, Donkin relents somewhat – he 'was really more concerned for the misguided rioters than he was aware; and he was aware of more interest than he cared to express' – and recommends another attorney, Edward Dawson.[49] Dawson has been Donkin's articled clerk, and is, says Donkin, 'a clever fellow, and has not too much practice' – it is perhaps not the most generous endorsement, but Dawson's cleverness may be evident in his subsequent efforts to assist Daniel.[50] Philip goes to see Dawson, but finds him out, 'making Mrs Dawson's will': there is a disquieting sense that Dawson's practice is sustained by family members.[51] Philip eventually succeeds in securing Dawson's services, but the novel does not depict further legal proceedings in any detail. Daniel is taken to York, stands trial there, and is found guilty; execution swiftly follows.

Although Gaskell offers us none of the details of the trial, Philip's conversation with Mr Donkin reveals the legal issues with complete clarity. Daniel is being charged under the Riot Act 1714, section 4:

> if any persons unlawfully, riotously and tumultuously assembled together, to the disturbance of the publick peace, shall unlawfully, and with force demolish or pull down, or begin to demolish or pull down any church or chapel, or any building for religious worship certified and registred according to the statute made in the first year of the reign of the late King William and Queen Mary, intituled, An act for exempting their Majesty's protestant subjects dissenting from the church of England from the penalties of certain laws or any dwelling-house, barn, stable, or other out-house, that then every such demolishing, or pulling down, or beginning to demolish, or pull down, shall be adjudged felony without benefit of clergy, and the offenders therein shall be adjudged felons, and shall suffer death as in case of felony, without benefit of clergy.

The first thing to notice here is that the offence Daniel is being charged with has nothing to do with the activities of the press-gang. Daniel thinks he has done 'a fine thing' by rescuing the impressed sailors; his wife and daughters regard his actions in doing so as 'a subject for just pride'; and, perhaps rather surprisingly, the charge he faces does not contest that view, but focuses on, and makes central, something that had appeared peripheral to the situation. The charge does not

[48] ibid 250.
[49] ibid.
[50] ibid 268.
[51] ibid 251.

even mention the physical attacks on the press-gang's members. It is impossible to imagine that Donkin could be ignorant of the context of the demolishing and pulling down: his unarticulated concern for the 'misguided rioters' suggests that he knows exactly what has been going on, and that his sympathies are with them. In any case, whether it is Donkin's decision to frame the charge in this way, or the decision of some more senior official, it is an exemplary legal manoeuvre. Quite plainly, the authorities do not want to proceed in a way that would implicitly put the legitimacy of the press-gang's activities on trial.[52] Instead, the way in which the charge is formulated takes control of the narrative: the press-gang's activities are rendered irrelevant, it does not matter *why* the building was damaged, all that matters is that the damage occurred. Donkin's comment that he drafted the charge, but his clerk would fill in the defendant's name later, enacts the point perfectly: the law expressed in this way does not care about an individual's circumstances, motivations or psychology. Such legal objectivity can appear desirable, but the apparent neutrality is, in reality, partisan – by adjudicating on relevance, and determining where the story begins (and ends), the law imposes a narrative frame, which the novelist's counter-narrative, characterised by its rich openness to individuality, is in constant tension with.

The statutory wording also casts light on Philip's discussions with Donkin about Daniel's sentence: execution is the default. Why, then, does Donkin speak of the judges being in a 'hanging mood'? By the late eighteenth century it was common, almost to the point of becoming a convention, for judges to be inclined to reduce death sentences to either transportation or imprisonment, particularly in respect of property offences. Daniel might stand to benefit from the exercise of this discretion – but, as Donkin hints, and events prove – mercy was not automatic. Daniel's offence is only against property, but its violent context, the fact that he was the instigator, and his lack of contrition, would make him less sympathetic to a sentencing judge.[53] Daniel is, thus, up against a formidable combination of legal rules and judicial discretions that not only do not favour him, they do not even allow him an opportunity to put forward what Gaskell has shown us are the salient points of his situation or to explain his motivations and justifications.

When we turn to examine the charge against Daniel Robson in more detail, this tension between the novelist's narrative and the law's becomes more pronounced. The legislation applies only to the demolition of certain kinds of buildings. The only two potentially relevant types in Daniel's case, as the charge correctly sets out, are dwelling-houses and outhouses. Daniel leads the mob through an outhouse to the backyard of the Randyvowse, but we are not told of any demolition of the

[52] C Lloyd, 'The Press Gang and the Law' (1967) 10 *History Today* 683, 684–85 describes the Solicitor General as advising against prosecutions involving impressment whenever the law was doubtful.

[53] D Hay, 'Property, Authority and the Criminal Law' in D Hay et al (ed), *Albion's Fatal Tree Crime and Society in Eighteenth-Century England* (Penguin, 1975) 17, particularly at 40–49 ('Mercy'). Note particularly that one of the factors Hay identifies (at 43) in inclining a judge to mercy would be that the crime did not require an exemplary hanging.

outhouse while he is there – on the contrary, access to the yard is gained by forcing open a wooden shutter in the outbuilding and climbing through the gap.[54] As for the Randyvowse, is it a dwelling-house? The tenant of the public-house seems to live there, but is this sufficient to make the entire building a dwelling-house? Its primary description is, surely, as an inn, or a business premises. Possibly it could be said that the section reserved for the tenant's living quarters is a 'dwelling-house'. Then there is the question whether the Randyvowse has been (or has begun to be) demolished? The facts here are perhaps left deliberately ambiguous: the mob storm the Randyvowse, free the sailors and destroy the furniture.[55] Dick Simpson, who was employed at the Randyvowse and will be a key prosecution witness, complains to Daniel about 'things' being destroyed,[56] and Daniel's own summary of what he has done seems to be informative:

> 'A've led a resky this neet, and saved nine or ten honest chaps as was pressed, and carried off to t' Randyvowse. Me and some others did it. And Hobbs' things and t' lieutenant's is a' burnt; and by this time I reckon t' Randyvowse is pretty nigh four walls, ready for a parish-pound.'
>
> 'Thou'rt niver for saying thou burnt it down wi' t' gang in it, for sure?' asked Bell.
>
> 'Na, na, not this time. T' gang fled up t' hill like coneys; and Hobbs and his folks carried off a bag o'money; but t'oud tumbledown place is just a heap o' brick and mortar; an' t' furniture is smoulderin' int' ashes;'[57]

'Things' have been burnt, 'furniture' is smouldering; but if all four walls are still standing, the Randyvowse has not been demolished. On the other hand, however, a couple of pages earlier, as Daniel looks back at Monkshaven while he is walking home, after the rescue, he sees 'a hot lurid mist against the hill-side beyond where the Mariners' Arms had stood.'[58] *Had* stood might be suggestive.

One possible explanation, borne out by the text, is that after Daniel has left, things have got out of hand.[59] Legally it is absolutely crucial whether this is so: as Philip's conversation with Donkin indicates, the key issue is whether Daniel was *present* aiding and abetting the demolition, or, at least, when the demolition was beginning. The reason presence is so crucial is that, under the general principles of criminal law as they then stood, principals in the second degree, who were subject to the same penalties as principals in the first degree (ie actual perpetrators), were defined only as those who were present aiding and abetting the offence. An accomplice who urged and encouraged a person to commit an offence later, when the accomplice was not present, was only an accessory before the fact, not a

[54] Gaskell, *Sylvia's Lovers* (n 3) 227.
[55] ibid 228.
[56] ibid. The significance of Simpson's evidence is highlighted at 277–78.
[57] ibid 234.
[58] ibid 231.
[59] ibid 247: 'The rescue of the sailors was a distinctly popular movement; the subsequent violence (which had, indeed, gone much further than has been described, after Daniel left it) was, in general, considered as only a kind of due punishment …'.

principal in the second degree.[60] In *R v Royce* it had been held that these general rules applied to the offence under the Riot Act 1714, section 4.[61] For Daniel, therefore, the legal question was whether he was, as charged, a principal in the second degree, or, merely, an accessory before the fact?

The evidence Gaskell gives us seems very much in favour of the latter alternative. As the furniture from the Randyvowse is smashed, Daniel cries out, excitedly – "If a was as young as onest a was, a'd have t'Randyvowse down and mak'a bonfire on it. We'd ring t'fire-bell then t'some purpose.'[62] 'No sooner said than done' says the narrator. But what is done? 'Their excitement was ready to take the slightest hint of mischief; old chairs, broken tables, odd drawers, smashed chests, were rapidly and skilfully heaped into a pyramid, and one, who at the first broaching of the idea had gone for live coals the speedier to light up the fire, came now through the crowd with a large shovelful of red-hot cinders.' This is not demolishing the building, nor even beginning to do so. The statutory requirements are not satisfied. How, then, does Daniel come to be convicted? The crucial witness evidence is that of Dick Simpson. Gaskell does not give us Simpson's testimony, but she does give us his confrontation with Daniel, which takes place immediately after the rescue, in the lane behind the Randyvowse: 'It was thee set 'm on – a heerd thee – a see'd thee a helping on 'em t' break in; they'd niver ha' thought on attackin' t' house, and settin' fire to yon things, if thou hadn't spoken on it.'[63] Simpson has seen the breaking in, and has seen the 'things' being set on fire – but this is not what Daniel is being charged with. Simpson has only 'heerd' the setting-on – ie the incitement to pull down the Randyvowse – and, crucially, he has not seen whether any demolition of the part of the Randyvowse that served as a dwelling-house began while Daniel was still present. It is easy to imagine counsel for the prosecution inviting a jury to infer that Daniel's incitement was acted on immediately, while he was still present; but we, the novel's readers, know better.

Given the emphasis on presence at any demolition in the indictment, it might, at first, appear surprising that Daniel's expensive attorney has not investigated this point. This may, however, be unfair to Mr Dawson. He reports to Philip that

> Daniel still retained his pride in his achievement, and could not be brought to understand the dangerous position in which he was placed; that when pressed and questioned as to circumstances that might possibly be used in his defence, he always wandered off to accounts of previous outrages committed by the press-gang, or to passionate abuse

[60] Sir Michael Foster, *A Report of Some Proceedings on the Commission for the Trial of the Rebels in the Year 1746, in the County of Surry, and of other Crown Cases: To which are added Discourses upon a Few Branches of the Crown Law*, 3rd edn (M Dodson (ed), Brooke, 1792) 347–50, especially at 349: 'He must be present at the perpetration, otherwise he can be no more than an accessary before the fact.' See also W Oldnall Russell, *A Treatise on Crimes and Indictable Misdemeanours*, 2nd edn (Joseph Butterworth, 1826) vol 1, 22ff, which reproduces and amplifies Foster's exposition.

[61] (1767) 4 Burr 2073.

[62] Gaskell, *Sylvia's Lovers* 228.

[63] ibid 230.

> of the trick by which men had been lured from their homes on the night in question to assist in putting out an imaginary fire, and then seized and carried off.[64]

The circumstances of what, exactly, Daniel had said, when he said it, whether it was acted on immediately, and the structural integrity of the Randyvowse when he left the scene of the rescue, may be exactly the kinds of things that his attorney is asking him about, and which Daniel regards as missing the point. It is the struggle for narrative dominance again. In domestic life we have seen Daniel being perhaps rather too accustomed to asserting his own versions of events – in his own home, the habit is merely irritating;[65] but his attempt to claim narrative sovereignty in the legal sphere will prove fatal.

VII

As can be seen, law figures in an extraordinary variety of ways in this turbulent, troubled novel. It can assert itself with the most devastating consequences (as in Daniel's trial), and, at the opposite end of the scale, be deliberately flouted to equally powerful effect (the press-gang's disregard of exemptions). In their most extreme incarnations in this novel, law and lawlessness make a terrifying alliance – they are not opposites, but, rather, complement each other, as legality is used to support overreaching or abuse of legal rights, and the legal language which, crucially, should define the limits of rights and liabilities, proves too weak to withstand the pressures placed on it by the reality of the legal system in operation. This 'lawless legality' (to borrow the phrase used by Terry Eagleton) is frequently experienced as a hostile, alien force, a calamity which befalls characters who have no way of avoiding it.[66] But there are also ways in which the law is not at odds with characters' values; indeed, there are ways in which law's ability to repress, and to suppress, are found congenial. Perhaps the best example is sedition: here we are told that confidences have been broken in order to bring prosecutions, and that this reduces all political discussion to idiotically patriotic inanity.[67] The law is, of course, in its terms, a repressive one, but it is the population's own enthusiastic co-opting of it that has given it its fearsome effectiveness. More than in Gaskell's other novels there is a disturbing sense that the law's repressiveness chimes with the instincts of her characters. This is particularly noticeable in two characters – William Coulson, a Quaker, and Philip Hepburn, who, though not a Quaker, has grown up among them. For instance, both men work themselves up about Charley Kinraid, who has previously courted Coulson's sister, Annie, before turning his attentions elsewhere. Annie, we are told, died within six months – '*she* forgave him, but it is beyond me',

[64] ibid 268.
[65] See eg ibid 35–36.
[66] Eagleton (n 1) 22.
[67] Gaskell, *Sylvia's Lovers* (n 3) 148–49, discussed in s V, above.

says Coulson.[68] Earlier Coulson has said that Kinraid murdered his sister.[69] He did no such thing, of course – law is being stretched to absurd lengths by characters who long to see Kinraid punished.

What Coulson and Hepburn want to repress here is Kinraid's spontaneity, charisma, and attractiveness to women (which they envy). The same holds true for Hepburn in respect of Sylvia's artless, captivating and capricious sexuality; although, once he has succeeded in marrying her, he wishes those qualities could return.[70] In one of the novel's most powerful moments he even upbraids Sylvia for having dreamt about her former lover – this truly is a kind of mania, an attempt at repression beyond all rational limits.[71] But the theme of repression is not limited to these two characters, it is a motif running, disturbingly, through the whole book. In one of the novel's most telling vignettes, Sylvia goes with Philip to a supper-party given by the Foster brothers, where she sits pale, silent and paralysed with fear about making a social gaffe; the brothers find her 'the best-behaved woman they had ever seen.'[72] There is a closely related oppressive obsession with cleanliness, ranging from Sylvia's mother's competitive cleaning, to Jeremiah Foster's house, which looks as if the bricks have been scrubbed.[73] A cautionary tale which Sylvia's mother tells Sylvia when she is trying to head off Sylvia's growing attraction to Kinraid combines both repression and the fixation with dirt. It is about a female servant whose head was turned by a sailor who never returned; its crucial dramatic moment occurs when immorality manifests itself as 'bingy' milk cans, which the girl has failed to clean properly, distracted as she is by love.[74] There is, in short, constant oppression, repression and, particularly in the final third of the book – confinement (when Sylvia moves from her father's farm to Philip's house). Against these forces, in which law plays such an active part, who, and what, is irrepressible? Clearly Kinraid – who returns from his enforced naval service a lieutenant; but Daniel is executed, Sylvia is tricked into her loveless marriage with Hepburn. Along with Kinraid, though, there is another force of nature that Gaskell describes as 'irrepressible': the fire that Daniel encourages at the Randyvowse.[75] If we wanted an optimistic reading of *Sylvia's Lovers* – and other readings are available – this unquenchable flame might represent a much-needed symbol of enduring hope and resistance against repression.

[68] ibid 169.
[69] ibid 76.
[70] ibid 298.
[71] ibid. On Hepburn's significance see further C Lansbury, *Elizabeth Gaskell The Novel of Social Crisis* (Paul Elek, 1975) 157–59 – discussing Gaskell's 'belief that the Calvinist's religious ethic was often a frustrated sexuality'.
[72] ibid 303.
[73] For Bell Robson's cleaning see ibid 34–35; for Jeremiah Foster's house: ibid 147.
[74] ibid 164–66.
[75] Gaskell, *Sylvia's Lovers* 228.

12

Conclusion

I

The close readings offered in earlier chapters of this book highlight the range, extent and originality of Gaskell's engagement with law. This concluding chapter has two aims. First, to draw together some general themes, ideas and preoccupations that run through the works already examined. Second, to consider moments in Gaskell's other works where law is involved and, in doing so, to reflect on what those moments add to our understanding of Gaskell's broader approach. The ultimate purpose of the chapter is to leave the reader with a complete picture of Gaskell and the law.

II

The work of this chapter has to some extent been anticipated in chapters seven and eight, where, although the main focus was *The Moorland Cottage* and *A Dark Night's Work*, material from Gaskell's other works dealing with attorneys provided a valuable frame and context. The attorneys highlighted in those earlier chapters were disruptive or troubled in ways that were central to the plots and psychology with which they were concerned, and so it is worth noticing that Gaskell could also create more genial lawyer characters. For instance, Mr Bullock in 'Mr Harrison's Confessions' is a country attorney of whom his wife says 'agriculture is his hobby, although law, horrid law, is his business.'[1] Bullock's pretensions to expertise in the theory of agriculture are comically deflated by his total ignorance of chemistry; fortunately he does no harm.[2] Similarly, in *Wives and Daughters* there is a brief appearance by a rather self-important Q.C.; again, he is harmless.[3]

The unnamed attorneys in *Wives and Daughters* are, by contrast, presented as shadowy, sinister figures. They are never seen directly, but are felt circling, like vultures. What has brought them to Hollingford is debt. The debtor is Osborne

[1] E Gaskell, 'Mr Harrison's Confessions' in *My Lady Ludlow and Other Stories* (E Wright (ed), Oxford University Press, 1989) 349 at 373.

[2] ibid 391: 'I can understand a good deal of this agricultural chemistry … [b]ut these unconnected letters puzzle me a little. I suppose they must have some meaning …'.

[3] E Gaskell, *Wives and Daughters* (P Morris (ed), Penguin, 2003) ch 38, 'Mr Kirkpatrick. Q.C.'

Hamley, whose father, Squire Hamley, holds the family estate; Osborne has borrowed money against the security of his inheritance, and the lender is evidently being careful to ensure that the security will cover the loan: 'certain disreputable attorneys were making inquiries as to the entail of the estate' and the age and health of the Squire.[4] It is the Squire's wife who provides this information, and it is worth pausing for a moment over her description of the attorneys as 'disreputable', for they are not acting unlawfully; indeed they seem to be dutifully protecting their clients' interests. What makes them 'disreputable' is that they facilitate transactions in which sons calculate on their fathers' deaths; family relationships are thus reduced to financial assets, to be monetised with unsentimental actuarial objectivity. Molly Gibson, the novel's heroine, finds such transactions 'shocking',[5] and Osborne's brother, Roger, refuses to believe that his brother could have done such a thing (although the evidence is damning).[6] But they are both naïve; the truth is that these are perfectly commonplace transactions. In a revealing passage of dialogue at the very end of the novel, Lady Harriet, a member of the aristocratic Cumnor family, is musing on what might happen if Osborne Hamley's young son (and heir) were to pass away, and is interrupted by her brother, who tells her – 'that's the worst of allowing yourself to plan far ahead for the future; you are sure to contemplate the death of some one, and to reckon on the contingency as affecting events.' 'As if lawyers were not always doing something of the kind' responds Lady Harriet. 'Leave it to those to whom it is necessary' replies her brother.[7] The passage perfectly captures an irresolvable contradiction: what the lawyers are doing is both 'necessary' and not to be spoken of, much less imitated, by lay people. There is a sense of polite society trying to have it both ways: deliberately closing its eyes to, and, at the same time, being entirely dependent upon, the economic realities and related legal transactions that sustain its existence. When Mrs Hamley speaks of the 'disreputable' attorneys she thus participates in this societal self-delusion: deploring the symptoms while denying the disease.

III

Gaskell's depiction of legal proceedings is consistently bleak and radically sceptical. As we have seen, in *Mary Barton* Jem Wilson is on the verge of being wrongly convicted of murder; in *Sylvia's Lovers* Daniel Robson is executed despite appearing to be innocent of the charge laid against him. Legal proceedings fail to find the truth; they impose their own distorting narrative, and it is for the novelist to show

[4] Gaskell, *Wives and Daughters* (n 3) 192. We later (at 248) hear about 'men' not specifically identified as attorneys, who have come to investigate the value of the trees on the Hamley estate in connection with 'the advances made to Osborne by the London money-lender.'

[5] ibid 203.

[6] ibid.

[7] ibid 621.

what really happened and to make sense of it. Elsewhere Gaskell eloquently develops this theme. In 'Lois the Witch' the story begins with Lois recollecting the trial by water of a suspected witch in the village where Lois grew up.[8] The pitiful and harrowing spectacle of this irrational mode of trial, in which there is no attempt to analyse evidence, turns out to be little different to the hysterical, entirely predetermined, judicial proceedings later brought against Lois for witchcraft. We have no idea whether the woman from Lois's village was guilty, but we are completely sure that Lois is innocent. There is a chilling inevitability in the way Gaskell shows a supposedly rational, objective legal system, conscientiously operated by dedicated judges, becoming malleable. Everything and anything – even a slight pause in reciting the Lord's Prayer – can be made evidence of guilt.[9]

Gaskell takes us straight to the heart of the problem:

> Where evidence takes a supernatural character, there is no disproving it. This argument comes up: 'You have only the natural powers; I have supernatural. You admit the existence of the supernatural by the condemnation of this very crime of witchcraft. You hardly know the limits of the natural powers; how then can you define the supernatural? I say that in the dead of night, when my body seemed to all present to be lying in quiet sleep, I was, in the most complete and wakeful consciousness, present in my body at an assembly of witches and wizards with Satan at their head; that I was by them tortured in my body, because my soul would not acknowledge him as its king; and that I witnessed such and such deeds. What the nature of the appearance was that took the semblance of myself, sleeping quietly in my bed, I know not; but admitting, as you do, the possibility of witchcraft, you cannot disprove my evidence.'[10]

The very idea of 'evidence' here is coming apart. Indeed, the first sentence of this passage should already set alarm bells ringing, for what kind of evidence is, by its very nature, incapable of being challenged?[11] We are already departing from the firm ground of legal rationality. As Gaskell goes on to remind us, these situations are all the more problematic when the accused has 'confessed' and is claiming to have supernatural powers; for then the sheer implausibility of what supposedly happened is no longer a factor in the accused's favour. The accused is effectively saying, as Gaskell imagines in the passage, that the ordinary rules of likelihood, probability and doubt, which presuppose ordinary, 'natural powers' are inapplicable to the assessment of her conduct. She convicts herself. In Gaskell's portrayal, the legal system is terrifyingly incapable of registering that its own methods are failing to elicit the truth.

In 'The Crooked Branch', legal processes do, at least, elicit the truth. They do so, however, at a price that the main characters find unbearable. The story revolves

[8] E Gaskell, 'Lois the Witch' in *Gothic Tales* (L Kranzler (ed), Penguin, 2000) 139.

[9] ibid 213.

[10] ibid 186.

[11] See eg the trenchant analysis of 'conclusive presumptions' in the law of evidence as effectively substituting proof of one fact for proof of another in S Greenleaf, *A Treatise on the Law of Evidence* 16th edn (JH Wigmore (ed), Little, Brown & Co, 1899) vol 1 at 108.

around a married couple, the Huntroyds, and their son, Benjamin. Benjamin takes his place in the line-up of Gaskell's attorney-criminals, joining Edward Browne (*The Moorland Cottage*), the draftsman of Sally's will in *Ruth*, and Edward Wilkins (*A Dark Night's Work*). He brings the profession into new depths of disrepute by preying on his own parents, culminating in him leading a robbery on the family home. The climax of the story comes when two of the gang are brought to trial, Benjamin having absconded. It seems, initially, as if the Huntroyds will be spared the ordeal of being called as witnesses at the trial, as there are others who can identify the gang members. The accuseds' lawyer, however, has heard from them of Benjamin's involvement, and sets out to show that his clients were 'but tools in the hands of one who had, from his superior knowledge of the premises and the daily customs of the inhabitants, been the originator and planner of the whole affair.'[12] The parents, who have heard Benjamin's voice during the robbery, are summoned.

First comes the father's evidence. He admits that the voice he heard sounded like Benjamin's adding, 'I'll tell yo' truth, though it kills me to speak it.'[13] Then comes the mother's. She manages to confirm that she heard her son's voice. But then she is asked what Benjamin said:

> Her face worked – her mouth opened two or three times as if to speak – she stretched out her arms imploringly; but no word came, and she fell back into the arms of those nearest to her. Nathan forced himself forward into the witness-box:
>
> 'My Lord Judge, a woman bore ye, as I reckon; it's a cruel shame to serve a mother so. It wur my son, my only child, as called out for us t' open door, and who shouted out for to hold th' oud woman's throat if she did na stop her noise, when hoo'd fain ha' cried for her niece to help. And now yo' ve truth, and a' th' truth, and I'll leave yo' to th' Judgment o' God for th' way yo' ve getten at it.'
>
> Before night the mother was stricken with paralysis, and lay on her death-bed. But the broken-hearted go Home, to be comforted of God.[14]

And this is the end of the story. It has become the parents' trial, culminating in the imposition of a capital sentence. Elsewhere in Gaskell, as we have already seen, the prospect of appearing at legal proceedings is painful and embarrassing for female characters;[15] and there is a special cruelty in forcing a mother to incriminate her own son.[16] 'The Crooked Branch' takes both concerns to their logical extremes, and it also, in Nathan Huntroyd's final line of dialogue, does something more radical. Witnesses swore on the Bible to state 'the truth, the whole truth', and in this case the legal requirement has been followed to the letter. Look at the results, Gaskell seems to be saying – the public exposure and humiliation that

[12] E Gaskell, 'The Crooked Branch' in *Gothic Tales* (n 8) 227 at 266.

[13] ibid 268.

[14] ibid, 270.

[15] See particularly *Mary Barton* (ch 2, s IV); Margaret Hale's fear of appearing at the inquest into Leonards' death in *North and South* (ch 4, s VII); Ellinor Wilkins' fear of public court proceedings in *A Dark Night's Work* (ch 8, s IV).

[16] cf Jane Wilson in *Mary Barton* discussed above in ch 2, s VI.

makes these victims of robbery victims a second time, and injures them far more painfully than the criminal offence ever did. On the facts such exposure is not strictly necessary – Gaskell has organised events such that Mrs Huntroyd's niece could have given evidence identifying Benjamin; the prisoners' counsel, unfortunately, does not realise this. But Gaskell's concern is, surely, a broader one. The law has to set out to ascertain the truth; neither Gaskell nor Nathan Huntroyd would deny that. It is 'th' way yo've getten at it' that is the problem: Gaskell shows us a system in which public trial, exposure and, perhaps, humiliation, is the only way the law can imagine to proceed with its inquiries. In the same way that we saw her troubled by the unrestrained investigative methods of the Detective Police, here Gaskell is protesting against legal processes that take no account of the collateral damage they cause.[17] It is not even as if the classic legal method of subjecting parties and witnesses to forensic questioning is infallible – 'Lois the Witch' very emphatically demonstrates that. What might be the alternative? Perhaps the kind of private, less formal procedure which Ellinor Wilkins makes use of at the end of *A Dark Night's Work*?[18] In any event, the law's commitment to truth does not, and should not, authorise it to deploy its most bruising machinery against people like the Huntroyds.

IV

Gaskell's interest in legal processes was always complemented by an interest in legal rules and their psychological consequences. In 'An Accursed Race', for example, she carefully traces the oppressive treatment of the Cagots in France from the middle ages to the eighteenth century.[19] Her account sets out some of the legal restrictions on what the Cagots could wear, where they were permitted to walk, etc, but it does not stop there. In later years, Gaskell explains, ostracism and discrimination continued despite the law prohibiting it. Thus, there was a long-running dispute over rights of sepulture, in which the curé refused to obey a court order, and was fined one hundred livres for every Cagot not interred in the right place. 'The inhabitants [of Biarritz] indemnified the curate for all these fines.'[20] Here law has initially reflected local prejudice, but it cannot carry the population with it when it tries to bring about a change in attitude. There is an echo here of the Manchester mill-owners' refusal to reduce their smoke emissions in *North and South*, with the legal rule precipitating not change, but entrenchment.[21] Clearly law has not solved the problem. As we shall see later in this chapter, Gaskell could

[17] For Gaskell's concerns about the Detective Police see *Mary Barton* and 'Disappearances' (discussed in ch 2, s VI above); and 'The Manchester Marriage' (discussed in ch 9, s I).
[18] See discussion in ch 8 above.
[19] E Gaskell, 'An Accursed Race' in *My Lady Ludlow and Other Stories* (n 1) 211.
[20] ibid 228.
[21] See discussion above in ch 4, s IV.

very occasionally, imagine law bringing about social change, but it would not achieve this by blunt orders.

One of the most original, and delightful ways in which Gaskell draws on legal rules is the way that she plays off legal status against her characters' sense of ties and relationships. We have already seen, for instance, Margaret Hale in *North and South* having to become a responsible parent-like figure to her mother and father; Thekla in *Six Weeks at Heppenheim* being maiden and mother, maid and manager; and in 'Libbie Marsh's Three Eras' Libbie finds her family when she meets a widow and her terminally ill young son.[22] The theme continues throughout Gaskell's work: in 'Lizzie Leigh', for example, Lizzie's illegitimate daughter is adopted and cared for by Susan Palmer; in 'The Well of Pen-Morfa' Nest Gwynn takes upon herself the care of Mary Williams, a very troubled woman with mental health difficulties.[23] Perhaps most strikingly, in 'The Grey Woman' the heroine flees her violent husband and sets up home with her maid, Amante, who is disguised as her male partner. After Amante's death the heroine 'marries' a doctor – both of them realising that the heroine is still legally married to her original husband.[24] The only legally recognised relationship is the one least worthy of any protection. Here we have a far more extreme version of one of the main themes of 'The Manchester Marriage' – there the bigamy is unwitting, the earlier marriage less than ideal rather than abusive.[25] In both (and in the other stories mentioned in this paragraph) characters very deliberately do not take their cue from the law: they have their own valuations, which they are to be applauded for acting on. It does not matter that the law does not recognise, or validate, these relationships.

The same underlying idea informs Gaskell's approach elsewhere. In *Wives and Daughters*, for instance, it is a telltale sign of a character's villainy that he regards himself as bound only by his legal obligations.[26] Gaskell's treatment of indebtedness in this connection is particularly interesting. Earlier, in *North and South*, we have seen how, at a moment of crisis when Thornton's business is on the verge of failure, he turns down a lucrative business opportunity.[27] If the venture fails, he explains, he will be unable to pay his creditors when their debts fall due. Thornton's attitude has, evidently, been formed by his mother's insistence that all debts incurred by Thornton's unhappy late father must be paid off in full. There is a morality of indebtedness, which extends far beyond one's strict legal obligations. In *Cranford*, Miss Matty can be seen to share Thornton's sense of morality: when

[22] See discussions in ch 5, s IV and ch 6, s II above.

[23] E Gaskell, 'Libbie Marsh's Three Eras' in E Gaskell, *A Dark Night's Work and Other Stories* (S Lewis (ed), Oxford University Press, 1993) 167; E Gaskell, 'The Well of Pen-Morfa' in E Gaskell, *The Moorland Cottage and Other Stories* (S Lewis (ed), Oxford University Press, 1995) 123.

[24] E Gaskell, 'The Grey Woman' in E Gaskell, *Gothic Tales* (L Kranzler (ed), Penguin, 2000) 287, 339.

[25] See discussion in ch 9 above.

[26] Preston's contemptuous offer of compensation of half-a-crown for any trespass on the Hamley estate by his workmen, and his taking the point that he is legally entitled to retain compromising letters written to him by Cynthia Fitzpatrick: *Wives and Daughters* (n 3) at 338 and 479 respectively.

[27] See above, ch 4, s VI.

she hears that a bank in which she has shares has stopped payment, she insists on giving her own money to a stranger whose attempt to use a bill drawn on the bank as payment has been refused.[28] That the bank has a separate legal identity to its shareholders, and that shareholders are not liable for the company's debts never crosses her mind.

In both of these situations Thornton and Matty suffer for staying true to their values in circumstances where the law would release them. In 'Morton Hall', Gaskell shows us a very different aspect of the morality of indebtedness when, after the death of a previous owner of the Hall, his creditors' fanatical insistence on their strict legal rights inflicts destitution on the debtor's innocent children:

> the creditors came down on the estate like wolves. It was entailed, and it could not be sold; but they put it into the hands of a lawyer, who was to get what he could out of it, and have no pity for the poor young squire, who had not a roof for his head. Miss Phillis went to live by herself in a little cottage in the village, at the end of the property, which the lawyer allowed her to have because he could not let it to anyone, it was so tumble-down and old.[29]

Here there is a strong sense of the law (and 'the lawyer') going too far – crushing the descendants by barring a sale (which seems the most rational solution), and throwing them into a way of life they are completely unprepared for. In this connection it is interesting to notice how Gaskell treats the one character in her fiction who seems to have taken the benefit of being declared bankrupt. That is Mr Palmer, the father of Susan Palmer (the woman who cares for Lizzie Leigh's illegitimate child):

> He had once been quite in a genteel line of business, but had failed for more money than any greengrocer he [Will Leigh, Lizzie's brother] had heard of; at least, any who did not mix up fish and game with greengrocery proper. This grand failure seemed to have been the event of his life, and one on which he dwelt with a strange kind of pride. It appeared as if he rested at present from his past exertions (in the bankrupt line), and depended on his daughter ...'[30]

Palmer evidently does not feel any of those ties of the extra-legal morality of indebtedness that bind Thornton and Matty, and the law encourages him to adopt this attitude. Part of Palmer's significance in 'Lizzie Leigh', of course, is to highlight the very different social standards brought to bear on Lizzie: she has a lifetime of shame for her error, he has a subject to boast about. It is a theme to which Gaskell would return at greater length in *Ruth*. But the contrast between Thornton and Palmer seems less than straightforward: is Palmer really so contemptible for availing himself of the legal mechanisms provided for his situation? Is there not

[28] E Gaskell, *Cranford* (E Porges Watson and D Birch (eds), Oxford University Press, 2011) ch XIII ('Stopped Payment').

[29] E Gaskell, 'Morton Hall' in *Cousin Phillis and Other Stories* (H Glen (ed), Oxford University Press, 2010) 32 at 46.

[30] E Gaskell, 'Lizzie Leigh' in *Cousin Phillis and Other Stories* (n 29) 3, 11.

something excessive, and oppressive, about Thornton's mother's rigid insistence that her son pay his father's debts? It is a situation where the idea of being 'a law unto himself' – which is so central in *Ruth* as well as in *North and South* – is peculiarly problematic and double-edged.

V

If stories like 'Libbie Marsh's Three Eras' and 'The Grey Woman' show women committing themselves to relationships beyond the law's recognition, and characters like Thornton and Palmer highlight the possibilities, and difficulties, of living by rules superior to the law, Gaskell could also create fictions driven by their antagonism towards law. In 'The Poor Clare', for example, the narrator (and a key character) is a lawyer who sets out, diligently, to tell his story in a rigorous, chronological fashion.[31] The story initially seems to lend itself to this narrative mode, concerning, as it does, the narrator's attempts to trace the heir to a large Irish estate. By careful genealogical research the narrator finds the heir, a young woman with whom the narrator starts to fall in love. But now the real difficulties begin, for Lucy has a terrible secret – she is haunted by a demonic double which is the result of a curse placed upon her father. Removal of the curse becomes the central focus of the story. The law's careful, analytical rationality – personified by the narrator – here comes into conflict with supernatural phenomena that he cannot explain, let alone combat. And in a story preoccupied with doubles, the law of succession also turns out to have its evil *alter ego* – the inevitable inheritance of Lucy's father's misdeeds – which nullifies the benefits she has acquired by her descent: 'The great Fitzgerald property was Lucy's, and that was all – was nothing' the narrator ruefully observes.[32]

Gaskell could also skilfully place her more realist fictions in settings where the characters retained their moral compasses whilst being simultaneously at odds with the law. Thornton and Frederick Hale in *North and South* are two powerful examples; Daniel Robson in *Sylvia's Lovers* another. One of Gaskell's earliest uses of this disorienting technique is 'The Heart of John Middleton'.[33] Middleton is a poor factory worker, whose drunken, abusive father has introduced his son to poaching, and has then absconded to avoid prosecution for some (unspecified) 'bad, cruel deed.'[34] The factory overlooker's son is quick to victimise John:

> The son of the overlooker at the mill never ceased twitting me with my father's crime; he now brought up his poaching against him, though I knew very well how many a good supper he himself had made on game which had been given him to make him and

[31] E Gaskell, 'The Poor Clare' in *Gothic Tales* (n 24) 49.
[32] ibid 90.
[33] E Gaskell, 'The Heart of John Middleton' in *The Moorland Cottage and Other Stories* (n 23) 145.
[34] ibid 149.

> his father wink at late hours in the morning. And how were such as my father to come honestly by game?[35]

The ambiguous status of poaching also comes through when John, having been dismissed during a slump in trade, tries to rejoin the poachers. He tells Jonah, a gang member, that although poaching is sinful he will do it anyway. Jonah's reply is forthright: 'Nay, lad … poaching is not sinful; it goes against man's laws, but not against God's.'[36] John, however, persists: 'I trusted to have been clear of it [ie, poaching] for the rest of my days. It led my father wrong at first. I have tried and striven. Now I give all up. Right or wrong shall be the same to me.'[37] But Jonah is unimpressed: 'I've no notion of taking such a spiritless chap as thou into the thick of it, with thy rights and thy wrongs. We don't trouble ourselves with such fine lawyer's stuff, and we bring down the 'varmint' all the better.'[38]

Jonah is a perfect illustration of the serenity that comes from being a law unto oneself. The 'fine lawyer's stuff' of property rights and trespass is not only irrelevant, it is bad for morale, and Jonah cannot risk a wavering colleague. Jonah's confidence, which echoes Margaret Hale's instinctive sympathy for poachers in *North and South*, rests on his understanding of 'God's laws'.[39] If he has some Scriptural reference in mind he does not mention it. This seems, rather, to be an instinctive understanding based on the nature of things – rather like the workers at the start of *Mary Barton* have claimed their holiday 'in right of nature'.[40] In that earlier novel there was, happily, no conflict between what was granted by nature and what granted by employers. But with poaching it is different, and Gaskell economically hints at the hypocrisies which follow when she gives us, in the passage quoted above, the overlooker's son's attitude. It was a theme she would return to, and elaborate on, in *Sylvia's Lovers*' depiction of smuggling.[41] As in that later novel, Gaskell is not dogmatic – she leaves the redistributive arguments hanging. John, for instance, is allowed to ask 'how were such as my father to come honestly by game?' as a rhetorical question. Perhaps in the background of both 'The Heart of John Middleton' and *Sylvia's Lovers* there is a radical presupposition about fair shares in life's good things, which gives the activities of the poachers and smugglers a supra-legal legitimacy.

John moves, in search of work, and finds it in Padiham, where '[we] saw … the grey stone houses … over which a black cloud hung, different from the blue wood or turf smoke about Sawley.' This is an early appearance of the 'unparliamentary smoke' of *North and South*; it makes Padiham seem unpromising, but John, and his wife, Nelly, live there happily until one day the past returns, in the form of the

[35] ibid.
[36] ibid 155.
[37] ibid.
[38] ibid 156.
[39] E Gaskell, *North and South* (A Shelston (ed), Norton, 2005) 51.
[40] See ch 2, s VIII.
[41] See ch 11, s III.

overlooker's son. He has been convicted of a crime, has been transported, but has returned early. Now the authorities are on his track, and he seeks shelter at the Middletons', not recognising John. John knows him, however, and plans revenge: he will offer shelter, wait until the returned convict has fallen asleep, then fetch a constable. His wife, however, sends their daughter to prevent John from carrying out the plan. The story ends with John, influenced by his wife's better nature, offering forgiveness. Just this bare description of the plot demonstrates the story's profound legal strangeness: to assist the authorities in apprehending a criminal is a temptation to be resisted; to frustrate the criminal law is to act well. We can, here, catch a glimpse of the attitude to informants that Gaskell would later develop in *North and South* in the despicable character of Leonards.[42] What makes John Middleton's story the more striking, though, is that for Middleton there is no thought of financial gain (Leonards is solely motivated by the reward), nor any sense that he would be betraying the overlooker's son (whereas Leonards and Frederick have been fellow-servicemen). Nor is there any suggestion that the overlooker's son has been wrongly, or unfairly convicted, whereas Frederick is facing charges of mutiny as a result of having acted nobly. For Middleton, morality and legality point in opposite directions, but there is only a momentary dilemma about which way to go.

VI

For law to obstruct, to repress, or to distract is almost a governing law of Gaskell's fiction. 'Almost' because, very occasionally, she could imagine law being helpful and facilitative. We shall conclude this study of law in Gaskell by looking at two of these uncharacteristically positive instances. The first is in 'Morton Hall', in which, as we have seen above, the tribulations of the owners of the Hall are traced across several generations.[43] The inability to dispose of entailed land inflicts cruel hardships on one generation; by the end of the story, however, the entail must have been barred, the land is being sold off for development, and Morton is becoming a suburb.

The second example is 'My Cousin Phillis', in which the narrator's father reaps the benefits of his inventions under the patent system. Here is the narrator's description of him:

> he was raising himself every year in men's consideration and respect. He was a mechanic by trade, but he had some inventive genius, and a great deal of perseverance, and had devised several valuable improvements in railway machinery. He did not do this for profit, though, as was reasonable, what came in the natural course of things was acceptable; he worked out his ideas because, as he said, 'until he could put them into shape, they plagued him by night and by day.'[44]

[42] See ch 4, ss IV and VII.
[43] Ch 12, s IV.
[44] E Gaskell, 'Cousin Phillis' in *Cousin Phillis and Other Stories* (n 29) 156.

It is worth pausing for a moment here to notice how very unlike other laws in Gaskell the patent system is. First, it corresponds perfectly with the narrator's father's own inclinations and priorities – ie to work out his own ideas. There is a painful contrast with, say, the effects of law on Mr Hale's activities as a clergyman in *North and South*. Second, the law is described as securing rewards that come 'in the natural course of things' – there is no conflict here between law and nature, and the effects are 'reasonable', not out of proportion. There is, admittedly, a certain artificiality about the 'natural course' that the patent system represents – another character gently reminds the narrator that 'we don't know who invented the alphabet' – but it is, crucially, a legal institution that aspires to facilitate.[45] For the narrator's father, social advancement seems to go hand in hand with creativity – he is offered a partnership with 'Ellison, of the Borough Green Works'. 'Mr Ellison the Justice?' replies his son, '– who lives in King Street? why he drives his carriage!'[46] Law, just this once, has secured someone what he deserves.

[45] ibid 171–72.
[46] ibid 184.

INDEX

NB

– Names of fictional characters are not inverted (e.g. Jem Wilson) unless these characters are mostly known by their honorific (e.g. Mr Bradshaw or Lady Ludlow) in which case they are alphabetised by surname.

– Titles of books are italicised (e.g. *Sylvia's Lovers*); those of short stories and articles are in single quotation marks (e.g. 'The Manchester Marriage')

www.ingramcontent.com/pod-product-compliance
Ingram Content Group UK Ltd.
Pitfield, Milton Keynes, MK11 3LW, UK
UKHW020820290926
15470UKWH00003B/1276

9 781509 939732